M000248164

GULF ISLANDS
CRUISING GUIDE

Destinations, Passages, Marinas,
Marine Parks and Anchorages

in the

Southern and Northern Gulf Islands

and on the adjacent

East Coast of Vancouver Island

PETER VASSILOPOULOS

www.marineguides.com

Contents copyright © 2006 Peter Vassilopoulos
Pacific Marine Publishing, Canada.
PO Box 1312 Stn A, Delta, BC V4M 3Y8
In the USA: PO Box 984, Point Roberts WA 98281-0984
Prepress graphics and production Pacific Marine Publishing.
Printed in India.
Photographs and illustrations by author unless indicated otherwise.

All information and illustrations in this book are provided without guarantee and it is up to the boat operator to ensure the proper use of navigational charts and other aids to navigation. Use of charts, depth sounders, BC Sailing Directions, Small Craft Guide and other sources is recommended. Hydrographic Charts and tide and current tables should be used at all times when navigating waterways, bays, coves, harbours and marinas. The publisher and author is not liable for marine operations leading to accident, damage or injury in any way connected with reference to this book.

Waypoints included were taken by the author at the point of reading, using a marine GPS unit. Every effort has been made to ensure accuracy but this is subject to transposition and final information cannot be guaranteed.

All rights reserved. No part of this book may be reproduced or transmitted in any form by any means without the permission of the publisher, except by a reviewer, who may show any two page sections in a review unless otherwise arranged with the publisher.
First Printing–May 2006.

Library and Archives Canada Cataloguing in Publication

Vassilopoulos, Peter, 1940-
Gulf Islands cruising guide / Peter Vassilopoulos, author, illustrator, photographer.
Includes bibliographical references and index.

ISBN 0-919317-38-3

1. Boats and boating--British Columbia--Gulf Islands--Guidebooks.
2. Gulf Islands (B.C.)--Guidebooks. I. Title.
FC3845.G8V38 2006   797.1'09711'2   C2005-906193-6

Copies available from marine stores, marinas and book stores. Distribution and acquisition enquiries to Pacific Marine Publishing. Phone (604) 943-4618.
website: *www.marineguides.com* email: *boating@dccnet.com*

The author and the boat he and his wife, Carla, use for cruising the BC coast. Below: Over the bow at Portland Island.

Peter Vassilopoulos is a veteran boater of over 30 years in the Pacific Northwest and British Columbia waters. He and Carla are well-known in western waters where they spend their time maintaining this and their other marine guides:
North of Desolation Sound, Docks and Destinations and **Anchorages and Marine Parks.**

The author wishes to express gratitude to those who assisted in the acquisition of material for this book. To Heinz Bold for making possible the updating of photographic files of the Southern Gulf Islands. To Chris Fraser and Robin Battley for the final proof reading. Special thanks to my wife Carla for her input and assistance in editing and proof reading and to marina owners and tenants for their input. A special tribute to the memory of Henry Karcz who enthusiastically assisted with the assembly of earlier illustrations.

Cover: *Telegraph Harbour set into a background showing a dramatic sunrise over the Gulf Islands–taken by the author from the docks at Canoe Cove in Sidney.*

GULF ISLANDS
CRUISING GUIDE

PETER VASSILOPOULOS

Other books by the same author
North of Desolation Sound
Docks and Destinations
Anchorages and Marine Parks
Antiques Afloat

Pacific Marine Publishing

Above: Looking north over the Southern Gulf Islands from above Saturna Island. The popular anchorage in Winter Cove lies in the foreground.

Below: A short cut between Bedwell Harbour and Port Browning in the Pender Islands, The Pender Canal is a man made passage that allows small to medium sized power craft through at all tides. Larger boats use it at higher tides. Sailboats should avoid it. There is a good temporary anchorage in Shark Cove opposite the white sandy beach. Small boats can be nosed up on shore on a rising tide.

GULF ISLANDS CRUISING GUIDE

Major marina and public dock locations

Throughout this guide icons are used to indicate anchoring locations, compass bearings, waterways, ferry landings and park facilities. These are added for graphic embellishment of illustrations and are not necessarily precise. Use official CHS nautical charts to determine depths and hazards. Shown to the right are some examples of the icons used in the unofficial, hand-drawn diagrams.

GOLF: See the book *Docks and Destinations* for available golf courses.

Blue dots indicate marinas or marina locations. ●

Ferry landings

Waterways

Anchorages

Campsites

CONTENTS

Foreword

It was about 30 years ago that I began cruising in the Gulf Islands, at first on brief overnight and weekend excursions and later for more extended periods.

I had recently arrived in Canada from Cape Town, South Africa where boating for me entailed quick trips in tenuously calm conditions. Weather changes were often sudden and dramatic in the open waters of the Atlantic and Indian Oceans. The coast was exposed to massive seas and frequent storm force winds. There was no shelter within range of my favourite departure points.

When I discovered the Gulf Islands, and other boating destinations in BC waters, I was hooked. From the first trip my wife Carla and I did into the Gulf Islands I began collecting knowledge, information and photographs. I knew I would eventually assemble these elements into a book. However, when Bill Wolferstan introduced his *Cruising the Gulf Islands* as the first in a series of cruising guides in the 1970s I shelved my book publishing plans.

Bill's books are still available but he is busy in Europe and has left the cruising guide business to others. Each guide on the market is different, reflecting the perspective of the individual author. I have taken an approach that guides the reader sequentially from south to north, island by island. This is intended to make it easy to follow and find your destination.

For those entering the Gulf Islands from Juan de Fuca Strait simply start at the beginning of the book. Those who are travelling through Gabriola, Active or Porlier Pass simply turn to the section and page forward or backward depending on whether you are heading north or south. Coming from the north, use the book back to front.

Rather than being very wordy, I have chosen to use lots of photographs, some of the same place from different angles. One quick look from the air says more than a lot of words.

Anchorages, waterways and places of interest referenced in this book are based on the explorations and findings of the author. Some suggestions included in this guide have been made by other mariners, authors and friends familiar with the area. There are many tiny nooks and coves in which to anchor, or places of interest to visit that are the personal findings or choices of some mariners who have visited the Islands or who will do so in the future. Due to space limitations every one of these places cannot be included in this guide. The author welcomes suggestions from mariners for future editions. Correspondence to PO Box 1312 Delta BC V4M 3Y8. Email: *boating@dccnet.com*

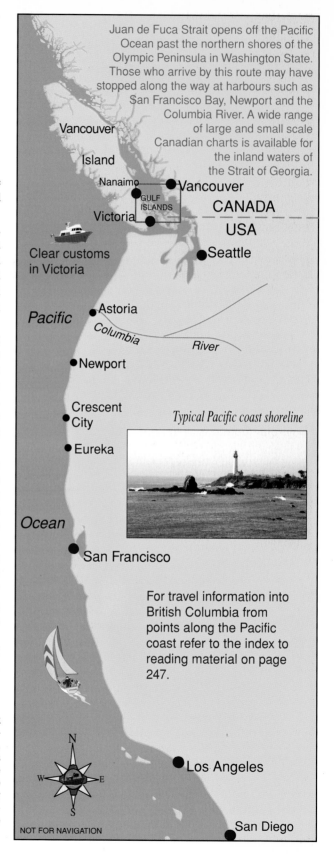

Juan de Fuca Strait opens off the Pacific Ocean past the northern shores of the Olympic Peninsula in Washington State. Those who arrive by this route may have stopped along the way at harbours such as San Francisco Bay, Newport and the Columbia River. A wide range of large and small scale Canadian charts is available for the inland waters of the Strait of Georgia.

Vancouver Island

Nanaimo

Vancouver

GULF ISLANDS

CANADA

USA

Victoria

Seattle

Clear customs in Victoria

Pacific

Astoria

Columbia

River

Newport

Crescent City

Typical Pacific coast shoreline

Eureka

Ocean

San Francisco

For travel information into British Columbia from points along the Pacific coast refer to the index to reading material on page 247.

Los Angeles

N

W E

S

NOT FOR NAVIGATION

San Diego

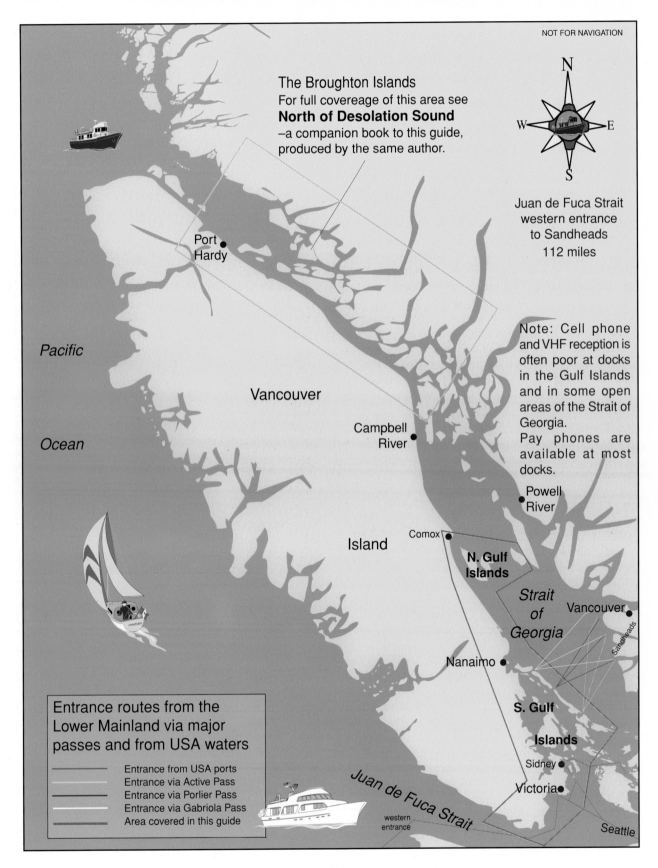

NOT FOR NAVIGATION

The Broughton Islands
For full covereage of this area see
North of Desolation Sound
–a companion book to this guide,
produced by the same author.

Juan de Fuca Strait
western entrance
to Sandheads
112 miles

Note: Cell phone
and VHF reception is
often poor at docks
in the Gulf Islands
and in some open
areas of the Strait of
Georgia.
Pay phones are
available at most
docks.

Port
Hardy

Pacific

Ocean

Vancouver

Campbell
River

Powell
River

Island

Comox

N. Gulf
Islands

Strait
of
Georgia

Vancouver

Sandheads

Nanaimo

S. Gulf

Islands

Sidney

Victoria

Seattle

Juan de Fuca Strait

western
entrance

Entrance routes from the
Lower Mainland via major
passes and from USA waters

Entrance from USA ports
Entrance via Active Pass
Entrance via Porlier Pass
Entrance via Gabriola Pass
Area covered in this guide

N
W E
S

Tidal Rapids in the Gulf Islands

Adapted from **Local Knowledge—A Skipper's Reference**
FineEdge Nautical Publishing. FineEdge.com
By Kevin Monahan.

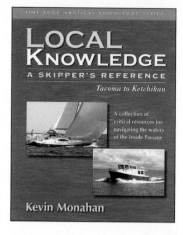

Twice each day, the sun and moon impel a vast mass of Pacific Ocean water toward the West Coast of North America. The mass of water floods into the Strait of Juan de Fuca and then piles up against the barrier formed by the Gulf Islands and San Juan Islands Archipelago. From there it forces itself through the passes of the Gulf Islands, floods the Georgia Basin to a height of five metres or more, and even reverses the flow of the mighty Fraser River as far upstream as Mission. But then again, twice each day, its force exhausted, the Pacific Ocean retreats, the massive "hill" of ocean water collapses, and the Strait of Georgia begins to drain through the Gulf Islands passes. This endless twice-daily cycle of astronomical proportions is the fundamental tidal cycle in the region, and the cause of the many tidal rapids in the Gulf Islands.

Turbulent Flow in Tidal Rapids

Pronounced irregularities in the sides or bottom of a channel deflect some of the current in a different direction than the rest of the stream. A single irregularity causes a single standing wave with localized turbulence. However, numerous irregularities or obstructions interfering with the flow of the current cause extensive turbulence—usually filling the channel from one side to the other and for a distance downstream. Where a restriction in a channel significantly interferes with the flow of water in a tidal channel, the result is a tidal rapids. There are a number of these turbulent tidal channels in the Gulf Islands. But the channel that deserves the most respect is Dodd Narrows.

At the interface between the smoothly flowing tongue and the surrounding water, a series of whirlpools and boils develops. Water subsiding in whirlpools is re-circulated to the surface in boils (upwellings); anything lost in a whirlpool will surface again in a boil, sometimes a long distance away.

From the upstream to the downstream side of the rapids the water flows down a slope. (If there were no difference in level there would be no tidal current.) A tongue of relatively smooth water flows through the opening, diminishing in width until it loses its identity in the general turbulence. This turbulence often extends downstream for several hundred meters.

Forming the boundary between the merely turbulent surrounding water and the relatively smooth tongue you will find a series of whirlpools (subsidences) and boils (upwellings). This area may be very hazardous to small craft, and is usually lower than the tongue.

Currents and Wind

When wind-driven waves are opposed by a current, they slow down and grow taller in response. In smoothly flowing passages the waves are uniformly retarded and inflated; at some point, as the current speed increases, the waves slow to a standstill. But in a turbulent passage, where the surface water may be moving in any direction, conditions can be extremely dangerous and chaotic.

In protected channels, this isn't usually a problem, but where a protected swift-water passage empties into an area that is exposed to wind, the effects can be devastating, especially if the passage is particularly turbulent—remember

FINE EDGE NAUTICAL KNOWLEDGE SERIES

LOCAL KNOWLEDGE
A SKIPPER'S REFERENCE
Tacoma to Ketchikan

A collection of critical resources for navigating the waters of the Inside Passage

Kevin Monahan

How to Read the Daily Tables
Using the Canadian Hydrographic Service Tide and Current Tables

Each line refers to a single ebb or flood current. To determine if the line refers to a flood or ebb current, refer to Column four. (*Ports and Passes* has a slightly different presentation, but the columns provide the same information as the CHS tables).

• **First Column**—Date and day of the week.
• **Second Column**—Time the current turns (**slack water**). (The *CHS Tide and Current Tables* must be adjusted for daylight time; when daylight time is in effect add 1 hour to all tabulated times. *Ports and Passes* has added the hour for you.)
• **Third Column**—The time of maximum speed (rate) for the cycle following the **slack water** in Column one.
• **Fourth Column**—Maximum current speed is given directly in Knots, followed by either a plus sign (+) for flood, or a minus sign (—) for ebb. This will indicate whether the slack water in Column one is **TTE** (**high water slack**) or **TTF** (**low water slack**).

"Obstructions in a narrow channel (such as Dodd Narrows or Boat Pass) restrict the tidal flow, thus causing a height difference that generates a tidal rapids. These rapids are characterised by a smooth flowing tongue surrounded by a series of whirlpools and upwellings (boils)."

the turbulence usually extends far downstream from the choke point in the channel. This means that you may transit a passage that seems mildly turbulent and relatively safe, until you are dumped into an exposed cauldron of chaotic waves, unable to turn around in the current and claw your way back upstream.

During storms, these chaotic conditions are often found throughout Porlier Pass, at either end of Active Pass, and at the northeast end of Gabriola Passage, Georgeson Passage and Boat Passage (Winter Cove); but also in the relatively protected waters at either end of Dodd Narrows.

In Dodd Narrows (which can flood at 9 knots on large tides) the channel is so narrow that wakes from larger vessels opposing a strong current can form standing waves in the narrows. These standing waves can swamp small boats.

During reasonable weather, conditions in many of the Gulf Islands' tidal channels are relatively benign. However, you must treat Dodd Narrows with respect under all weather conditions. This means you should only transit the narrows at or near slack water.

Remember to treat all tidal passages with caution; even those you know well can surprise you in certain weather conditions. In the Gulf Islands, you will eventually have to use one or more of the tidal channels to reach your destination. Learn to use the current tables to predict times of slack water, and plan your travels around the times of slack water. The old adage "Time and tide wait for no one." is nowhere more true than it is in the tidal passes of the BC coast.

General Rules for Transiting Tidal Narrows

• In especially narrow rapids such as Dodd Narrows, broadcast your intention to enter the rapids a few minutes before you do so. If you receive an answer you will not be surprised to meet someone heading the other way. Usually vessels transiting from the upstream side will go first, on the last of the dying current. Then, as slack water approaches, when you are fairly certain it is clear (you can never know for sure) enter the rapids yourself.

• When you first transit a tidal narrows, do so only at slack water.

• Duration of slack water is usually just a few minutes. In certain high-velocity rapids the change of direction may be virtually instantaneous. Make sure you are in position to take advantage of the slack when it occurs.

• If you wish to challenge the current in the Narrows, the first time you do so should be shortly before slack water at the tail end of an opposing current. If you get into difficulties, the current will be abating, not increasing, and you can always cut and run the way you came with the current behind you.

• Never challenge a flood or ebb current for the first time on a large tide, the rapids may rapidly reach maximum speed.

• With the experience you have gained you will then be able to challenge the rapids a longer time before slack water. As you gain confidence you can increase the time before (or after) slack water.

Timing of Slack Water

Slack water is a time of weak or insignificant current that occurs when the tidal current changes direction. When the current turns from ebb to flood, (**Turn to Flood—TTF**) it is low water slack; from flood to ebb, (**Turn to Ebb—TTE**) it is high water slack. Slack water may last only an instant or it may last for 15 minutes or more. Usually slack water lasts longer when the tides (and thus current speeds) are smaller. You can find the times of slack water in the Gulf Islands passes in Table 4 of Volume V of the Canadian Hydrographic Service's (CHS) *Tide and Current Tables* or in *Ports and Passes*, by Chyna Seas Publishing.

Daily current predictions are tabulated only for certain **reference current stations.** If the channel you are interested in is a **reference station**, you need simply read off the times the current turns and the times and speed (rate) of maximum flow. Other tidal channels are considered **secondary stations**; the time the current turns and the time of maximum flow are shown as time differences from a specific **reference station**. It may seem that the time of slack water should be the same time as high or low tide, but don't believe it for a moment. The time of slack water varies widely from the time of high or low water. Never use the *Tide Tables* to estimate the time of slack water. Use the *Current Tables* only.

GPS References

By Kevin Monahan and Don Douglass
Published by FineEdge.com
Anacortes, WA

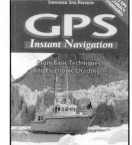

*Kevin Monahan of Shipwrite Productions and author of the book, **GPS–Instant Navigation,** has kindly written the following about the use of the GPS coordinates in this guide:*

Latitude and Longitude—It's not quite that simple

Boaters using a modern GPS receiver can probably determine their position more accurately than was possible even for map-makers until just a few years ago. An unassisted GPS can now resolve a position to within 10 to 15 metres, 95% of the time. As a result, your GPS may be more accurate than your chart. As if this wasn't enough, the chart may also be drawn to a different horizontal datum than is used in your GPS, resulting in errors of up to 200 metres in Northern BC.

A datum is simply a reference point from which latitude and longitude are measured.

In 1927, map-makers in North America established the first truly continental datum at Meade's Ranch in Kansas. This datum was known as North American Datum 1927 (NAD27).

By 1983, using satellite telemetry data scientists had learned enough about the shape of the earth, that they were able to accurately model the surface of the earth. This allowed a new horizontal datum to be developed in North America—(NAD1983)—a datum that did not depend on any physical reference point.

When charts were drawn to the new datum, cartographers discovered that the positions of geographic features on older charts could not be reconciled with their positions on new charts—the lines of latitude and longitude on the older charts were in the wrong places. In many areas of the continent, these differences are minimal—just a few metres—but in northern B.C. and Alaska, the difference between NAD27 and NAD83 is over 200 metres.

Now that world-wide satellite positioning is available, GPS uses a truly universal chart datum—World Geodetic Survey 1984 (WGS84). In North America, WGS84 is equivalent to NAD83.

So much for the idea that latitude and longitude are absolute. Any one location can be represented by different lat/long co-ordinates, depending on the datum that is used. So in order to accurately identify a position, you must know not only the latitude and longitude, but the horizontal datum used as well.

The positions of the various docks etc. in this guide have been taken directly from a Garmin GPS set to the WGS84 Horizontal Datum.

In general, it is best to match the datum your GPS reads out to the datum of the chart you are using. Thus if you are working with a chart drawn to NAD27, you should set your GPS to the same datum. Every chart should incorporate a Horizontal Datum note describing the datum used in that particular chart and the corrections to be applied to convert to NAD83 (or NAD27 as the case may be).

Boaters using electronic navigation systems with electronic charts will find that all their electronic charts have been compensated to read out in NAD83, and should simply ensure that their GPS is set to NAD83 at all times.

However, if you are using paper charts drawn to NAD27 and have set your GPS to the same datum, the latitudes and longitudes here in this guide will not match the positions on the chart, nor will they match the readings on your GPS. The only way to resolve this is to convert the latitudes and longitudes using the conversion factors in the Horizontal Datum note. —Kevin Monahan

For more information on GPS and Horizontal Datums, visit *www.shipwrite.bc.ca*

Conversion Tables   1 nautical mile = 6,067.11 feet (1 land mile = 5,280 feet).

Measures:

1 US gallon	0.833 Imperial gallon
1 US gallon	3.785 litres
1 Imperial gallon	1.201 US gallons
1 Imperial gallon	4.546 litres
1 litre	0.264 US gallon
2 pints	1 quart
4 quarts	1 gallon
1 litre	1.0567 quarts
1 quart	0.9463 litre

Mariners' Measures:

6 feet	1 fathom
1 metre	39.37 inches (1.0936 yards)
120 fathoms	1 cable (length)
5,280 feet	1 statute mile
6,067.11 feet	1 nautical mile

Linear Measure:

1 metre	39.37 inches (1.0936 yards)
1 kilometre	0.621 mile
1 mile	1.609 kilometres

Temperatures:

A Fahrenheit is smaller than a Centigrade (Celsius) degree. It is 5/9 of a Celsius degree.

Conversion method

To convert Celsius to Fahrenheit multiply by 9, divide by 5 and add 32.
To convert Fahrenheit to Celsius, subtract 32, multiply by 5 and divide by 9.

A simple variation for an approximate conversion:
Celsius to Fahrenheit–Multiply by two and add 32.
Fahrenheit to Celsius–Subtract 32 and divide by two.
For example:
Fahrenheit–72° minus 32 = 40 divided by 2 = 20°C.
Celsius–10° multiplied by 2 = 20 plus 32 = 52°F

Throughout this guide chart distance references have been made in nautical miles and depths in metres. Tides affect depths and therefore all suggested anchoring depths are approximate. More precise measurements, if needed, can be calculated with the use of your nautical charts or taken from official publications such as the *BC Sailing Directions*. The above suggested method of conversion is intended as a quick way for the mariner to convert measures and distances to their preferred standard.

Customs information

The master of any pleasure boat must report to Customs immediately after arriving in Canada or the United States and must report any foreign merchandise that is subject to duty. The report should include the name of the boat, its nationality, name of the master, place of docking and arrival time. If an inspection is required, the Customs officer will direct the vessel to an inspection area. The vessel must make formal entry with Customs within 48 hours.

It is now recommended that passports be carried when crossing the border in either direction.

Vessels entering the USA that are 30 feet or longer in length must pay an annual fee to enter the USA. Vessels under 30 feet with nothing to declare are not subject to the fee. The fee may be paid annually, by credit card over the phone, and a decal will be issued.

The I-68 or NEXUS programs allows small craft entry to the USA. Anyone seeking entry to the United States must report their arrivals. Boaters participating in the I-68 or NEXUS programs must report but may do so by phone at a designated point of entry (telephones are available at ports of entry or use your cellular phone when you have docked).

Call 1-800-562-5943. Provide the following information to the customs officer: • Vessel name and length • Registration Number • User fee decal number (if applicable) • Date of your intended departure.

You will be given a release number which you should enter in your logbook along with the time of clearance and place of reporting.

In Canada the Automated Customs Information Service (ACIS) system now called Border Information Service (BIS) is reflected on the Internet, intranet, and in CBSA publications. The Border Information Service Online, or BIS Online, provides access to all the recorded phone information from the BIS telephone system in a convenient, navigable format. Use one of the categories below and follow the links to answer many basic border services questions:

For in-depth enquiries, call the BIS phone service during regular business hours - Monday to Friday (except holidays) from 8:00-16:00 local time, and press 0 to speak to an agent: From within Canada, call: 1 800-461-9999 (toll free). From outside Canada, call: 204-983-3500 or 506-636-5064 (long-distance charges apply).

U.S Customs and Border Protection

U.S. citizens are now urged to carry proof of citizenship by way of a valid passport. Canadian citizens should present proof of Canadian citizenship (passport).

If your boat has anchored or tied up, you are considered to have entered the United States. No one may board or leave the boat without first completing customs processing, unless permission to do so is granted by the Customs officer in charge. The only exception to this requirement is for the captain to report arrival.

If it is necessary for someone to leave the boat to report arrival to U.S. Customs, he or she must return to the boat after reporting and remain on board. No one who arrived in that boat may leave until the Customs officer grants permission to go ashore. Violations may result in substantial penalties and forfeiture of the boat. Reporting is required after having been at any foreign port or place and/or having had contact with any hovering vessel.

Canada Customs

All vessels arriving in Canada from across the border must clear customs immediately after docking. The master or his designated representative must report in person or by telephone. No one else may leave the vessel and no merchandise or luggage may be removed until it has been cleared.

The master may call at 1-888-226-7277 or from a Customs Direct line phone. Canpass members phone 1-888-CANPASS (226-7277). Canpass may be used only if all on board are members. You will still have to stop at a Canpass designated reporting station, but processing is quick.

It is recommended that you have a passport. US citizens may use photo identification. Citizens of other countries need passports and sometimes visas, and birth certificates for minors on board. Documentation for non-related children is required for crossing the border.

When you report by telephone you may be directed to a customs port where an officer is present and able to conduct an inspection of your vessel.

You may be asked for all or some of the following:
• Vessel Name, length and registration numbers
• Names, birth dates, addresses and citizenship of everyone on board.
• Estimated time of departure (boats returning to the US).

You will be given a clearance number which should be posted in a side window. Keep a logged record of this number, with the date, place and time of clearance.

Designated US Ports of Entry

Report your arrival in the United States to U.S. Customs nearest your point of entry.

Weekday Phone Numbers:

Anacortes	360-532-2030
Bellingham	360-734-5463
Blaine	360-332-6318
Everett	425-259-0246
Friday/Roche Hbr	360-378-2080
Longview	360-425-3710
Neah Bay	206-645-2311
Olympia	253-593-6338
Point Roberts	360-945-2314
Port Angeles	360-457-4311

Designated BC Ports of Entry (southern waters)

Report your arrival in Canada at the following ports of entry:

Bedwell Harbour:	Customs dock–Phone in.
Cabbage Island	Permit only.
Ganges	Permit only.
Horton Bay	Permit only.
Miners Bay	Permit only.
Montague Harbour	Seasonal May 1 to Sept 30 or by permit.
Port Browning	Permit only.
Nanaimo:	Nanaimo Port Authority Basin, Brechin Point Marina. Townsite Marina–permit only.
Sidney:	Angler's Anchorage Marina, Canoe Cove Marina, Port Sidney Marina, Royal Victoria Yacht Club (Tsehum Harbour), Van Isle Marina.
Victoria:	Royal Victoria Yacht Club (Cadboro Bay), Victoria Inner Harbour customs dock, Oak Bay Marina. Canadian Forces Sailing Association (Members only)

Contact Canada Customs toll free at 1-888-226-7277
Vancouver: Call 604-278-1825 or 604-278-7422   www.cbsa.gc.ca

Preface

There are many ways to reach the Gulf Islands. This guide is primarily for the mariner cruising into the southern Strait of Georgia. It is intended to show the many anchorages and marinas where safe and secluded overnight moorage is available. It includes information about where provisions, services and fuel can be found. It also provides information to those who arrive by ferry or by small boat, canoe or kayak, on the type of facilities available for them at waterfront marine establishments and about some of the many parks and shoreline campgrounds scattered throughout the islands.

Mariners arriving in British Columbia from off shore enter the inland waters of the Straight of Georgia by way of Juan de Fuca Strait. This wide passage opens off the Pacific Ocean past the northern shores of the Olympic Peninsula in Washington State. Those who arrive by this route may have stopped along the way at harbours such as San Francisco Bay, Newport and the Columbia River. Their first landfalls in the relatively protected Juan de Fuca Strait may be made at the sheltered Washington harbours of Neah Bay or Port Angeles. They may stop at Port Renfrew or the haven of Sooke only after clearing customs in Victoria. For those en route to the West Coast of Vancouver Island, Port Renfrew is a relatively safe haven from a sometimes rough Juan de Fuca Strait. Port Renfrew and other outer Juan de Fuca Strait ports are beyond the scope of this book.

Sooke is a destination in its own right and may be visited after stopping in Victoria. It serves in this guide as a destination for mariners seeking a sampling of west coast navigation and ambience while remaining within the general environs of a large boating region bordering on the fringes of a large community.

Approaching Victoria from Puget Sound mariners from offshore waters may deviate along the northern shores of the Olympic Peninsula and cross Juan de Fuca Strait from Port Angeles or Neah Bay before continuing to the British Columbia capital. Or travel to Sooke from Victoria before returning to Puget Sound after a sojourn in the Gulf Islands. Locally the routes to the islands begin at some large centres and at ferry terminals on Vancouver Island and the BC lower mainland. These include Tsawwassen, Swartz Bay, Nanaimo, Crofton and Chemainus. Ferries from Anacortes in Washington State travel through the lower Gulf Islands to drop off passengers at Sidney, bound for Vancouver Island as well as Gulf Islands destinations. Inter island ferries move passengers between the major islands in the archipelago.

Each summer sees hordes of vacationers and weekenders arriving by ferry or by private boat or yacht, or paddling across calm passages into the islands. There are many establishments on the islands catering to those who stay overnight. Many bed and breakfast facilities exist along the shorelines, providing magnificent views of the waterways and the passing traffic, of the nearby islands and of Mount Baker looming over the mainland, to the east.

Marine Parks in the Gulf Islands, as in the San Juan Islands and elsewhere in British Columbia, offer tranquil and delightful moorage. They have been established for use by the general public and attract hikers, backpackers, cyclists, RV campers and mariners. Many parks have picnic and overnight camp sites with trails and beaches. Some have docks adequate to moor dinghies only, some to moor a number of small to medium sized craft and others none at all. Some have mooring buoys for safe overnight moorage. Flat fees are levied for use of docks or mooring buoys. These change periodically and the charges usually apply after 6 pm.

The authorities ask that parks be respected and kept clean. Garbage should not be disposed of unless there is a specific disposal station. Sewage should not be discharged in marine park anchorages and noise should be limited to daylight hours. There are marine park hosts at some and their presence will be indicated by the flying of a BC Parks Marine Park Host burgee. The host is usually a member of a power squadron, a yacht club, a sailing association or is an individual who has volunteered to assist visitors in the parks.

See page 92 in the Southern Gulf Islands section for a diagram and information on the National Parks Reserve. For more information on marine parks in British Columbia, see BC Parks' website page at *www.bcparks.ca*.

Diagrams used throughout the guide are meant to assist readers when referencing official nautical charts. They include information and selected distances between points in blue type and notices in red. In the text and diagrams sometimes specific navigational aids have been referenced. This is when they are considered significant for easy and safe passage in areas where description alone may not be clear.

GPS readings are approximate and close to major points, entrances or installations. They are meant only for general reference. Chart numbers are provided at the beginning of each section. Where groups of charts are listed they are provided largest to smallest scale. However, the first chart number in and adjacent to the Southern Gulf Islands is the Chart Book 3313.

Boating in the Gulf Islands

Collectively, when it comes to boating destinations, the Gulf Islands are the jewel of British Columbia. The islands have a Mediterranean climate with less annual rainfall than the rest of the province. This influences a landscape of wildflower meadows and forests of Garry oak and coniferous timberlands. The Gulf Islands offer mariners a wide choice of anchorages, moorage and cruising destinations with the choice of peace and tranquility away from the crowds. The small town communities and island settlements of artists, artisans and aesetics hold numerous social events and annual attractions. Most of them celebrate holidays and weekends with festivals and functions that showcase the culture, history and talents of the people.

This area of the British Columbia coast was strongly influenced by British colonization. The major seaport of Victoria, which was to become the province's capital, was named for the reigning monarch, and nearby Albert Head for her royal consort. Many other place names were derived from names of ships of her majesty's navy and for the men in them or for significant people back home in England. The trend to name landfalls, islands, rocks and reefs throughout the Gulf Islands and all the waterways explored by Captain Vancouver in his ships *Discovery* and *Chatham* continued throughout the new world. Most place names are discussed in Captain Walbran's book, *British Columbia Coast Names*.

The fabled Gulf Islands are steeped in history and folklore and there are books on many subjects dealing with these fascinating islands as well as the nearby San Juan Islands. This guide encourages you to pick up the works of other authors who have spent time researching those subjects. See the list of recommended books at the end of this guide.

As you make passage along the east shore of Vancouver Island, stopping possibly in Victoria or Sidney to clear customs, you will encounter places of interest and people of charm and character. Stop and take in their ambience and uniqueness. You may prefer to tie up at a dock and enjoy the local facilities. Victoria has the charm of British styled stores, pubs and restaurants. British imports are the speciality and if the atmosphere of old England does not strike you immediately, go and reserve afternoon tea at the Empress Hotel. Tourists flock to Victoria each summer. They are attracted by the Royal BC Museum, the Art Gallery of Greater Victoria, the parliament buildings, the Royal London Wax Museum, undersea gardens, scenic London-bus tours and much more.

Visit also Vancouver Island destinations such as Port Sidney where several major marina facilities offer good access to restaurants, services and places where you can sit and take in the magnificent crimson summer sunsets.

In Saanich Inlet stop at one of the marinas and take your dinghy around to Butchart Gardens for a day of strolling in one of the most exquisite masterpieces of landscaping anywhere. Stay overnight and watch the fireworks displays on summer weekends.

Continue along the coast taking in Chemainus and its artistic wall murals. Continue to Nanaimo and then to Comox and the northern Gulf Islands. Visit the marine parks and tranquil anchorages along the way. No matter your destination in this renowned cruising area you are bound to experience all that your interest in boating ever promised.

The Gulf Islands lie adjacent to the fascinating east coast of Vancouver Island. The nearest islands to this shoreline are no more than a short paddle away from places such as Sidney, Maple Bay, Ladysmith and Nanaimo. Salt Spring Island is the largest of the Gulf Islands and is divided from Vancouver Island by Sansum Narrows at its closest point. On Salt Spring Island, the town of Ganges with its Saturday morning market is the hub of the islands and attracts a large number of vessels throughout the summer.

The Pender Islands, not far to the east of Salt Spring Island, offer several well-protected marinas. As you travel through the archipelago you will discover many anchorages and sheltered coves where you can spend time enjoying the ambiance of the best of the British Columbia coast, its coastal communities, its marine life and the indigenous fauna and flora. Most anchorages depicted in photographs, diagrams and text in this book are popular places where mariners spend weekends or longer durations away from home.

Active Pass is a major passage between the Gulf Islands and the Strait of Georgia. To its north, Galiano Island stretches along the outer eastern edge of the islands to form a breakwater for them. This island is divided from Valdes Island by Porlier Passage which opens off the Strait as another major gateway to the Gulf Islands. It gives quick access to nearby destinations

Marine Parks

The popularity of the Gulf Islands stems from their mild, Mediterranean climate. Visitors and residents cherish the islands for their fir and oak forestation and their habitat for a variety of waterfowl and marine life including the great blue heron, bald eagles, killer whales, sea lions, dolphins and harbour seals.

The guide includes the marine parks of the islands. These, in many cases, also serve as protected anchorages recommended en route between points or as cruising destinations in themselves.

The British Columbia provincial government signed an agreement with the national government in Ottawa in 2003 setting aside 26 square kilometres on 15 islands in the Strait of Georgia as national parks. Parks on Sidney Island, Saturna Island, Mayne Island, Prevost Island and the Pender Islands as well as all of Tumbo and Portland Islands are included in the package. The setting aside of this marine conservation area is aimed at preserving the pristine wilderness nature of the islands. Parks Canada has a mandate to manage national parks so as to preserve their environment. Boat operators are called on to respect the environment by helping prevent pollution of the waters.

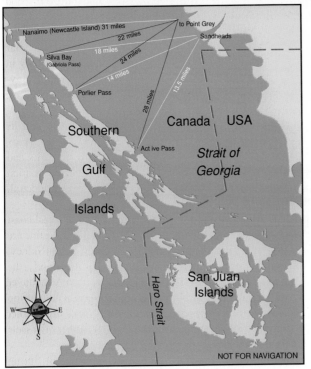

NOT FOR NAVIGATION

including Thetis and Kuper islands. These two islands form a breakwater to Telegraph Harbour, another of the most popular destinations in the Gulf Islands. The harbour has two ample marinas in a very sheltered bay. Telegraph Harbour lies in close proximity to other popular anchorages and to Vancouver Island landfalls. Gabriola Island is among the northernmost of the Southern Gulf Islands. Its harbours include the prominent Silva Bay and snug Degnan Bay. It forms the north shore of another major entrance to the Gulf Islands–Gabriola Pass–and lies in close proximity to yet another–Dodd Narrows to the west. In the Northern Gulf Islands I have included Denman, Hornby and Lasqueti islands and the adjacent Vancouver Island shore from Nanaimo to Comox.

Tides and Currents

"Many currents are asymmetrical in nature. The speed of the flow may slowly increase to a maximum, then decrease rapidly toward the turn. Or, they may increase relatively quickly, then decrease more slowly toward the turn. This asymmetrical character generally occurs on the ebb tidal flow and is predominant at Porlier Pass, Gabriola Passage and Dodd Narrows as well as other locations on the west coast. In these areas, mariners should take caution while transiting the passages because the velocity of the current could change more rapidly than expected."

—*Norm and Jodi Brochno, Ports and Passes.*

Above: Anderson Cove, a protected anchorage with an entrance at its north side, opens off the south shore of Sooke Basin. Mariners drop anchor at the eastern side or in the centre of the cove. Below: A view of Cooper Cove anchorage at the east side of Sooke Basin.

Vancouver Island South

Western entrance to the Strait of Georgia and the Gulf Islands–Juan de Fuca Strait to Victoria

Charts 3313, 3411, 3410, 3440, 3461, 3462, 3606

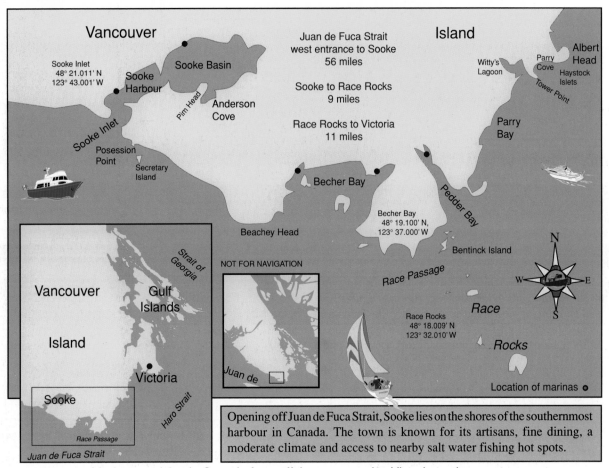

Opening off Juan de Fuca Strait, Sooke lies on the shores of the southernmost harbour in Canada. The town is known for its artisans, fine dining, a moderate climate and access to nearby salt water fishing hot spots.

Mariners arriving in Canada from offshore proceed to Victoria to clear customs.

Sooke to Victoria

The town of Sooke lies on the west shore of Sooke Harbour. Sooke Inlet entrance opens widely off Juan de Fuca Strait. But it narrows fast with **Whiffen Spit** protruding across the entrance from the west. Use the range markers to guide you in. There are currents to 4 knots through the entrance at times and care should be exercised when approaching, entering and leaving. Check the depths and the tide tables for tidal currents.

Passage is mostly mid channel to the point of the spit, passing close to its tip before edging off slightly and taking a course determined by the markers in its lee. Pass Woodward Point and proceed to channel marker VA. Continue to V4, V5

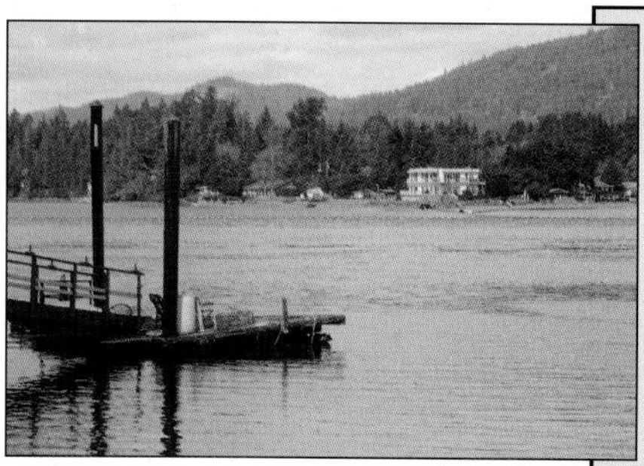

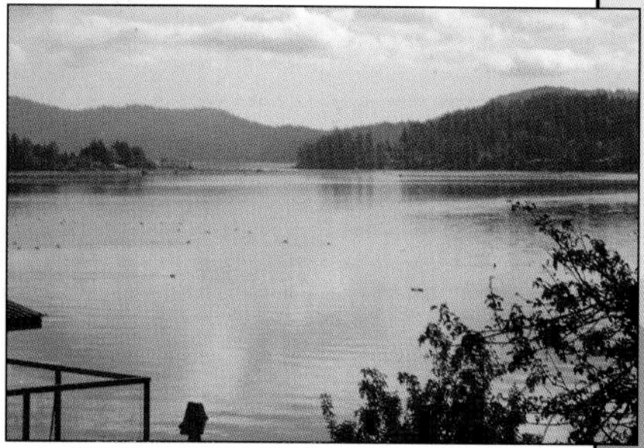

Two views of Billings Spit. Top photo taken from wharf on opposite shore. Bottom photo looking towards Sooke Basin from Sooke.

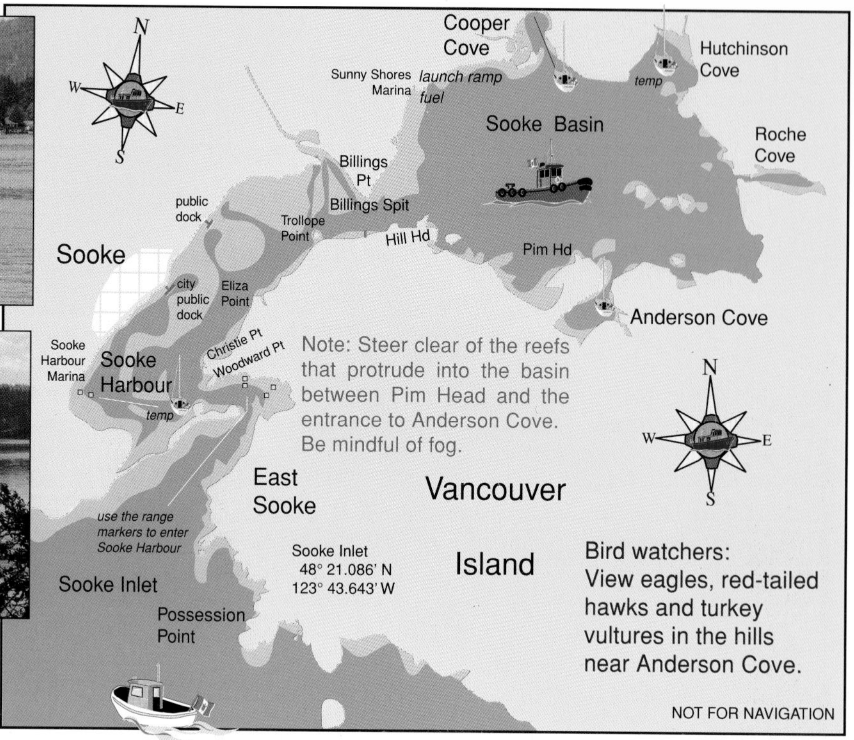
N
W
E
S
Cooper Cove
Sunny Shores Marina
launch ramp
fuel
Hutchinson Cove
temp
Sooke Basin
Roche Cove
Billings Pt
Billings Spit
public dock
Trollope Point
Hill Hd
Pim Hd
Sooke
city public dock
Eliza Point
Anderson Cove
Sooke Harbour Marina
Sooke Harbour
Christie Pt
Woodward Pt
temp
Note: Steer clear of the reefs that protrude into the basin between Pim Head and the entrance to Anderson Cove. Be mindful of fog.
East Sooke
Vancouver
Island
use the range markers to enter Sooke Harbour
Sooke Inlet
48° 21.086' N
123° 43.643' W
Sooke Inlet
Possession Point
Bird watchers:
View eagles, red-tailed hawks and turkey vultures in the hills near Anderson Cove.
NOT FOR NAVIGATION

and into the channel that runs parallel to the shore. It is possible to stop temporarily off Whiffen Spit. Use your judgement regarding depths and weather conditions. The markers direct traffic to the **public dock** on the west shore, just south of the town of Sooke. It's a beautiful passage with pleasant surrounding scenery at the entrance. Private moorage at Sooke Harbour Marina along the west side of the harbour can be reached by marked passages to the west of the sand bars and charted middle ground. A passage leads into the harbour and inner harbour from Woodward Point beginning to the east of channel marker VA followed by VB.

Sooke River flows into the harbour over a shallow delta that lies west of Billings Point. This promontory protrudes deep into the harbour to divide the southwestern section from the larger and deeper Sooke Basin. After clearing the centre of Sooke Harbour take care travelling into Sooke Basin, passing off Eliza Point and east of channel marker V13. Pass very close to Trollope Point opposite Middle Ground where the passage low tide depth drops to about 1.2 metres, and follow the east shoreline past Hill Head into the Inner Basin.

Sunny Shores Marina to the west of Goodridge Peninsula at the far end of Sooke Basin caters to small craft, some moored year round and others in for the season. It is mostly for guests at the adjacent campground. Beyond the peninsula, **Cooper Cove** may be entered with care along its east shore. Anchorage may be taken over rock, mud and gravel in the shallows well inside the cove opposite a restaurant with its own landing. Beyond this cove is **Hutchinson Cove** which is open and exposed to winds across the basin. **Roche Cove** is a small inlet that opens on the east shore of the basin, with a low road bridge over the entrance. It is not suitable for anything but small boats.

The favoured anchorage in Sooke Basin can be found inside **Anderson Cove** which opens off the south shore beyond Pim Head. Steer clear of the reefs that protrude into the basin between Pim Head and the entrance to Anderson Cove. There are private docks inside on the west shore and anchorage is usually taken in the centre and on the east side of the cove. Beware of submerged power lines, indicated by markings on shore in alignment with their location.

Poking around in small boats near shore and avoiding the fog bank that hovers across the harbour. Fog is often a factor at Sooke.

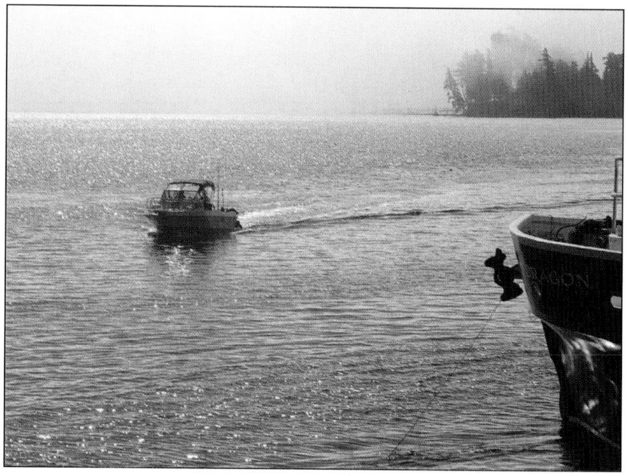

Above: Whiffen Spit at the entrance to Sooke Harbour. Below, left: A private dock near the entrance to the harbour. Below, right: The dock at Sunny Shores Marina. Bottom: The harbour from Cooper's Cove Guest House, overlooking Sooke.

Whiffen Spit is popular for walking, bird watching and family open-air outings.
There is a trail along its ridge with sandy beaches, shrubs, salt flats and the lighthouse at its far end marking the harbour entrance.

Above: Fishing boats tied up at the Sooke Public docks. Right and below: The public docks at Sooke Harbour. It is a busy place with lots of fishing boats. Space may be limited at times and rafting is permitted. There is an interesting marine store nearby and more stores uptown.

A tranquil anchorage off the eastern shore of Anderson Cove. This is the most recognised anchorage in Sooke Harbour.

Below: The Rotary Pier near the Sooke Public Marina is used mostly for recreational line fishing. Access by land is from Ed Macgregor Park near the town centre.

Sooke Public Docks Phone: 250-642-4431
Transient moorage. Garbage disposal. Water, power. Short walk to city centre to washrooms and showers at public pool. Security key available for marina gate.

Sooke Harbour Resort & Marina
6971 West Coast Rd, Sooke BC V0S 1N0
Phone: 250-642-3236 VHF 66A
Limited summer transient moorage.

Sunny Shores Marina
5621 Sooke Rd, Sooke V0S 1N0 Phone: 250-642-5731
Fuel. Limited summer transient moorage.

Ed Macgregor Park overlooks Sooke Harbour above the Rotary Pier (left). The dock is not meant for large vessels and is used mostly by locals for relaxing in the sun and by kids for line fishing. Access it by dinghy to visit the park.

From Sooke Harbour to Victoria requires passage around Beechey Head and through Race Passage past William Head, Albert Head and Esquimalt Harbour. En route, pass either side of Secretary Island. The first possible sheltered stop is at **Becher Bay** where anchorage should be considered temporary. For protected moorage small boats may go to Becher Bay Marina in **Campbell Cove** or most sizes to Cheanuh Marina on the northwest side of Becher Bay. Here mariners can replenish some supplies, including fuel.

Anchorage is semi protected in the lee of **Wolf Island** or **Frazer Island**. The former island forms the east shore of **Murder Bay**, named as such because of the murder of a white resident there. Becher Bay saw other incidents of great drama such as the massacre of a Becher First Nations band by the Clallam and Nitinat natives some 200 years ago.

Fair weather anchorage can be taken in the lee of the **Village Islands** east of Frazer Island or **Large Bedford Island** in the group of islands at the southeast entrance of Becher Bay. Use caution and a large scale chart negotiating these waters.

With time and the inclination mariners should take in **Whirl Bay**. It lies about midway between Becher Bay and Race Passage and it is worthwhile stopping in good conditions for a temporary anchorage east of **Shelter Island**. Here and from all points along the southern tip of Vancouver Island there is a magnificent view of the Olympic Peninsula with its tall, imposing mountains on the American side of Juan de Fuca Strait.

*Above: Cheanuh Marina.
The view takes in Frazer
Island and the entrance to
Becher Bay.
Right: Docks at Becher Bay
Marina.
Below: Dolphin Loustalot
in the store at Becher Bay
Marina. The two marinas
are well protected from
most wind and sea
conditions.*

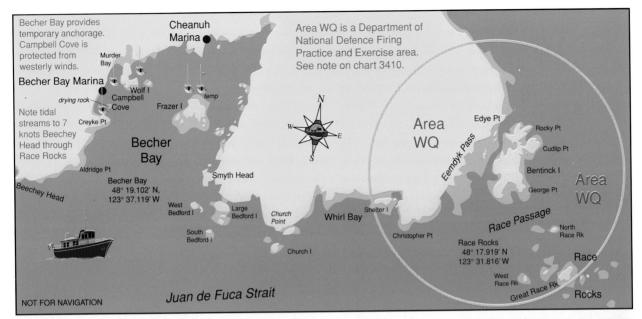

Becher Bay provides temporary anchorage. Campbell Cove is protected from westerly winds.

Murder Bay

Becher Bay Marina

drying rock

Wolf I

Campbell Cove

Frazer I

temp

Creyke Pt

Note tidal streams to 7 knots Beechey Head through Race Rocks

Cheanuh Marina

Becher Bay

Area WQ is a Department of National Defence Firing Practice and Exercise area. See note on chart 3410.

Area WQ

Edye Pt

Rocky Pt

Cudlip Pt

Bentinck I

George Pt

Area WQ

Aldridge Pt

Becher Bay 48° 19.102' N, 123° 37.119' W

Smyth Head

Beechey Head

West Bedford I

Large Bedford I

Church Point

Whirl Bay

Shelter I

Race Passage

North Race Rk

South Bedford I

Church I

Christopher Pt

Race Rocks 48° 17.919' N 123° 31.816' W

Race

West Race Rk

NOT FOR NAVIGATION

Juan de Fuca Strait

Great Race Rk

Rocks

Becher Bay Marina (closed in winter)

241 Becher Bay Rd, Sooke BC V0S 1N0
Phone: 250-642-3816 VHF 66A
Transient moorage. Mostly smaller boats. Water, power. An RV campground and facilities are adjacent to the marina. The Smokin Tuna family-run restaurant on the waterfront is alongside a large launching ramp.

Cheanuh Marina

4901 East Sooke Rd, Sooke BC V0S 1N0
Located in Becher Bay
Ph: 250-478-4880 Fax: 250-478-5800 VHF 66A
Fuel–gas only. Limited summer transient moorage. Laundry, washrooms and showers. Bait available.

Pedder Bay Marina

12-925 Pedder Bay Dr, Metchosin BC V9C 4H1
Ph: 250-478-1771 Fax: 250-478-26895 VHF 66A
www.obmg.com
Limited summer transient moorage. Washrooms, showers and laundry. Rental boats and fishing guides available. Mini chandlery and store.
Caution: Reef at entrance.

Race Passage and Race Rocks

The historic lighthouse on the fabled rocks stands tall to starboard as you pass eastbound through Race Passage. Currents run to 6 knots with tide rips and breaking waves. This is a strategic waterway in the great annual Swiftsure sailboat race every Spring. Seasoned sailors use the tides

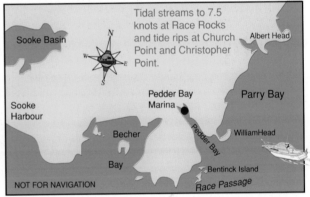

Tidal streams to 7.5 knots at Race Rocks and tide rips at Church Point and Christopher Point.

Sooke Basin

Albert Head

Pedder Bay Marina

Parry Bay

Sooke Harbour

Becher Bay

Bay

Pedder Bay

William Head

Bentinck Island

NOT FOR NAVIGATION

Race Passage

and currents to their advantage and know the best place to be or where not to be to benefit from the swirling, rushing waters. Travelling through the passage, it is best for smaller craft to pass near George Point on Bentinck Island then Cudlip Point and Rocky Point for Pedder Bay and Victoria. Avoid **Eemdyk Pass** unless you have a small, powerful boat, lots of time, a good chart and fair weather. It is full of shoals, rocks and reefs and runs at speeds to about 4 knots. **Bentinck Island** is used for testing explosives. Keep 1,500 metres clear of the island when red flags are flying. Like D'Arcy Island (see page 36), Bentinck Island was once a leper colony.

Pedder Bay is fairly protected against all but occasional southeasterly winds. It has a sheltered marina at its head. A marked reef protrudes from the western shore of Rocky Point between Weir and Watt Points about midway. Some mariners use the Rocky Point shore for temporary anchorage, particularly in the vicinity of Manor Point. The **Pearson College** dock, on the north shore beyond Weir Point, is private. Pedder Bay Marina, beyond, has available moorage and facilities for mariners, including fuel.

Above: Looking across Becher Bay from its northern shoreline. The bay is open but there is protected anchorage behind the islands. Right: A view of the marina at Pedder Bay from Pearson College on the east shore of the bay.

William Head is the site of a medium security prison. **Quarantine Cove**, which opens at the south end of Parry Bay, has anchoring restrictions with controls on approaching too close to the shore. Temporary stopping in the western portion of the cove and off Weir Beach is possible, but beware of underwater cables which extend into Parker Bay.

Parry Bay

Parry Bay is shallow at the north end, with shoals extending from **Witty's Lagoon**. This is a regional park. Some vessels are known to anchor off the shallows in good weather but dropping the hook south of Haystock Islets is prohibited. Submerged cables extend along the subtidal zone and these are meant to be protected by the restriction. Those who know the area tend to anchor in **Parry Cove** between the islands. Or stop just off the shallows outside Witty's Lagoon and row into the lagoon at high tide slack. The area is home to a wide variety of birds including bald eagles, herons and Canada geese. If you do enter the lagoon at high tide do so under your own power as any form of motor is prohibited. Look for a picturesque waterfall, known as The Sitting Lady, near Whitney-Griffiths Point. There is a kayak launch at Pine Sand Beach.

The cove in the nook north of **Albert Head** is a good anchorage, other than in a northerly blow. Such breezes seldom affect the cove during summer.

Angle across Royal Roads (roadstead) to Victoria or continue along the shore taking in its rugged features. Anchorage is possible on the approaches to Victoria Harbour at Fleming Bay or temporarily in the lee of the Fisgard light.

Esquimalt Lagoon is best left to paddlers. A narrow,

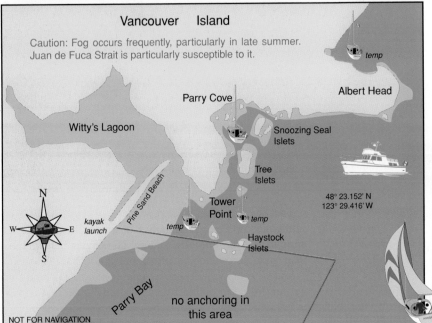

NOT FOR NAVIGATION

Vancouver Island

Caution: Fog occurs frequently, particularly in late summer.
Juan de Fuca Strait is particularly susceptible to it.

Parry Cove

Witty's Lagoon

Albert Head

temp

Snoozing Seal
Islets

Tree
Islets

Pine Sand Beach

kayak
launch

Tower
Point

temp

temp

Haystock
Islets

48° 23.152' N
123° 29.416' W

Parry Bay

no anchoring in
this area

NOT FOR NAVIGATION

Above, left: The marina at Pedder Bay.
Above, right: A young woman explores the
waters off the ruins of the old guard house
at Cole Island in Esquimalt Harbour.
Cole Island is said to have been used for
munitions storage during World War I as
part of Fort Rodd Hill territory.

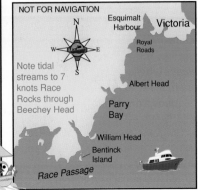

NOT FOR NAVIGATION

Esquimalt
Harbour

Victoria

Royal
Roads

Note tidal
streams to 7
knots Race
Rocks through
Beechey Head

Albert Head

Parry
Bay

William Head

Bentinck
Island

Race Passage

shallow passage under a low road bridge allows the lagoon to empty and fill during tidal changes, but passage is complicated and the lagoon is a wildlife refuge. Along the outside of the **Coburg Peninsula** temporary anchorage may be taken but is not recommended due to its exposure to southerly winds. The lagoon is a scenic place to visit by paddle boat and a sanctuary for birds and wildlife. Observe regulations for operating a boat in a sanctuary.

Esquimalt

Esquimalt Harbour (see diagram page 29) opens to the northwest as you approach Victoria. Its entrance lies adjacent to the historic Fisgard Light at Fort Rodd Hill. Inside and on the opposite side of the harbour is a Canadian naval base, with dry docks, berths and naval installations in and near **Constance Cove**. Day boaters out of Victoria sometimes cruise up towards the shoals, busy with waterfowl, at the head of the harbour, passing Inskip Islands to starboard and ending at **Limekiln Cove**, **Tovey Bay** or scenic **Cole Island**. The Harbour has a number of obvious restrictions including anchoring. Your best bet is at Cole Island. When entering the harbour call the harbour master on channel 10. Remain clear of any military installations and expect the harbour patrol to check on your movements within the harbour.

The Fisgard Lighthouse at Fort Rodd Hill can be seen in the distance after passing through Race Passage in Juan de Fuca Strait. It was constructed in 1859 and is now a national historic site.

The Fisgard Lighthouse at Fort Rodd Hill is Canada's oldest west coast lighthouse. It is now a museum of the history of shipwrecks and lifesaving. The structure includes the rampart of three artillery batteries complete with the original guns, underground magazines and camouflaged searchlight emplacements. Phone: 250-478-5849. *www.pc.gc.ca/fortrodhill*

*Above: Fisgard light
stands as a sentinel at
the entrance to
Esquimalt Harbour,
from the beach at
Coburg Peninsula.
Left: Esquimalt Harbour
with Cole Island in the
foreground.
Bottom: Off Fleming
Bay on the approaches
to Victoria.*

Continue in the direction of Victoria. Pass outside of Brothers Islands and beware of the reefs around the Gillingham Islands outside Fleming Bay.

Fleming Bay is protected by a substantial breakwater and has a small float and a good launch ramp, meant for small boat use. There is a pleasant beach and park area in the cove. The bay, busy with trailerable boats in summer, is very compact, making the anchorage rather tight. The best spot to drop the hook is in the lee of the breakwater using a stern line to prevent swinging in the confined space.

Victoria to Haro Strait

The Southern Saanich Peninsula–Victoria to D'Arcy Island Marine Park

Charts 3313, 3412, 3419, 3424, 3440, 3441, 3461, 3462, 3606

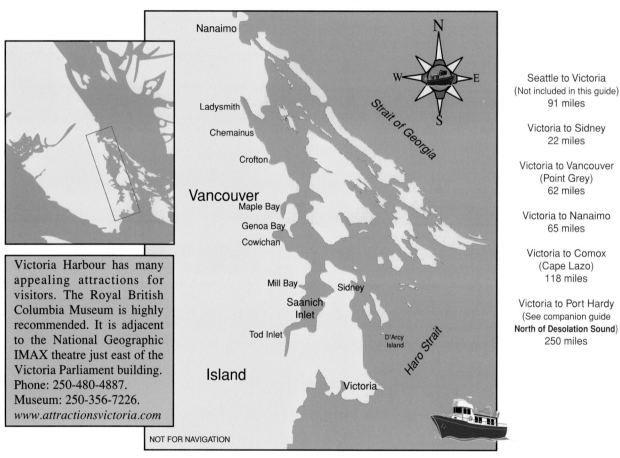

Victoria Harbour has many appealing attractions for visitors. The Royal British Columbia Museum is highly recommended. It is adjacent to the National Geographic IMAX theatre just east of the Victoria Parliament building.
Phone: 250-480-4887.
Museum: 250-356-7226.
www.attractionsvictoria.com

Seattle to Victoria
(Not included in this guide)
91 miles

Victoria to Sidney
22 miles

Victoria to Vancouver
(Point Grey)
62 miles

Victoria to Nanaimo
65 miles

Victoria to Comox
(Cape Lazo)
118 miles

Victoria to Port Hardy
(See companion guide
North of Desolation Sound)
250 miles

NOT FOR NAVIGATION

Victoria and vicinity

After crossing the waters of Royal Roads off Esquimalt Harbour, and passing Macaulay Point, enter Victoria Harbour between McLoughlin Point and the Ogden Point breakwater. Vessels arriving from across Juan de Fuca Strait or points east, pass Brotchie Ledge keeping clear of the shallows near the light. In summer the prevailing southwesterly winds can become quite strong around Victoria so plan your arrival and departure according to wind predictions. A substantial cruise ships terminal is located at Ogden Point. A floatplane zone exists between **Laurel Point** and Shoal Point. Be wary passing the wharves when cruise ships are moving, and watch

for other large vessels arriving and departing the harbour.

Mariners arriving from US waters should proceed to the customs dock alongside the public marina at Wharf Street. After clearing customs find a slip at the adjacent docks, or at the nearby docks in front of the Empress Hotel. Other moorage is available at the Coast Hotel marina or the large Fisherman's Wharf marina west of Raymur Point between Shoal Point and Laurel Point. There is a 7 knot speed limit approaching the main harbour and a 5 knot limit in the harbour. A small ferry carries passengers between a number of points around Victoria's convoluted shoreline.

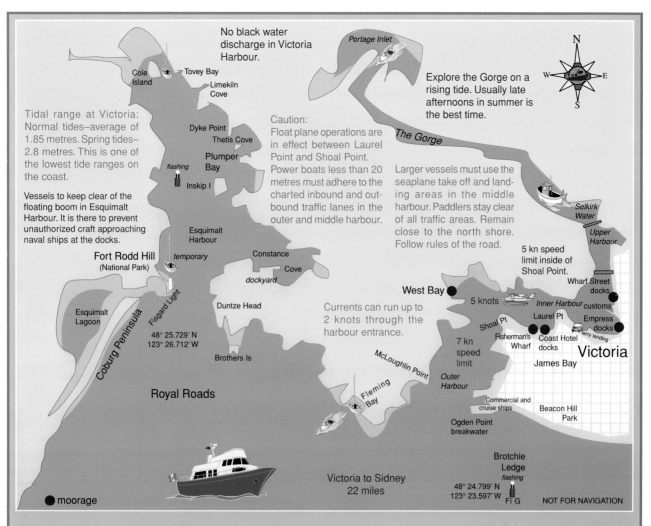

No black water discharge in Victoria Harbour.

Portage Inlet

Explore the Gorge on a rising tide. Usually late afternoons in summer is the best time.

Cole Island

Tovey Bay

Limekiln Cove

Tidal range at Victoria: Normal tides–average of 1.85 metres. Spring tides–2.8 metres. This is one of the lowest tide ranges on the coast.

Dyke Point

Thetis Cove

Plumper Bay

flashing

Inskip I

The Gorge

Caution:
Float plane operations are in effect between Laurel Point and Shoal Point. Power boats less than 20 metres must adhere to the charted inbound and outbound traffic lanes in the outer and middle harbour.

Larger vessels must use the seaplane take off and landing areas in the middle harbour. Paddlers stay clear of all traffic areas. Remain close to the north shore. Follow rules of the road.

Selkirk Water

Upper Harbour

Vessels to keep clear of the floating boom in Esquimalt Harbour. It is there to prevent unauthorized craft approaching naval ships at the docks.

Esquimalt Harbour

Constance Cove

dockyard

5 kn speed limit inside of Shoal Point.

Wharf Street docks

Fort Rodd Hill
(National Park)

temporary

West Bay

5 knots

Inner Harbour

customs

Laurel Pt

Empress docks

ferry landing

Duntze Head

Currents can run up to 2 knots through the harbour entrance.

Shoal Pt

Fisherman's Wharf

Coast Hotel docks

Victoria

Esquimalt Lagoon

Fisgard Light

48° 25.729' N
123° 26.712' W

Brothers Is

7 kn speed limit

James Bay

McLoughlin Point

Outer Harbour

Royal Roads

Fleming Bay

Commercial and cruise ships

Beacon Hill Park

Ogden Point breakwater

Brotchie Ledge

flashing

Victoria to Sidney
22 miles

48° 24.799' N
123° 23.597' W   Fl G

NOT FOR NAVIGATION

● moorage

Coast Victoria Harbourside Hotel and Marina

VHF 66A

48° 25.420' N
123° 22.788' W
Charts 3313, 3441, 3412 (replaces 3415)

146 Kingston St, Victoria BC V8V 1V4
Phone: 250-360-1211 Fax: 250-360-1418
www.coasthotels.com/home/sites/victoria
Moorage and Services: Gas and diesel fuels available at the adjacent fuel dock. Permanent moorage and overnight slips. Reservations required. Power: 30, 50 amp. Water, dry cleaning, showers, washrooms available to guests. Pumpout station. Garbage disposal.
Award winning restaurant in hotel. Dock service to marina guests. Complimentary shuttle to the city. Whale watching tours and other local attractions.

Right: The docks at the Coast Victoria Harbourside Hotel and Marina.

Top: Government Street floats in the Victoria inner harbour.
Above left: Historic homes in nearby residential neighbourhoods.
Above right: The public Fishmerman's dock.

The marina at **West Bay**, has limited transient moorage. Entrance is opposite Shoal Point around navigational aid V23 which marks a reef off the northeast end of Berens Island. A strobe on the island is for float plane operations. A dredged channel is marked by pilings along its north perimeter and a log breakwater extends along the edge of a mud bank opposite the marina. **West Bay Marina** has laundry and showers as well as a quaint restaurant which is open long hours. There is an adjacent RV park and a waterside walkway extending along the north shore to downtown. This walk along the harbour has breathtaking views of the city.

Victoria, BC's capital, is a major harbour with many and varied city attractions within walking distance of its docks. The city's charm is exemplified by the old fashioned horse-drawn carriages, London buses and British style shops. Tourists arrive every summer by air, water and road to visit this British inspired city that was founded as a fort and trading post by the Hudson's Bay Company in 1843. It became the centre of government for the province and is home to the imposing parliament building and Empress Hotel as well as a renowned art gallery, the highly regarded Royal BC Museum of natural history, a wax museum, undersea gardens, maritime museum, and the provincial archives.

Beyond the Johnson Street blue bridge is the **Upper**

West Bay Marina
Phone: 250-385-1831
Some transient moorage. Reservations recommended. Restaurant, washrooms, showers, laundry.

Greater Victoria Harbour Authority
Goverment St Floats (at Empress Hotel)
Phone: 250-383-8326 Fax: 250-383-8306
www.victoriaharbour.org
Transient moorage. Reservations. Water, 30 amp power, laundry, washrooms and showers. Adjacent city centre.

Wharf Street Floats
Phone: 250-383-8326 Fax: 250-383-8306
www.victoriaharbour.org
Transient moorage. Reservations. Water, 20 and 50 amp power, laundry, washrooms and showers. Adjacent city centre.

Fisherman's Wharf (Erie Street)
Phone: 250-383-8326 Fax: 250-383-8306
www.victoriaharbour.org
Transient moorage. Reservations taken for boats 20 m and over. Water, 20 amp power, laundry, washrooms and showers. Fuel dock adjacent. Tidal grid. Garbage disposal. Reservations are required for special events and holidays. Administration offices at 202-468 Bellville St Victoria V8V 1W9.

Top: The public docks at Wharf Street, Victoria. They are home to many visiting boats during the summer as well as to the Victoria floating boat show in April each year. Above: A view of the docks at Laurel Point from the Coast Victoria Harbourside Hotel and Marina.

Above: A moonlit scene across Victoria Harbour from West Bay.

Harbour, **Selkirk Water**, **The Gorge** and **Portage Inlet**. Selkirk Water extends from the Johnson Street bridge to the Bay Street bridge. The Gorge goes from this point to the Tilikum bridge and extends beyond that to Craigflower Park. A small, narrow, tidal entrance leads into Portage Inlet but this is where most, even the smallest boats, turn around. Much of the waterway is subject to tidal current so care should be taken when navigating in The Gorge. Watch out for rowboats and racing skulls that use the waterway frequently. Mind the currents, particularly at the narrows.

The coast from Victoria to Sidney requires passage around the Trial Islands and past Oak Bay. Leaving Victoria, pass Ogden Point and the reefs at Brotchie Ledge following a route around the south end of Trial Islands or carefully chart a course to their north using Enterprise Channel between them and the nearby shore of Vancouver Island. Pass midway between Harling Point and the islands and turn into the passage only when well clear of the north end of Trial Islands to avoid a reef that extends into **McNeill Bay**. Passage should be taken with great care, using the large scale chart 3424.

At high tide the shallows in McNeill Bay indicated on the chart are well covered so steer clear of them and also Mouat Reef as you pass through the east side of the channel. As you approach McMicking Point you will be heading

straight for Mouat Reef and encountering some tide rips, which are quite strong during tidal exchanges. It is safest to travel out of Enterprise Channel until abeam of the northernmost of the Trial Islands before turning east and then heading north for Mayor Channel.

If you are continuing north take a course between Lee Rock and Great Chain Island passing west of the marker at Lewis Reef and then east of Fiddle Reef. Change course for Baynes Channel and keep well off Jemmy Jones Island. Continue into and through Baynes Channel or, to find marina moorage in Oak Bay or anchorage in Cadboro Bay, turn west south of Fiddle Reef.

Oak Bay

To enter Oak Bay, where a substantial marina offers overnight moorage for visitors, rather than cruise through Mayor Channel go the the west of Lee Rock north of Gonzales Point, proceed west of Harris Island and the beacon south of Emily Islet to enter the marina between its breakwater and Mary Tod Island. Here you will find services such as a marine chandlery and a well established restaurant. This is also a recognized customs port.

Take anchorage in **Cadboro Bay** rather than Oak Bay. It is a deeper, more sheltered spot with an easy entrance off

Right: Looking out over Enterprise Channel towards Trial Islands. Passage is possible this side of the islands but care should be taken, especially of Mouat Reef marked by YB at its south end.

Baynes Channel. While occasional south easterly blows will cause some disturbance in the bay, the anchorage is not subject to much danger of dragging. The best anchorage is at the head of the bay over a muddy bottom. Use the south passage to enter the bay when approaching from the east, or from the north around Jemmy Jones Island. For those with reciprocal moorage privileges, the **Royal Victoria Yacht Club** is located in Cadboro Bay. Watch for markers and buoys located in the bay. Oak Bay is not a suitable anchorage.

Discovery and Chatham Islands

Discovery Island and the pristine Chatham Islands, located a mere two miles from Oak Bay, lie at the south end of Haro Strait. This sometimes busy body of water forms the border between Canada and the United States, with the Saanich Peninsula on the western side and the San Juan Islands to the east. It is the route used by large ships to reach Vancouver and other large harbours on the inside passage.

There is no moorage or safe overnight anchorage among them, but they are beautiful, natural islands that justifiably form part of the marine parks system.

Discovery Island is not developed but has some trails for walking. The park has limited facilities such as toilets and wilderness camping but no potable water. Camping fees are in effect. Kayaking is popular in the area and the wilderness camping areas are used largely by visiting paddlers.

Temporary anchorage can be taken in **Rudlin Bay**, **Puget Cove**, off Alpha Islet and in the locally named **Arbutus Cove**.

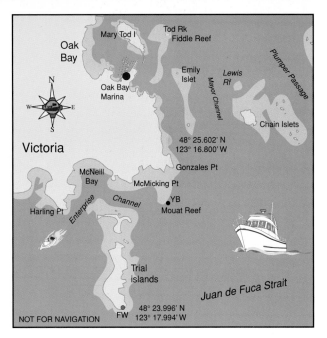

The northern part of Discovery Island and some of the nearby smaller islands are First Nations reserves and should be respected.

Discovery Island was formerly owned by Captain E.G. Beaumont who donated the property to the Parks Branch. An important lighthouse is located at Sea Bird Point for navigation in the tidal waters of the adjacent channels.

Above: Trial Islands from Gonzales Bay showing the east side of Enterprise Channel. Left: From the air, Enterprise Channel is seen clearly with a small boat having just been through. Travel well off the reefs, indicated on chart 3424.

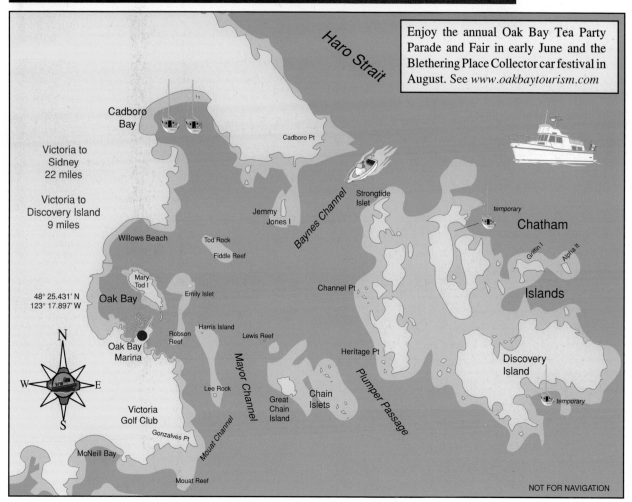

Haro Strait

Enjoy the annual Oak Bay Tea Party Parade and Fair in early June and the Blethering Place Collector car festival in August. See *www.oakbaytourism.com*

Cadboro Bay

Cadboro Pt

Victoria to Sidney 22 miles

Victoria to Discovery Island 9 miles

Strongtide Islet

temporary

Chatham

Jemmy Jones I

Baynes Channel

Griffin I

Alpha It

Willows Beach

Tod Rock

Fiddle Reef

48° 25.431' N
123° 17.897' W

Mary Tod I

Emily Islet

Channel Pt

Islands

Oak Bay

Harris Island

Lewis Reef

Robson Reef

N

Oak Bay Marina

Heritage Pt

Discovery Island

W   E

Mayor Channel

Lee Rock

Chain Islets

Plumper Passage

temporary

S

Victoria Golf Club

Great Chain Island

Gonzalves Pt

Mouat Channel

McNeill Bay

Mouat Reef

NOT FOR NAVIGATION

33

Oak Bay Marina

48° 25.431' N
123° 17.897' W

1327 Beach Dr
Victoria BC V8S 2N4   VHF 66A
Ph: 250-598-3369 Fax: 250-598-1361
www.obmg.com
Charts 3313, 3440, 3424, 3462
Hazard: Rocky entrance. Shoals and shallows–marked with buoys. Consult charts.
Moorage and Services:
Fuel: gas and diesel available at marina fuel dock. Customs phone-in. Permanent moorage and overnight slips. Water and 15 and 30 amp power. Reservations recommended. Mechanic available. Laundry, showers and washrooms are available at the nearby village, on Oak Bay Avenue, a 15 minute walk away. Chandlery, tackle shop, gift shops and others within easy walking distance of the marina. Restaurant, sushi bar, coffee shop. Pleasant views along the waterfront road sidewalks and adjacent Willows Beach.
www.oakbaytourism.com

Above: Oak Bay Marina. Note the entrance past the breakwater off Mary Tod Island. Lower, left: Across Oak Bay towards Baynes Channel. The tip of Mary Tod Island with its FIR (flashing red) light can be seen to the left. Bottom: Oak Bay with boats moored adjacent to the shallows near the beach. Not suitable as an anchorage.
Bird watchers: More than 240 species of birds frequent Oak Bay.

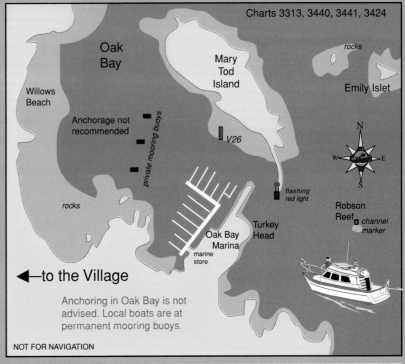

Charts 3313, 3440, 3441, 3424

Oak Bay

Mary Tod Island

rocks

Emily Islet

Willows Beach

Anchorage not recommended

private mooring buoys

V26

rocks

flashing red light

Robson Reef

channel marker

Oak Bay Marina

Turkey Head

marine store

←to the Village

Anchoring in Oak Bay is not advised. Local boats are at permanent mooring buoys.

NOT FOR NAVIGATION

Left: Rudlin Bay, at the bottom of the photograph, is a temporary anchorage off Discovery Island Marine Park. The Chatham Islands, beyond, have lots of rocks and reefs. Baynes Passage and Cadboro Point lie to their northwest.

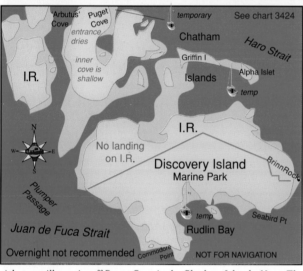

A large sailboat sits off Puget Cove in the Chatham Islands. Note: The channel between the northern Chatham Island is navigable for small boats but is very shallow with drying reefs.

Discovery Island Marine Park can be entered from Plumper Passage by going wide around Commodore Point into Rudlin Bay, or from the east around Sea Bird Point at the south end of Haro Strait. Beware of rocks and shallows in Rudlin Bay and Virtue Rock in Plumper Passage.

You could easily spend lots of time poking around the Chatham Islands and you will find solitude at anchor in a rocky bottomed Rudlin Bay. Enter the anchorage north of Discovery Island by passing south of Alpha Islet where there is temporary shelter for anchoring.

Note the drying rock off Alpha Islet. When travelling along the east side of Discovery Island be aware of the possibility of strong tide rips near the shore.

The closest safe harbour to Discovery Island is Oak Bay. Also nearby is Victoria with its multitude of marinas and docks, commercial and private. When wind conditions are uncomfortable take shelter at a marina.

If you are leaving Cadboro Bay and Oak Bay, continue past the Chatham Islands into Haro Strait for passage to Sidney. Pass Cadboro Point and travel north to Sidney or the

35

Above and left: There are mooring buoys at D'Arcy Island. Approach the temporary anchorage from the west south of the light at the tip of D'Arcy Island. It is a marine park and a noted kayaking destination and has camping facilities for those who plan to stay overnight.

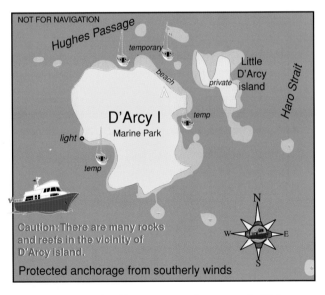

NOT FOR NAVIGATION

Hughes Passage

temporary

beach

Little D'Arcy island

private

Haro Strait

D'Arcy I

Marine Park

temp

light

temp

Caution: There are many rocks and reefs in the vicinity of D'Arcy Island.

Protected anchorage from southerly winds

nearby islands passing Johnstone Reef either side. Pass between Little Zero Rock and Zero Rock, keeping well over towards the larger of the two. Use D'Arcy Shoals as a bearing for the centre of Sidney Channel if you are continuing to the town of Sidney or Sidney Spit, or as a reference for avoiding the drying rock off the northwest side of D'Arcy Island. Pass either side of Little D'Arcy Rock for a heading through Cordova Channel en route to Saanichton Bay or Sidney.

D'Arcy Island

The first anchorage you reach travelling north in Haro Strait is a temporary one, located at D'Arcy Island and Little D'Arcy Island. D'Arcy Island was used in the early part of last century as a leper colony. There are practically no lingering traces of inhabitation.

The island is just south of James and Sidney Islands on the south side of Hughes Passage. To reach D'Arcy Island anchorage approach from the west to the south of the lighthouse. Use great caution as there are numerous reefs and shoals in the vicinity. Other temporary anchorages are found at the north and east sides. This small island is not for

mariners in search of long term anchorage or facilities.

It is preferred by campers who will find nothing more than wilderness camping facilities. Camp fees are in effect. There is no fresh water available on the island.

Little D'Arcy Island is private. Marine parks such as Discovery and D'Arcy are for nature lovers. Birds, marine mammals and other wildlife can be observed close up in these parks. Scuba divers will see some of British Columbia's unique marine creatures in local waters. Limited temporary moorage is available in nearby **Saanichton Bay**.

Sidney Area

Haro Strait, Sidney Island, Rum Island and waterways off Sidney

Charts 3313, 3476, 3441, 3462

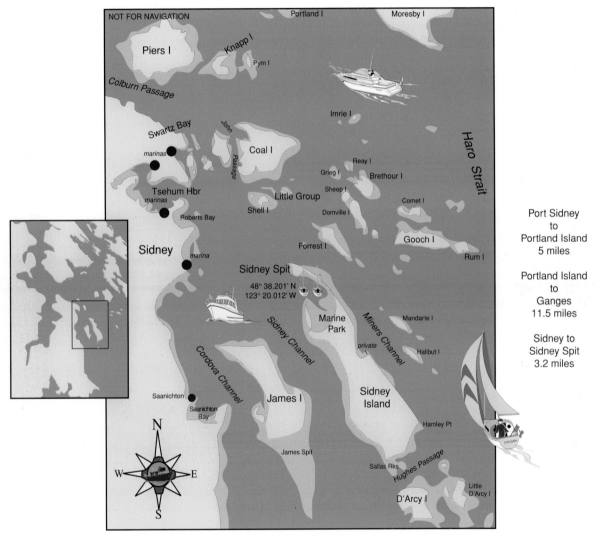

Port Sidney
to
Portland Island
5 miles

Portland Island
to
Ganges
11.5 miles

Sidney to
Sidney Spit
3.2 miles

Sidney Spit

Sidney Island lies between Miners Channel and Sidney Channel. Despite the threat sometimes of a bumpy night, the anchorage at Sidney Spit holds a powerful attraction for most. It is entered from Sidney Channel and although very shallow at places, especially during a low tide, all but very large pleasure boats should be able to slip well into the lee of the spit with little danger of touching bottom. There is one shallow bank that will nearly dry at low tide. It is located on the outskirts of the buoyed area and is shown clearly, as a shallow patch, on the chart. All vessels should consult the large scale chart for the anchorage to avoid this and other shallow areas. There is a lot of activity, small boats and

Above: Sidney Island anchorage lies in the protection of the Spit.
Right: Boats moored in the shallow basin.
Below: A boat lies at anchor close to shore off Sidney Spit.

Part of the land on Sidney Island comprises a popular marine park. The island is located at the west side of Haro Strait, to the east of the town of Sidney. Cordova Channel, James Island and Sidney Channel separate it from Vancouver Island. The long shallow spit at its north end is mostly covered at high tide, but forms a beautiful beach for walking, particularly at low tide.

dinghies in the anchorage and children at the beach so be careful when navigating around the moorings. There are numerous mooring buoys and a dock with space for a limited number of small craft and dinghy mooring. Anchoring in the area is safe and fairly protected although some winds cause discomfort, especially early in the season. It is recommended that you monitor wind forecasts for the area before settling in for a night's sleep at anchor.

A small dock remains in the bight of the spit where an island brickworks loaded bricks for shipping to nearby towns for use in construction. The brickworks were a short way along the path from the dock and pieces of brick can still be found lying in the field. The dock now is used at high tide for temporary stops and landing.

With a short row from a mooring buoy to the docks, which are in place only during summer months, it is a simple matter to go ashore. At weekends in summer a foot passenger ferry from Sidney lands at a designated dock regularly carrying campers and other visitors back and forth. Swimming is a popular pastime at Sidney Spit. There are literally thousands of metres of sandy beach areas and summertime sees beachcombers, scores of sunbathers, day visitors and overnight campers arriving at the park for weekends or longer periods.

The national park reserve area covers the northern third of Sidney Island. This well-preserved marine park is among the best anywhere with its long, shady walk along the water's edge and through the middle of large expansive meadows of Douglas fir and arbutus or madrona trees, with deer roaming freely on the open plain. Campers love this graceful island for its peacefulness so close to the bustle of Sidney and the

nearby ferry landing and island highway traffic. On the west side of the park, overlooking the anchorage, there are camping and picnic facilities including some for groups. The views from Sidney Island are spectacular with the Washington State ferry from Anacortes passing Sidney Spit

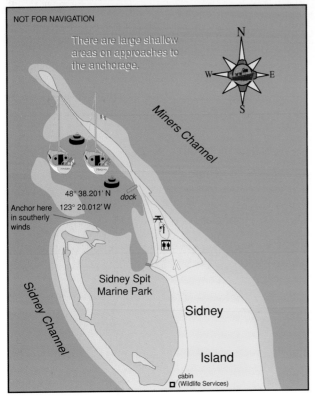

NOT FOR NAVIGATION

There are large shallow areas on approaches to the anchorage.

N
W   E
S

Miners Channel

48° 38.201' N
123° 20.012' W

dock

Anchor here in southerly winds

Sidney Spit Marine Park

Sidney Channel

Sidney

Island

cabin
(Wildlife Services)

Above: The dock at Sidney Spit.

Opposite page top: Sidney Spit points towards Miners Channel where the Anacortes-Sidney ferry runs its daily schedule between US and Canadian ports. Centre: Views across Miners Channel of Forrest, Domville and Gooch Islands and Mandarte Island (on right).

Opposite page, Bottom: The park ranger's boat.

and the sail boats and large visiting American pleasure yachts slipping by en route to and from Port Sidney across the way. An advantage of Sidney Island is that it is very close to downtown Sidney, a distinctively favourite place for mariners who have done any cruising in local waters and know the town.

Haro Strait

Beyond Sidney and Sidney Island there is a group of islands lying north of the Saanich Peninsula (Sidney) and along the west side of Haro Strait. Rum Island and its attached neighbour, Gooch Island, lie east of the town of Sidney. Anchorage between them is temporary.

The group of islands includes a marine park at Portland Island which is included in the Gulf Islands section on page 94. The best anchorage in the group is at Princess Cove on the southeast side of Portland Island.

The former Canadian naval vessel,
MacKenzie, *being sunk as an artificial reef off Rum Island in 1995. It lies about 10 metres beneath the surface off Rum Island and scuba diving activities may be in progress.*

To contact the Gulf Islands National Parks Reserve call 250-654-4000 or see *www.pc.gc.ca/gulf/*

Gooch island is adjacent to Haro Strait and Prevost Passage and can be reached via Haro Strait quite easily. From the anchorage at Sidney Island, pass Sidney Spit and cruise north past the west end of Forrest Island keeping well clear of the rock clearly marked on the chart and visible by the kelp attached to it. Alternatively, passage may be made around the top of John Island or to the south of it taking care to use a large scale chart

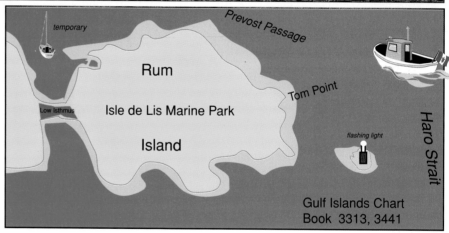

temporary

Prevost Passage

Rum

Isle de Lis Marine Park

Island

Low Isthmus

Tom Point

flashing light

Haro Strait

Gulf Islands Chart
Book 3313, 3441

DIAGRAMS ARE NOT FOR NAVIGATION

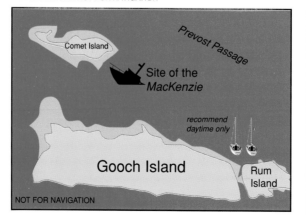

Comet Island

Prevost Passage

Site of the
MacKenzie

recommend
daytime only

Gooch Island

Rum
Island

NOT FOR NAVIGATION

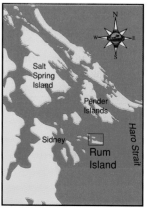

Salt Spring Island

Pender Islands

Sidney

Rum Island

Haro Strait

Rum Island (Isle de Lis), appears attached to Gooch Island (centre top of photo). MacKenzie, pictured at the sinking (opposite page), lies between Gooch and Comet Island (above, centre–marked X). Domville Island is in the foreground, Haro Strait and the San Juan Islands in the distance.

for reef and submerged rock avoidance in the Little Group. Most submerged rocks or reefs are marked by navigational aids, but some reefs extending from protruding rocks are dangerous, especially at low tides.

For a pleasant passage pass between Greig Island and the small island off Domville Island's west side. Then turn east down the passage between Domville and Brethour Island. You may pass between Domville Island and the small island on its west side, but do so with utmost care, slowing down to a no-wake speed in consideration of a small landing serving the private ownership of the island.

Approach Gooch Island and Rum Island either side of Comet Island. Use caution if you take the passage between the two islands, watching for the indicated rocks and shallows in the middle.

Rum Island

It is easy to visit Rum Island and the neighbouring islets while stationed or anchored in Sidney and Sidney Spit. Approach Rum Island from Miners Channel off Sidney Island being mindful of reefs such as South and North Cod Reefs.

From the San Juan Islands Rum Island is almost on the border between Canadian and US waters. Mind the open stretch of water when crossing Haro Strait during windy periods especially if there is a large tide change. Best passages are at slack or near slack tides.

The entire island is a popular park, known as **Isle de Lis Marine Park** and is especially suitable for paddlers.

The park has three walk-in campsites, a park host, points of interest, toilets, hiking, kayaking, fishing, and good nearby scuba diving. It has beach access with a walking trail and a gentle shoreline.

Apart from tenting and relaxing on the island, scuba divers are visiting the area in large numbers since the sinking off Rum Island in September 1995 of the decommissioned *MacKenzie*, a 120 metre former escort ship of the Canadian Navy. It lies in about 10 metres of water beneath the surface.

The adjacent anchorage is best used temporarily during daylight. Most mariners drop the hook just north or south of the drying passage between Rum Island and Gooch Island. Scuba divers exploring the *MacKenzie* use mooring buoys at the site while diving.

Watch for the red and white divers' flag indicating underwater activity and the presense of divers nearby.

Above: The waterfront at Sidney has seen significant changes in recent years. There is a walk along the shore that links the marina with the downtown main street and restaurants, with views over Haro Strait. Opposite page: A view of the large Port Sidney Marina. It has many permanent moored vessels and lots of room for visitors. Summers are very crowded. Make reservations for an overnight stay. There are many things to do in the town of Sidney.

Passage to Portland Island

From Rum Island, pass to the west of Cooper Reef and Arachne Reef then pass Imrie Island to the north taking a course across Prevost Passage and Moresby Passage for the south end of Portland Island. **Moresby Island** has no landings or facilities for boaters. Some indents on its shoreline are used by mariners as temporary anchorages. These are mostly on the northwest and east sides of the island. Two points on Moresby Island, at its north and south ends are its only shoreline features of note. At the south end, Point Fairfax, which juts into Boundary Pass and faces across Haro Strait towards Washington waters, has a prominent international boundary marker. There is no suitable anchorage here but some mariners stop briefly in nooks along the northeast side of the island. Others drop anchor temporarily in the bight of Reynard Point which faces west across Moresby Passage towards Portland Island. This open nook is exposed to westerly winds. The best place to stop is between the reefs and rocks midway beyond the curve of the bight at the north end and Seymour Point to the south.

Continuing from Sidney Spit northwards, it is an easy passage to **Portland Island**, one of the southernmost of the Gulf Islands (see page 94). Travel straight up Moresby Passage between the Little Group and Sunk Rock off Forrest Island. Interestingly at one time a sandy beach, clearly seen on a small pair of islands as you pass by, was used for hauling boats. It is known as Dock Island, now part of the National Parks Reserve of Canada. Other islands in the area that are part of the reserve are Imrie Island, Reay Island, Greig Island and the islets of the Little Group. Access to these is limited and used mostly as stops for paddlers.

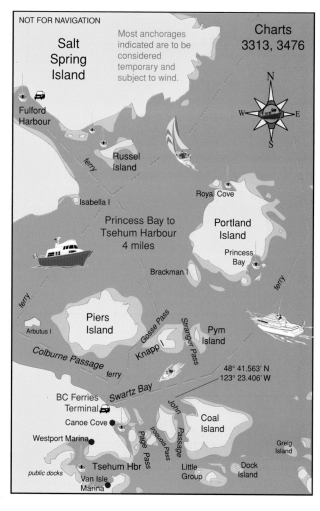

Port Sidney Marina

9835 Seaport Place
Sidney BC V8L 4X3   VHF 66A
Phone: 250-655-3711 Fax: 250-655-3771
www.portsidney.com

48° 39.104' N
123° 23.491' W
Charts 3313, 3476, 3441, 3462

Sidney Events
Sidney Days includes
Canada Day on July 1.
Phone: 250-656-4365.
Summer Market on
Beacon Ave–Thursday
nights 5.30 to 8.30.
Bandstand concerts.
Saanich Fair every
September.

Marina services:

Shorepower at the docks: 15, 30 and 50 amp service. An activities dock may be reserved for group functions.

There are washrooms, laundry, showers and a large office with gifts and souvenirs.

Customs service is available at check in. BroadbandXpress internet service is available. Cable TV is available at most slips. Restaurants are located adjacent and uptown. Consider the restaurants at Tsehum Harbour, Canoe Cove or at the Sidney waterfront where you will find an eclectic selection of establishments. A water taxi service is available to other, nearby marinas. Stores in Sidney include supermarkets, book shops and marine hardware. Ferries nearby to BC mainland and US ports. For anchorage try Sidney Spit, located in Sidney.

Saanichton

Transport Canada public dock
Charts 3313, 3441, 3462
Float length 10 metres with lights on the dock. It is located to the south of Sidney in Saanichton Bay. For shops, medical centre and all amenities, go to Sidney (not within easy walking distance).

Above: The marina at Sidney. It is a large, complete facility with many slips and is located close to shops and services.
Left: The public docks in Tsehum Harbour.
Below, left: One of the private docks in busy Tsehum Harbour.

Sidney

Caution: Do not attempt to enter or leave Sidney Marina by way of the opening at the north end of the docks. It is foul with a lot of rocks. Ignore local operators with small boats who sometimes use this reef-filled passage. Always travel by way of the breakwater entrance using the navigational aids to clear the reefs.

The town of Sidney is a popular tourist destination. It is accessible by road on Vancouver Island and is a busy centre for residential shopping and tourism. A large, modern marina near the foot of the town's main road serves mariners seeking overnight moorage with power, water, cable TV hook-up and access to service and supplies. The marina provides moorage for boats and larger yachts. It gives immediate adjacent access to the uptown stores, restaurants and other services. These include artisan centres, marine stores and book sellers. Visit the Marine Ecology Station at Port Sidney Marina.

This is a town that one can visit by water and obtain a totally different feeling of where they are compared with arriving by land. It is picturesque with waterfront hotel, restaurants, a museum and shopping centres. Canoe, kayak and small boat rentals are available. A new Marine Centre is due to open in the Spring of 2007.

Other marinas are located a short distance north at Tsehum Harbour and Canoe Cove where fuel and marine services are available. Customs docks are provided at these marinas. The Victoria airport is located at Sidney and fly-in cruising guests can easily reach you when they are invited to joint you at the marina.

Sidney Events

Sidney Days includes Canada Day on July 1. Thursday nights Summer Market on Beacon Ave–5.30 to 8.30. Bandstand concerts. Saanich Fair every September. Phone: 250-652-3314.

Van Isle Marina is a large home port with many available overnight slips for summer visitors. Check in at the fuel dock on the outer finger at left in the photograph.

Van Isle Marina

2320 Harbour Rd, Sidney BC V8L 2P6   VHF 66A
Phone: 250-656-1138 Fax: 250-656-0182
www.vanislemarina.com

Marina services: Shore power at the docks: 15, 20, 30, 50 and 100 amp service. 120 and 208 volt available. Marine store on fuel dock. Waste oil disposal, holding tank pumpout. Ice, charts, books, fishing tackle, licences, bait and some marine items–life jackets etc. Washrooms, laundry, showers. Yacht broker. Marine mechanical service available. BroadbandXpress wireless internet. Customs service and check in. Dine at the award winning Dock 503 waterfront restaurant–Phone: 250-656-0828. The Latch or Blue Peter restaurants are also nearby. Philbrooks Shipyards adjacent for repairs and modifications. Phone: 250-656-1157.

48° 40.158' N (off breakwater)
123° 24.378' W
Charts 3313, 3476, 3441, 3462

Fuel dock
48° 40.279' N
123° 24.439' W

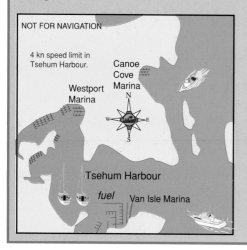

NOT FOR NAVIGATION

4 kn speed limit in Tsehum Harbour.

Westport Marina

Canoe Cove Marina

N
W E
S

Tsehum Harbour

fuel Van Isle Marina

Right: The fuel dock at Van Isle Marina. Overnight moorage and friendly service.

48

Top: Looking north across Tsehum Harbour, the fuel dock lies in the foreground with the anchorage beyond (also middle photo). The public docks are located southwest (left) of the anchorage. More marinas plus some overnight facilities at Westport Marina are in the north end of the harbour. Note Salt Spring Island in the background beyond Satellite Channel.

Bottom: Westport Marina at the head of the harbour. Beyond lies the road to the ferry terminal in Swartz Bay. A boat enters Blue Heron Basin opening off Tsehum Harbour to the west.

Westport Marina
2075 Tryon Rd,
Sidney BC V8L 3X9
Phone: 250-656-2832
www.thunderbirdmarine.com

Tsehum Harbour
Tsehum Harbour Authority
Public Wharf
PO Box 2636
Sidney BC V8L 4C1
Phone: 250-655-4496
www.haa.bc.ca
Floats length is 318 metres. Launch ramp, breakwater, garbage and waste oil disposal, parking, water, lights, power, telephone, washrooms • Adjacent marinas, restaurants, chandlery, haulouts, marine repairs and full shipyard services.

Tsehum Harbour

Tsehum Harbour lies beyond Roberts Point just north of the Sidney breakwater. Beware of Graham Rock as you pass. Enter the wide opening of the harbour between Armstrong Point and Curteis Point off Haro Strait before reaching Fernie Island. Navigate wide around Graham Rock at the tip and south side of the entrance. Slow down to no wake speeds as you approach and enter beyond the breakwater that shelters Van Isle Marina. Here you will find a well equipped fuel

A large power yacht slips along slowly in Iroquois Passage off Goudge Island. Slow down to avoid creating a wash.

and customs dock. The marina offers overnight moorage to all sizes of pleasure yachts. It is well protected from the weather and has all services, yacht brokerage and facilities for mariners. A large adjacent shipyard, Philbrooks, does major overhauls and refits and builds custom yachts. There is The Dock 503 restaurant at the marina and others nearby.

Farther into Tsehum Harbour there are other marinas including Westport Marina which offers space at unoccupied tenants' slips. This marina has a large workyard, a ways and a well-stocked marine chandlery.

Canoe Bay

There are some shallows off Curteis Point to be avoided at extreme low tides. Just south of Canoe Cove Marina is an anchorage known as Canoe Bay. It is sheltered from most conditions year round, but winter winds can cause some discomfort at times. Anchor in locations away from obvious boat passages accessing the marina. Mind the private mooring buoys and anchor in about 2.7 metres, indicated on the chart.

The anchorage should be reached by passage between the Canoe Cove Marina and Kolb Island. There are some obstacles in the adjacent Page and Iroquis Passages when approaching Canoe Cove. Use a large scale chart and exercise great caution. The passages are good between some of the rocks and reefs but be mindful of the currents during tidal

exchanges. For moving between Swartz Bay and Tsehum Harbour the fastest and easiest route is **John Passage**. Some rocks on the approaches to the docks are marked with stakes.

Canoe Cove Marina, located in Canoe Bay, is a long established facility for resident and some transient mariners. The Cove has been associated for many years with the manufacture of pleasure boats which bear its name.

Facilities at Canoe Cove include the Stonehouse Pub, restaurant, yacht brokerage, service and chandlery. There is a resident artist, Morgan Warren, whose work is widely known, located in an A-frame building on the property. A fuel dock can be reached down a long narrow passage alongside C dock. The marina office, located across the parking lot, will be able to allocate moorage, if there is any available, to visiting yachtsmen.

The alternative passages from Canoe Cove into Colburne Passage and Swartz Bay, include a narrow, shallow channel following the shore of the cove northwards immediately west of Swartz Head. There are some boats on mooring buoys off Canoe Cove Marina. Pass them and turn north between the shore and a row of rocks that divide the channel from the outer passages. Colburne Passage runs between the Saanich Peninsula and Piers and Knapp Islands. This is a very high traffic area with ferries arriving and departing frequently. Pass the ferry terminal with care and continue west through

Canoe Cove Marina

2300 Canoe Cove Rd, North Saanich BC V8L 3X9
Phone: 250-656-5566
Fax: 250-655-7197
Service department 250-656-5515
www.canoecovemarina.com

48° 40.966' N
123° 24.025' W
Charts 3313, 3476, 3462, 3441

Moorage and Services: This cosy marina is a classic, with many permanent resident boats and little room for guests. Mariners stop in for fuel at the dock tucked away between docks C and D or to clear customs. There is a homey cafe for breakfast or lunch and early light dinners. For finer fare the Stonehouse Pub a short way behind the marina has an atmosphere that matches its good dining. Special events are celebrated at the restaurant with appropriate meals for the occasion. A water taxi runs from Canoe Cove to Sidney.

The large, full facility boat yard adjacent to the marina has haulout and dry storage space and is operated by the marina. The ways will allow haulouts of larger vessels to 65 tons and the travel lift caters to more average sized boats to 35 tons. A chandlery situated near the cafe carries a wide range of items for repairs, service and annual maintenance.

The property is extensive with a resident artist, the Canoe Cove yacht building yard and yacht sales located on it. Many boat owners at the marina commute by ferry from the mainland and other parts, taking advantage of the marina's close proximity to some of the most favoured cruising destinations on the coast and in the nearby islands. There is a trail from the marina to the BC Ferries harbour.

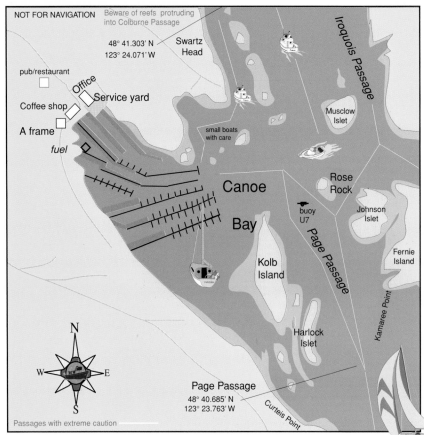

NOT FOR NAVIGATION Beware of reefs protruding
into Colburne Passage

48° 41.303' N
123° 24.071' W

Swartz
Head

Iroquois Passage

pub/restaurant

Office

Service yard

Coffee shop

A frame

fuel

small boats
with care

Musclow
Islet

Canoe

Bay

Rose
Rock

buoy
U7

Johnson
Islet

Page Passage

Kolb
Island

Kamaree Point

Fernie
Island

Harlock
Islet

N
W   E
S

Page Passage
48° 40.685' N
123° 23.763' W

Curteis Point

Passages with extreme caution

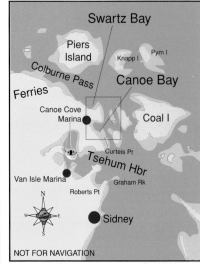

Swartz Bay

Piers
Island

Knapp I   Pym I

Colburne Pass

Canoe Bay

Ferries

Canoe Cove
Marina

Coal I

Curteis Pt

Tsehum Hbr

Van Isle Marina

Graham Rk

Roberts Pt

N
W   E
S

Sidney

NOT FOR NAVIGATION

Diagram of Canoe Bay. There is room to anchor in Canoe Bay and nearby Tsehum Harbour. The passage off Swartz Head is narrow and shallow, for small boats only. Continue well clear of the exit from the passage, northbound, before turning.

Canoe Cove
to
Princess Cove
3 miles

Tsehum Harbour
to
Bedwell Harbour
9 miles

Below: Rocks and reefs on approaches to and in Canoe Bay. Several passages can be used. Refer to chart book 3313, page 7.

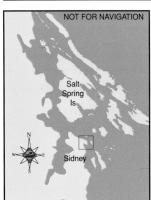

NOT FOR NAVIGATION

Salt
Spring
Is

N
W   E
S

Sidney

Piers Island

This is a Transport Canada public dock
Charts 3313, 3476, 3441, 3462
Piers Island has a manager and is used
primarily for local residents' access.
It is located opposite the BC Ferries Swartz
Bay terminal (Sidney).

Opposite page: Canoe Bay and Canoe Cove Marina. This large permanent mooring marina also offers some overnight moorage. There is a fuel dock and marine store as well as a cosy cafe. The marina has haul out and service facilities as well as a large work yard.

The passages leading to the marina appear intimidating until you have navigated them. Use large scale charts and travel slowly to avoid causing a wash. There are private moorings on some of the small islands adjacent to the waterways.

Photos left show rocks and islets in and adjacent to Iroquois Passage and Page Passage. See diagram on page 52.

Scuba divers enjoy the underwater terrain at Arbutus Island in Satellite Channel. This island lies at the west end of Colbourne Passage and is subject to the wash of ferries passing it en route to Active Pass.

the passage to emerge past Arbutus Island into the eastern reaches of Satellite Channel. Alongside the ferry terminal is a 26 metre public dock with no facilities.

Follow the shore of the peninsula and navigate into Saanich Inlet. If you are travelling into the Gulf Islands from Canoe Cove and Sidney, take Goose Passage between Piers Island and Knapp Island. Smaller boats can run through east of Knapp Island, or take the passage north of Coal Island into Prevost Passage. This leads to Moresby Passage which connects to Portland Island or Salt Spring Island and beyond to the Pender Islands via Haro Strait.

Top: Early morning at Canoe Bay.
Right: Boats tied up at the dock in Deep Cove on the west side of the Saanich Peninsula.
Below: Looking over Moresby island from above the Pender Islands. The view includes Portland Island to the right with Hood Island off its tip, Sidney is to the far right beyond Portland Island. Tiny Imrie Island can be seen beyond Moresby Island.

Saanich Inlet

North Shore of Saanich Peninsula, Saanich Inlet to Cowichan Bay

Charts 3313, 3476, 3478, 3441, 3442, 3462

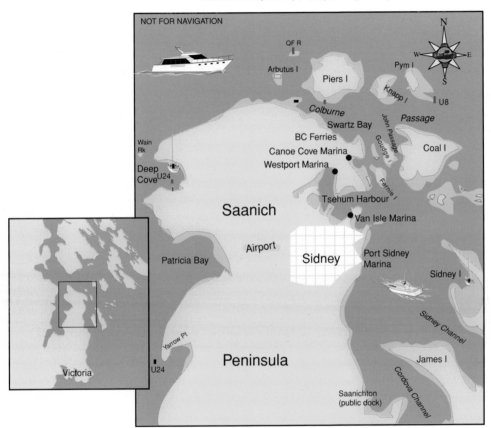

NOT FOR NAVIGATION

Sidney
to Brentwood Bay
12 miles

Brentwood Bay
to Mill Bay
6 miles

Mill Bay
to Cowichan
8 miles

Note:
Speeds should be limited
to 7 knots in Swartz Bay
and the adjacent narrow
passages.

Saanich Inlet

Depart Swartz Bay past **Arbutus Island** into Satellite Channel. You may, however, want to stop at Arbutus Island if you are into scuba diving. It has a most interesting underwater terrain, with a drop off going down the south slope of the east side of the island into a gully covered with huge plumose anemones. Or just drop anchor in the shallows nearby for a lunch break.

Continue around Moses Point at the north end of the Saanich Peninsula into **Deep Cove**. Wain Rock has good water on either side and local fishermen know the virtues of fishing in the vicinity. There is a marina in Deep Cove that offers limited moorage. **Deep Cove Marina** is alongside a large landing located on the south shore of the cove. The dock manager can be reached at 250-656-0060 for more

information. Keep an eye on your chart and depth sounder as there is a drying rock and a reef nearby. Note the red buoy U24 marking the reef and the beacon indicating the rock off the end of the docks. Anchor on the north side of the bay to escape northerly or easterly winds.

Past Coal Point at the south side of Deep Cove lies **Patricia Bay (Pat Bay)**. This is a large open bay with a substantial dock protruding from the centre shoreline. Pat Bay is the location of the Institute of Ocean Sciences which has been the Canadian government hydrographic service headquarters for local marine chart compilation and distribution since the 1960s. There is no facility for pleasure craft at the dock, which lies almost directly under the flight path of the Victoria International airport.

Patricia Bay

Top: The west shore of the Saanich Peninsula (the east shore of Saanich Inlet) looking north. The island in the right foreground is Senanus Island, just north of Brentwood Bay. The deep indentation to the left, beyond Coles Bay and Yarrow Point is Patricia Bay (Pat Bay).
Above: Brentwood Bay with Willis Point in the right foreground. Pass this point eastbound to enter Tod Inlet and visit the Butchart Gardens.

Brentwood Bay

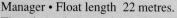

Saanich Inlet
Transport Canada dock
Charts 3313, 3441, 3462
Manager • Float length 22 metres.
There is a private marina and Anglers Anchorage Marina located nearby. Enjoy a walk in adjacent park. This dock is used mostly by commercial traffic for loading and unloading. Holding tank pumpout in south Saanich Inlet is available from Pumpty-Dumpty mobile services. Ph: 250-480-9292. VHF 16 and 66A.

Travel across Saanich Inlet to Mill Bay for fuel, groceries, marina services and moorage. Or head south to Brentwood Bay. Pass Yarrow Point and enter **Coles Bay** for conditional anchorage. Be cautious passing the shoals off Dyer Rocks. Continuing south, pass Henderson Point either side of the marker U23. Stay far enough off the private docks along the shore. Slow down to reduce or eliminate wash.

Enter Brentwood Bay east of Senanus Island and slow down as you approach Slugget Point well before the marina. A reef runs along the outside of the breakwater at the Brentwood Bay Lodge and Spa Marina. It is marked by a red buoy U22 that should be kept to your starboard as you approach the outer dock. The reef lies south of the entrance and should not be overlooked when leaving. Do not pass south of the marker. A ferry landing wharf protrudes from shore immediately north of the marina, and smaller marina installations are located to the north.

Cruise south into **Tod Inlet.** Anchor and dinghy ashore to the Butchart Gardens. Or pass Willis Point to reach the gardens if approaching from Finlayson Arm.

Above: Brentwood Bay Lodge's docks.
Left: View from the lodge restaurant at Brentwood Bay.

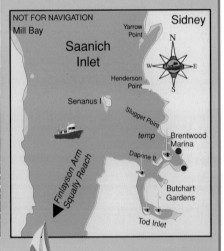

NOT FOR NAVIGATION

Brentwood Bay Lodge & Spa

849 Verdier Ave, Victoria BC V8M 1C5
Toll Free: 1-888-544.2079
Phone: 250-544-2079 Fax: 250-544-2069
www.brentwoodbaylodge.com

48° 34.617' N
123° 28.022' W
Charts 3313, 3441, 3462

Moorage and Services:

Luxury facilities can be found at the waterfront resort overlooking the marina. These include a comfortable lounge and pub, convenience store where ice, fishing tackle, licences, bait, and some provisions are available. Adjacent there is a waterfront restaurant with a magnificent view. The deck is open in good weather and a coffee bar is in operation 7 days a week in summer. Access to pool and jaccuzzi.

The marina is a 65 slip facility with overnight moorage to 80 feet. Reservations are recommended. Wireless Broadband internet access. There is water and 15, 30 and 50 amp power at the dock. Showers, laundry and washrooms are provided. Mechanic and services are available from local and nearby marine operators. There are walking trails or road access and some beach front and parkland walks. Professional fishing guides and rental kayaks are available.

A water taxi is available for access to the historic Butchart Gardens. An alternative is to dinghy in and tie up at the Gardens' dinghy dock. There are fireworks worth attending inside the Gardens on Saturday nights in summer.

Bus, taxi and rentals will get you to downtown Sidney. There is easy access to Victoria, the airport and the BC ferries. Golf, tennis and other recreation can be found nearby. Adjacent to the resort marina is a restaurant with a dock for boat-in customers.

Fuel is available at Mill Bay, Goldstream or Sidney. A launch Ramp is located nearby on First Nations land.

Top: Brentwood Bay with Senanus Island to the left.
Centre, right: Shipyard alongside the Brentwood Bay wharf.
Right, bottom: At the Brentwood Bay Lodge & Spa dock.
Above: The lounge and an art display in the lodge.
Opposite page: Angler's Anchorage Marina.

Angler's Anchorage Marina

48° 34.340' N
123° 27.874' W

Charts 3313, 3441, 3462

933 Marchant Rd,
Brentwood Bay BC V8M 1B5
Phone: 250-652-3531 Fax: 250-652-9923

Marina Entrance:
Deep water moorage–refer to chart 3313 for navigation to avoid shallows.

Moorage and Services:
This is a large permanent marina with limited overnight moorage slips. There is water and 15 or 30 amp power at the docks.

Nearby you will find restaurants and the historic Butchart Gardens. This marina is the closest facility to the Gardens. Stop at the marina, where some overnight moorage is available, and take your dinghy to the dock at the small cove off Tod Inlet.

Bus, taxi and car rentals are available for excursion to downtown Sidney, Victoria, the airport and the BC ferries. There are pleasant walking trails or road access and some beachfront walks. Golf, tennis and other recreation can also be found nearby.

Goldstream Boathouse

48° 29.907' N
123° 33.117' W

3540 Trans Canada Highway
Victoria BC V9B 6H6
Phone: 250-478-4407 Fax: 250-478-6882
Charts 3313, 3441, 3462 **VHF 66A**

This is the site of an historic landmark boathouse built in the 1930s. It is located at the southern tip of Finlayson Arm, well beyond the facilities at Brentwood Bay. Fuel is available as well as some overnight moorage. Water and power are available at the dock. A two-lane marine repair facility offers haulouts to 50 feet.

Photo Carla Vassilopoulos

Butchart Gardens

Butchart Gardens dinghy dock in Butchart Cove. Opposite: A small portion of the gardens.

Passage beyond the marina at Brentwood is uncomplicated and clearly marked as you approach Angler's Anchorage Marina and Tod Inlet beyond. Bby way of either side of Daphne Islet, move to **Tod Inlet** where you can drop anchor in about 5 metres over a muddy bottom and stern tie along the west shore. Mind the rock marked by the green can buoy U21. From Tod Inlet it is possible to watch the fireworks display at Butchart Gardens on Saturday nights in the summertime. Alternatively, you can go by dinghy to the Gardens' dinghy dock in **Butchart Cove** and tour the grounds, taking in the display from the Gardens' spectator area. There are four mooring buoys and space for several boats to drop anchor on the north side of Butchart Cove.

If you decide to venture farther down Saanich Inlet, pass Willis Point to your port and take Squally Reach into Findlayson Arm. Continue to the protected waters of the shallows in the southern extremity where you will find **Goldstream Boathouse**, a marina that caters primarily to permanent moorage customers. It sells fuel and services. There is possible moorage for several boats. Because of its remote location, overnight guests are not frequent and it is best to call ahead to make reservations if you want to stay.

On the west side of Saanich Inlet is **Bamberton**. It is a provincial park with a campground and picnic tables. In good weather a temporary stop off the shallows abutting Johns Creek will provide dinghy access to the beach.

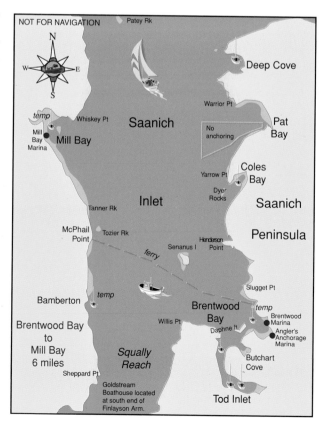

Photos Carla Vassilopoulos

Butchart Gardens Phone Toll Free: **1-866-652-4422**
or visit their site at *www.butchartgardens.com*

The docks at Mill Bay. Plans for big changes to the waterfront were made by new ownership in 2006.

Mill Bay

On the return trip up Saanich Inlet, a fairly straight, open run will get you to the docks at Mill Bay Marina on the western shore. Clear Tozier Rock off the McPhail Point BC Ferries landing. Mill Bay and the marina are sheltered from northwesterly winds in summer, and the breakwater at the marina offers a comfortable stay at the docks even if it is windy. The marina offers fuel at a long, easy to negotiate dock. There is a chandlery at the head of the dock where you can check in for overnight moorage and guest services. A small public dock lies in the shallows just south of the marina. It is too small for any useful purpose. Walk up to the local shopping centre for a tasty cappuccino or shopping at the well-stocked Thrifty Foods market.

There are mooring buoys in the sweep of the bay. These are private and care should be taken to avoid running into them. Temporary anchorage may be taken in 10 to 15 metres over mud and sand.

Saanich Inlet meets Satellite Channel just north of Mill Bay. Cruise into the channel either side of Patey Rock. If your destination is Musgrave Landing or Maple Bay on Salt Spring Island a mid channel course will take you to the north of Separation Point. A course along the Vancouver Island shore passes a private marina at **Cherry Point** that may welcome and accommodate a few small boats overnight. Phone 250-748-0453. Boatswain Bank protrudes well into the channel just beyond Cherry Point Marina but it is deep enough for pleasure craft as long as you do not venture too far into the bight west of the point. Continue into Cowichan Bay following the shoreline along the south shore of Satellite Channel until you reach a large wooden breakwater.

The marina at Mill Bay. There are two launch ramps alongside and it is a short walk to a large shopping centre.

Mill Bay Marina

48° 38.987' N
123° 33.087' W

Charts 3313, 3441, 3462

740 Handy Road, PO Box 231
Mill Bay BC V0R 2P0   VHF 66A
Phone: 250-743-4112 Fax: 250-743-4122
www.millbaymarina.com

Moorage and Services:
There is gas and diesel fuel and water available at the dock. Power is 15 amps at multiple outlets throughout the marina. Laundry, showers and washrooms are also available. Portahead dump. A store at the head of the dock sells marine supplies, fishing tackle and bait and specialises in prawning equipment. Marina and customer services include boats for rent and charters. Mechanic and services can be arranged. The marina has 600' of overnight moorage. Reservations are recommended. Immediate road access and some nearby river and beach trails for walking. There are two launch ramps adjacent to the marina.

The nearby shopping centre has a variety of stores and the grocery store (Thrifty Foods) will deliver purchases to your boat. Private liquor store 7 days a week.

On arrival check in on VHF or at the fuel dock on the south side of the marina for moorage allocation.

Development at and adjacent to this marina was in the works. Expect changes plus new facilities.

Cowichan to Nanaimo

Cowichan Bay, Genoa Bay, Maple Bay, Crofton, Chemainus, Ladysmith, Nanaimo

Charts 3313, 3478, 3475, 3447, 3441, 3442, 3443, 3462, 3463

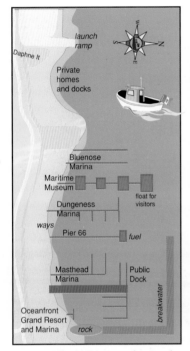

Above: Diagram showing the breakwater and approximate layout of marinas on the Cowichan waterfront.

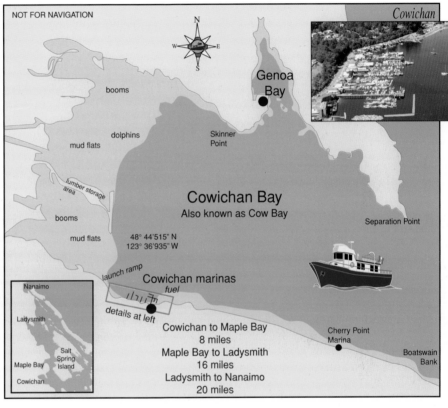

Cowichan Bay

The village of Cowichan Bay is a colourful place with stores, restaurants and marinas lining the waterfront. The docks, many of which have retained a heritage atmosphere, accommodate a large number of local boats as well as some liveaboard vessels and floathomes. Most of these marinas are private and fully occupied by permanent moorage boats and float homes. Visitor moorage is limited but constantly being upgraded.

The large, substantial breakwater added in 2005 has prompted development of the marinas in the bay. Notably, Dungeness Marina, formerly known as Beachcomber Marina, has new, improved docks and additional facilities for visiting boats. Other marinas along the waterfront are also being upgraded. Dungeness Marina docks have a 192

foot float dedicated to transient moorage year round. Check out the community website *www.cowichanbay.com* for local attractions.

The public dock now has an open vista with the removal of a high plank breakwater that used to serve as a protective wall against wind and waves. When the fishing fleet is out there is usually lots of room at the public dock at the east side of town. If the marina is full, moorage may be taken alongside another boat. The outer floats to the west of the wharf are used primarily for visitors and recreational craft. The marina manager's office is located on the wharf and is distinguished by its barnlike appearance.

There is a large modern hotel on the water's edge, facing the entrance to the marina. It has a small dock out front and

mariners visiting the facility as restaurant guests have been welcomed to use it for landing in their dinghies.

Just up from the docks the wharf leads to the main street. There is a selection of restaurants which includes the Masthead Restaurant. It is located in the 1868 building that was originally the Columbia Hotel. The hotel was built by Giovanni Ordano, a settler who established a store, the Cowichan Shipyard and other prominent businesses.

The cosy restaurant is a remnant of the era. It has a reputation for fine food to satisfy the most descriminating of gourmet tastes and a view to match. The wine list includes selections from a nearby vineyard.

The main street of the town is a few blocks long with a selection of book shops, hardware and grocery stores, ice cream vendors, a bakery and cheese store and a liquor store.

Cowichan was a popular recreational fishing centre long before Campbell River and attracted some interesting people. Among them were Bing Crosby, William Boyd (Hopalong Cassidy), Bob Hope, and John Wayne. They would converge on the Buena Vista Hotel, a super luxury establishment that is the present day Cowichan Bay Arms. The shipyard produced boats for the use of these and other visiting sports fishing enthusiasts.

The fascinating Cowichan Bay Maritime Centre (see *www.classicboats.org*), occupies a series of buildings strung out along a pier that stands out as one of the more recently constructed features of the waterfront. It houses very interesting collections of antique outboard motors,

Top and above: In 2005 a breakwater was added to the public marina at Cowichan. Changes are constant and mariners visiting the bay can expect to find new and upgraded facilities at most docks. The maritime museum and tours of nearby vineyards are popular attractions.

commercial fishing equipment, small boat and model displays, marine artifacts and historic photographs.

Private residences built out over the water line the shore west of the marinas and a there is a launch ramp at the far end of these structures. It draws many Vancouver Islanders to launch their trailerable boats on busy sunny weekends.

At the head of Cowichan Bay is the large drying delta of the Cowichan and Koksilah rivers. Abutting the shores are tracts of First Nations land and in mid summer you may be treated to some of their colourful festive days marked by events such as canoe races and the annual regatta off Cowichan Bay village. Another big attraction is the Cowichan Wooden Boat Festival.

Above: View of the new breakwater from the restaurant in the waterfront hotel. Note the open vista from the docks. Left: These are the visitor floats, west of the wharf at the public docks.

Cowichan Bay public docks

Immediately inside the breakwater.
1699 Cowichan Bay Rd, Cowichan BC
V0R 1N1 Phone: 250-746-5911
Overnight moorage available. Use docks on west side behind the breakwater, or as directed. Washrooms, showers, laundry on site. Water, 20 amp power service at docks. Marine repairs, ways, restaurants, shops, and accommodations nearby.

Dungeness Marina

1759 Cowichan Bay Rd, Cow Bay
BC V0R 1N1 Phone: 250-748-6789
www.dungenessmarina.com
Docks with a 192 foot float dedicated to transient moorage year round. Water and 30 amp power at the docks. Washrooms. Showers. Nearby restaurants and stores. Fuel at Pier 66.

Masthead Marina

1705 Cowichan Bay Rd, Cow Bay
BC V0R 1N1 Phone: 250-246-6702
Mostly for permanent moorage. Adjacent to stores, restaurants and facilities. Historic Masthead Restaurant building at the head of the wharf.

Pier 66 Marina

1745 Cowichan Bay Rd, Cow Bay
BC V0R 1N1 Phone: 250-748-8444
www.pier66marina.com
Overnight moorage available. Check in on arrival or reserve. Fuel dock serves gas and diesel fuels, oil, premix, ice and bait. Water and 15 amp power at the dock. Take-out restaurant, whale watching charters and a fish market. Liquor and grocery store adjacent. Close to shops.

Cowichan Boat Festival

www.classicboats.org
—on the third Sunday every June.
Cow Bay Improvement Association:
www.cowichanbay.com

Bluenose Marina

1765 Cowichan Bay Rd, Cow Bay
BC V0R 1N1 Phone: 800-663-7898
Overnight moorage available. Check in on arrival or reserve. Washrooms. Power and water at the dock. Garbage disposal. Kayak sales, rentals, lessons. Restaurant Greek food 250-748-2841.

Oceanfront Grand Resort & Marina

1681 Botwood Lane, Cowichan Bay
BC V0R 1N1 Ph: 1-800-663-7898
www.thegrandresort.com
Small dock located inside breakwater for hotel guests. Hotel, restaurant and all facilities. Near stores and marine services. Pool use for a small fee.

Cowichan is a working harbour. The atmosphere is captivating and visitors are welcome to stop and experience its ambience. Moor at local marinas or the public docks.
Top: The wharf and the barn-like office structure at the public dock.
Centre: Masthead Marina and the historic Masthead restaurant.
Right: The maritime museum at Cow Bay has a day use visitors' float.

There is lots of space for visitors at Dungeness Marina.

Deep traditions

On Vancouver Island, few words carry as much allure as "Cowichan," which means "warm land" in the local First Nation's language. Today, the Cowichan (or Quw'utsun') people who have called the area home from time immemorial still share their name with the lake, river, bay and valley that shape their culture and define the local landscape. European settlers started to arrive soon after Sir Francis Drake's arrival on the shores of Vancouver Island in the early 1700s. Today the Cowichan Valley is home to over 3500 Quw'utsun' First Nations people, the largest tribe in British Columbia. The Cowichan area's scenic beauty, relaxed lifestyle, abundant natural resources and year-round seasonable weather draw visitors from the world over, including many who are pleasantly surprised to learn of the region's rich history and cultural dynamics.

–Courtesy Cowichan Tourism and the Bceh.com Travel Website Network

Photographs left show progress in upgrading docks and creating more space for visitors.
Above: The waterfront Grand Resort and Marina from the public dock at the Cowichan Bay public marina.
Below: Part of the exhibit at the maritime museum in Cowichan Bay.

Genoa Bay Marina

48° 45.468' N   **VHF 66A**

123° 35.738' W

Charts 3313, 3478, 3441, 3442, 3462

1-5100 Genoa Bay Rd, Duncan BC V9L 5Y8

Phone/Fax: 250-746-7621

Toll Free: 1-800-572-6481

www.genoabaymarina.com

Hazard: Entering the bay keep to port of day beacon.
Avoid shore-side marked reef.

Marina services:

This is a large marina with permanent and transient moorage. There is water and 15 and 30 amp power at docks, plus laundry, showers and washrooms. A small but well stocked general store is located on the docks. It has groceries, fishing gear, licences, fresh baked goods and ice. A party dock in the marina will accommodate up to about 60 people. Marine repair service is available. Genoa Bay Cafe, a licensed restaurant with patio service, is directly up the dock on the waterfront. Genoa Bay Art Gallery is located on the docks. There is a barbecue area for guests. Historic Captain Morgan's home bed & breakfast and gift shop overlooks the marina.

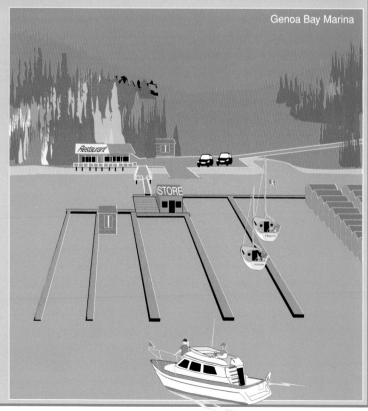

Genoa Bay Marina

The marina at Genoa Bay has a store and an art gallery on the floats.

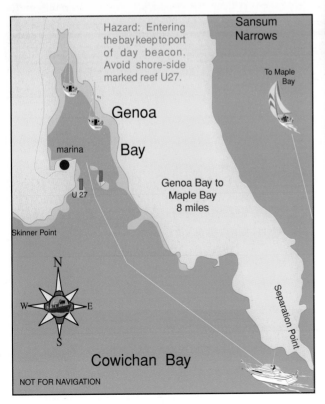

Hazard: Entering the bay keep to port of day beacon. Avoid shore-side marked reef U27.

Sansum Narrows

To Maple Bay

Genoa

Bay

marina

U 27

Genoa Bay to Maple Bay 8 miles

Skinner Point

Separation Point

N
W E
S

Cowichan Bay

NOT FOR NAVIGATION

Genoa Bay

The next port of call after Cowichan Bay is Genoa Bay. Cross Cowichan Bay and enter Genoa Bay between Skinner Point and Separation Point. If you travel via Satellite Channel around the south of Salt Spring Island and are not planning to visit Cowichan Bay you may want to look for moorage or anchorage in the shelter of Genoa Bay. When entering steer clear of the shallows, rocks and reefs in the entrance as indicated on your large scale chart. Keep the near-shore black can buoy reef marker U 27 to port and the red triangular day beacon channel marker to starboard. It is an easy entrance.

There is lots of room to anchor in the bay although the marina will be pleased to have you as a mooring customer.

Above: The entrance to Genoa Bay has a reef to starboard (southeast) and another marked by U 27 to port. Good anchorage is available as seen in the above and right photos.

There is usually space available. A restaurant on the adjacent shore offers meals throughout the day. There is a launch ramp immediatly adjacent to Genoa Bay Marina.

Genoa Bay was named by the Cowichan settler, Giovanni Ordano. His grandson, Ray Ordano, long-time member of Burrard Yacht Club and a good friend of this author, says Genoa Bay was named for Genoa in Italy, Giovanni's birthplace. He lived in Genoa Bay while conducting his substantial businesses in Cowichan Bay.

Genoa Bay has long been a popular anchorage and the site of a busy marina. Genoa Bay Marina sees a flow of visitors year round. It has a store and an art gallery on the docks and a restaurant at the head of the dock. The facilities serving the marina are located ashore, just back of the launch ramp and adjacent to the parking lot.

The renowned historic home, Captain Morgan's, is perched on the rise overlooking the marina and the entrance to the bay. It is a bed and breakfast establishment and has a regular clientele of visitors by land and by water. All guests, including, with reservations, those staying on their boats overnight at the marina, will find a good breakfast menu awaiting them. The house has a large living room with many interesting pieces of art and antiques, and a large sailboat, without the mast of course, suspended from the ceiling. Contact them at *captainmorgans@uniserve.com.*

Satellite Channel

From Saanich Inlet to Cowichan and across to the south side of Salt Spring Island, Satellite Channel is a fairly open stretch of water. It can be rough when the wind blows from the west or east. **Burgoyne Bay** and **Musgrave Landing** are located off Sansum Narrows on the west side of Salt Spring Island. You will pass these two places as you travel through Sansum Narrows. Both have small public docks with somewhat exposed moorage. There is more on Sansum Narrows in the section on Salt Spring Island–(see page 115).

Refuge may be taken at Musgrave Landing, which is a nice spot to visit in summer. It has a small public dock that can accommodate several medium sized boats, but due to its popularity among a regular crowd of visitors, early arrival is necessary to secure a space. The marina on the opposite side of the cove is private.

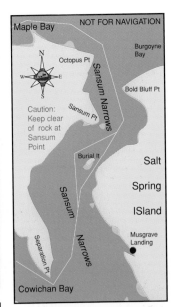

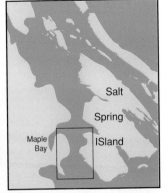

Sansum Narrows

Entering Sansum Narrows after rounding Separation Point east of Genoa Bay take passage either side of Musgrave Rock and then Burial Islet. En route to Maple Bay keep well clear of Sansum Point as the drying rock indicated protrudes farther off than it may appear on your chart. Strong currents run through Sansum Narrows causing whirlpools and eddies between Bold Bluff Point on Salt Spring Island and Sansum Point. It is possible to steer clear of much of the disturbed water by keeping out of the centre of the passage. Your best bet in a slow boat is to avoid maximum flood and ebb.

Top and centre left: Views of Genoa Bay Marina and adjacent anchorage.
Above: Looking south down Sansum Narrows from Maple Bay.
Centre: An antique piano at Captain Morgan's B&B at Genoa Bay
Left: views of the store and the art gallery on the docks.

Right: Bird's Eye Cove and Maple Bay with the lagoon and Chisholm Island in the middle foreground.

Above: The public float at Maple Bay is in the outer bay before approaching Bird's Eye Cove. A shallow patch lies south of the dock.
Left: A view of the docks at Maple Bay Marina.
Bottom: Bird's Eye Cove Marina and Cove Yachts facilities.
Supplies are available at Maple Bay Marina.

Maple Bay

Municipal dock. Phone: 250-715-8186
This is a wharfinger managed float with a total length of 46 metres–see photograph above. Water, lights and public phone are available. There is a restaurant overlooking the bay and a pub a short walk away. A launch ramp is located nearby.

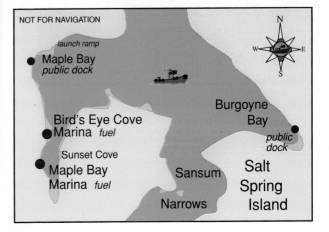

NOT FOR NAVIGATION

launch ramp

Maple Bay
public dock

Bird's Eye Cove
Marina *fuel*

Sunset Cove
Maple Bay
Marina *fuel*

Burgoyne
Bay

public dock

Sansum

Narrows

Salt
Spring
Island

Maple Bay Marina

48° 47.743' N
123° 36.010' W
Charts 3313, 3478, 3441, 3442, 3462

6145 Genoa Bay Rd Duncan BC V9L 5T7   VHF 66A
Phone: 250-746-8482 Fax: 250-746-8490
www.maplebaymarina.com

Moorage and Services: This is a well-known fuel stop serving the Gulf Islands. It has gas, diesel, CNG and propane. Water and 15, 30 and 50 amp power at the docks. Laundry, showers and very clean washrooms are available for guest and permanent moorage customers. Ashore there is the Shipyard Pub & Restaurant with patio service, licenced and open daily year round. The marina complex includes a general store and chandlery, Internet and Broadband services and yacht brokerage. A 50 ton travelift is run by the marine supply store. B&B accommodations are available nearby. Pizza delivery is available after 4 pm. A coffee bar and convenience store is located at the marina. The annual Classic and Wooden Boat Festival is a popular attraction on the May long weekend every spring. Walk or cycle on the adjacent narrow country road. Courtesy van and trips can be arranged to Duncan and nearby golf courses.

There is scheduled float plane service to Vancouver and Salt Spring Island. Car rentals are available.

Maple Bay Marina

Above: Crofton with the ferry landing and public docks behind the breakwater.

Maple Bay

After passing through Sansum Narrows travel along the shore beyond Octopus Point and turn south into Maple Bay. The public dock is located on the west side of the bay. At the head of this dock is a restaurant that is well worth a visit. The pub is a five minute walk away.

As you enter the tapering Bird's Eye Cove you will pass the Maple Bay Yacht Club to your starboard. A large float in the centre of the entrance calls for no wake so slow right down. There are floating homes, fuel docks and boathouses in the cove that should be given due consideration. Beyond the yacht club is Bird's Eye Cove Marina and fuel dock, Cove Yachts marine service facility and beyond, in Bird's Eye Cove, is Maple Bay Marina with its stores and services. Transport can be arranged for excursions into nearby Duncan.

The annual wooden boat festival held at the marina in spring every year attracts many mariners.

Anchorage just off the marina floats and at **Sunset Cove** on the east side of Maple Bay is protected from most winds. However, northwesterly winds can cause a stir.

The lagoon beyond Chisholm Island is too shallow for navigation but is popular among paddlers.

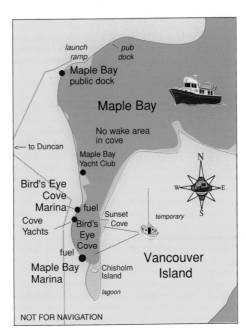

Along the shores of Vancouver Island after departing Maple Bay there is the choice of crossing over to Salt Spring Island or continuing to Crofton. Here a ferry leaves regularly for Vesuvius on Salt Spring Island (see page 114).

An overnight stop at the sheltered harbours of Crofton and Chemainus can be a memorable experience. **Crofton** is a mill town. It has a public marina protected by a large rock breakwater and is usually occupied by fishing boats. When they are away, however, small to medium sized boats can stop to visit the local community. The government docks have room for transient boats in the summer. Off season if there is no room to tie up it is possible, preferably for not too long a stay, to come alongside a docked fishing boat. Fishermen generally do not object to having a boat moored temporarily alongside them. However you may prefer to be tied directly to the dock for easier access to and from your moored boat. The Crofton mill offers free tours. Ask the dock manager for information.

Passage from Crofton to the next refuge along the coast is short but requires staying clear of the substantial shallows around the

New layout of docks 2006

Above: Bare Point serves as a breakwater to Chemainus Bay.
Top: The public dock at Chemainus is located immediately
south of the landing that serves the ferry to Thetis and Kuper islands.
There is limited space at the marina but the harbourmaster will make
an effort to accommodate visitors.

Chemainus named for tribal chief

Tsa-meeun-is, meaning Broken Chest, was a legendary shaman and prophet who survived a massive chest wound and later became chief. His people took his name to identify their own tribal group. By the time of the arrival of the first Europeans the Tsa-meeun-is people had spread from Kulleet Bay and had many villages on the nearby Gulf Islands.

Shoal Islands of which Willy Island is the largest and most prominent. The edge of the shoal is well marked with buoys but to stay clear it is a good idea to take careful bearings on Sharpe Point at the entrance to Ladysmith Harbour.

Chemainus

On coming abeam of Bare Point about two miles beyond the Shoal Islands, a hard turn to port will take you into Chemainus. The small harbour in this quaint town is busy but the wharfinger will direct you to a slip and help you into it. Alternatively find a suitable boat to tie alongside.

After its heyday from the 1800s to mid 1900s, with logging, fishing and mining, the town faced an uncertain future. Chemainus is now famous for its more than 30 artistic murals. It was the first in the region to have these murals, a major feature that has contributed to the town's well-being and success as a tourist destination.

Crofton

Municipal dock. Phone: 250-246-4655
Wharfinger-managed floats (above). Power: 20 and 30 amps and water at the dock. The ferry landing and a launch ramp are adjacent to the marina. Washrooms and showers at Infocentre. A laundry is uptown nearby. Nearby playground, swimming pool and tennis.

Chemainus

Municipal dock. Phone: 250-246-4655
This is a wharfinger-managed float. Water, 30 amp lights and public phone are available. There are restaurants and stores at the historic town centre a short walk away. The docks are adjacent to the Thetis/Kuper Islands ferry landing. Chemainus is on the 49th Parrallel.

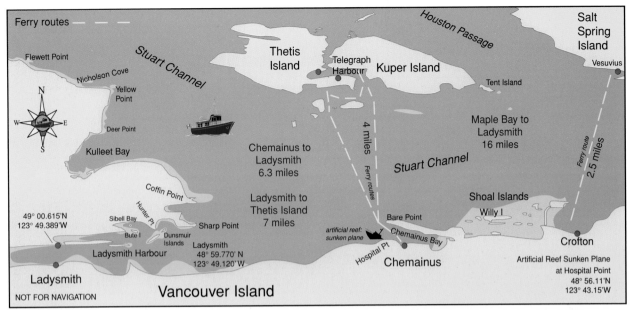

Houston Passage

Salt Spring Island

Stuart Channel

Thetis Island

Telegraph Harbour

Kuper Island

Vesuvius

Flewett Point

Nicholson Cove

Yellow Point

Deer Point

Kulleet Bay

Tent Island

Maple Bay to Ladysmith
16 miles

4 miles

Chemainus to Ladysmith
6.3 miles

Stuart Channel

Ferry route 2.5 miles

Ferry routes

Coffin Point

Ladysmith to Thetis Island
7 miles

Shoal Islands

Willy I

49° 00.615'N
123° 49.389'W

Hunter Pt.

Sibell Bay

Sharp Point

Bare Point

Crofton

Bute I

Dunsmuir Islands

Ladysmith
48° 59.770' N
123° 49.120' W

artificial reef:
sunken plane

Chemainus Bay

Ladysmith Harbour

Hospital Pt

Artificial Reef Sunken Plane
at Hospital Point
48° 56.11'N
123° 43.15'W

Ladysmith

Chemainus

NOT FOR NAVIGATION

Vancouver Island

Below: Scenes on walls of town buildings. These are a sample of more than 35 murals and 13 sculptures that may be found at Chemainus. They depict the history of the town from its First Nations beginnings to its pioneer mining and logging heyday. Today the town is a major tourist destination on Vancouver Island. Its close proximity to the centre of the Gulf Islands makes it easy to reach by water, either directly into its small marina or by ferry from Thetis Island while visiting one of the marinas in Telegraph Harbour.

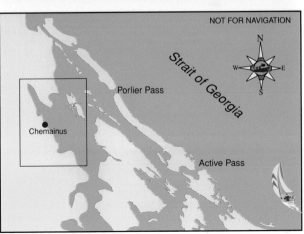

Strait of Georgia

NOT FOR NAVIGATION

Porlier Pass

Chemainus

Active Pass

This town is alive with visitors and year round activity. In summer there are craft sales, flea markets, a steamboat meet and heritage boat show, wine and musical festivals and horse drawn tours. The Chemainus Theatre has regular performances. There is also a well-organized museum a short way into town. Phone the Visitor's Bureau at 250-246-3944 for more information or check out *www.chemainus.com*.

Above: Road access to the docks at Chemainus public marina. New floats have increased dock space. Note the BC Ferries passenger lounge overlooking the marina as well as the ramp to the ferry landing. The marina office is on the wharf.
Right: Nearby anchorage is located beyond Hospital Point. It is mostly shallow and exposed but some mariners take temporary refuge in this bay when the winds are favourable. Note the reefs and shallows, dictating where anchorage is safest. An aircraft artifical reef is underwater to the right.
Below: The anchorage at Sibell Bay. The bay is to the left in the photo. Additional anchorage is found in the lee of the Dunsmuir Islands, right.

48° 56.11'N
123° 43.15'W
Aircraft artificial reef

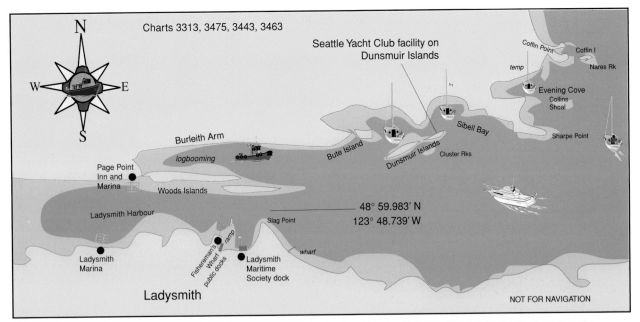

Charts 3313, 3475, 3443, 3463

Seattle Yacht Club facility on
Dunsmuir Islands

Coffin Point   Coffin I

temp   Nares Rk

Evening Cove
Collins
Shoal

Burleith Arm

logbooming

Bute Island   Sibell Bay   Sharpe Point

Dunsmuir Islands   Cluster Rks

Page Point
Inn and
Marina

Woods Islands

48° 59.983' N
123° 48.739' W

Ladysmith Harbour

Slag Point

wharf

Ladysmith
Marina

Fisherman's Wharf   ramp
public docks

Ladysmith
Maritime
Society dock

Ladysmith

NOT FOR NAVIGATION

Below: Anchorage behind the Dunsmuir Islands in Ladysmith Harbour with Bute Island to the left and the Dunsmuir Islands to the right.

Above: Anchorage between the Dunsmuir Islands and Bute Island. Note Ladysmith public docks and the Ladysmith Maritime Society at upper right (see also photo on page 80).

If space is not available at the Chemainus public dock a visit to nearby Thetis Island (see page 174) will afford the opportunity of a short ferry ride to Chemainus.

Ladysmith

It is a short trip along Stuart Channel to Ladysmith and its variety of restaurants and stores. The harbour opens off Stuart Channel which washes the east shore of Vancouver Island and the western shores of Thetis and Kuper islands.

Although open to wind, there are several spots to anchor in the harbour that are somewhat protected. These are in the lee of the rocky islets and reefs that run close along its outer shores. The most popular anchorage is between Bute Island and the **Dunsmuir Islands** or in **Sibell Bay**. Take care and

use a large scale chart for navigating into the cove off Bute Island. Anchor in Sibell Bay or off **Bute Island** in the lee of the Dunsmuir Islands. Respect the adjacent private and First Nations Reserve property. If you are looking for overnight moorage, continue past Slag Point to the inner part of the harbour to Page Point Marina or Ladysmith Marina. An alternative is to stop at Ladysmith Maritime Society dock or the public dock near the entrance to Ladysmith Harbour.

There is a great deal to see and do at Ladysmith. To go ashore and readily reach the town on foot it is easiest to tie up at the substantial government dock to port as you pass the narrows at the harbour entrance. This dock is sometimes occupied with fish boats. A long flight of steps begins the walk to town where you will find all services from banks to

Top: Anchorage behind the Dunsmuir Islands in Ladysmith Harbour with Bute Island in the centre. Bottom: Ladysmith public docks at far right. Entrance is to the west around the north side of the rock breakwater. The Ladysmith Maritime Society, left of public docks, also has overnight moorage available. A drying reef extending to the breakwater from alongside the launch ramp divides the two facilities.

post office, supermarket, bakery, hardware and buildings dating back to the turn of the previous century. Ladysmith is an old coal mining town named for its South African namesake which was under siege during the Boer War before being relieved by British troops. The event was coincidental to the founding of Ladysmith in BC. Its naming also honoured the charitable wife of Sir Harry Smith, governor of the Cape Province of South Africa. The town has seen the days of the importance of coal mining and lumber in the early part of the century give way to the tourism industry.

There are beach areas along the substantial shores of the harbour, a launch ramp and park areas with walking paths. The island highway runs along the shore between the harbour and the town. Take care crossing the road to reach the shopping centres.

Across the harbour Page Point Marina is most hospitable to recreational boats. During summer a steady stream of craft call at the lodge for overnight moorage, fuel and supplies. Also a regular clientele check in for the sumptuous meals served at the lodge. Moorage is sheltered and the docks are available for local and visiting boats.

From Ladysmith there are several outstanding Gulf Island destinations close by. Among them are Telegraph Harbour, Wallace Island and Pirate's Cove.

Continuing northwards along the east coast of Vancouver Island from Ladysmith make a wide pass around Coffin Island and the shallows that surround Nares Rock. **Kulleet Bay** and **Nicholson Cove** are exposed with little protection from windy weather. The dock at Yellow Point is used by guests of the Inn of the Sea. Their toll free number is 1-877-384-3456. There is a shallow bay just beyond Yellow Point where elegant waterfront properties have their private

Page Point Inn and Marina offers overnight sheltered moorage, fuel, restaurant and many amenities.

Page Point Inn and Marina

49° 00.615 N
123° 49.389' W
Charts 3313, 3475, 3443, 3463   VHF 66A

4760 Brenton-Page Road
Ladysmith BC V9G 1L7
Phone: 250-245-2312 Fax: 250-245-7546
Toll free 1-877-860-6866
www.pagepointinn.com
Moorage and Services:
Gas and diesel fuel are available. The large marina includes lots of guest moorage space. Power is provided at the dock. Laundry, showers and washrooms are also provided
The licensed restaurant offers fine dining and patio service. It is open during summer months. Walking, cycling and golf nearby afford exercise or recreational excursions. Bed and breakfast accommodations and a fine gift shop are available at the lodge overlooking the marina.

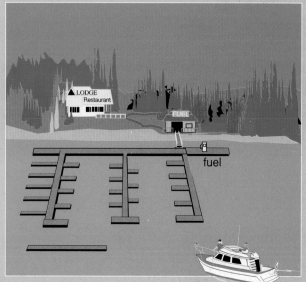

The docks shown at left are at Page Point Inn and Marina with fuel dock and available guest moorage.

Ladysmith Marina

| 49° 00.386' N | Charts 3313, 3475, 3443, |
| 123° 49.618' W | 3463   **VHF 66A** |

12335 Rocky Creek Rd, Ladysmith BC V9G 1K4
Phone: 250-245-4521   Fax: 250-245-4538
Moorage and services: 15 amp power at the docks.
Showers, washrooms and laundry are available in summer.
There is a chandlery, a coffee shop, boat top repair shop
and a welding repair facility. Haulout and boat repairs,
marine services are all available at the marina. Docking to
15.4 metres and marine lift to 9.2 metres'. It is about a one
kilometre walk into town. *www.obmg.com*

Ladysmith Maritime Society dock
Ladysmith BC V9G 1A7 Phone: 250-616-6433.
Close to town–300 metres transient moorage, 15, 30
amp power, washrooms. *www.ladysmithmaritimemuseum.ca*

Ladysmith Fisherman's Wharf
Phone: 250-245-7747. The dock has 615 metres of
dock behind a substantial breakwater. Amenities include
a 4-lane launch ramp, tidal grid, power, water and lights
on the docks, garbage drop and oil disposal. Near
restaurants and shops. *www.ladysmithfishermanswharf.com*

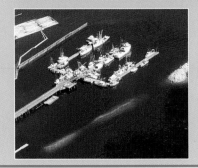

*On the west side of
Ladysmith Harbour,
Ladysmith Marina, above,
offers some overnight
moorage. The public dock,
left, has a large launch
ramp and is near city
amenities.*

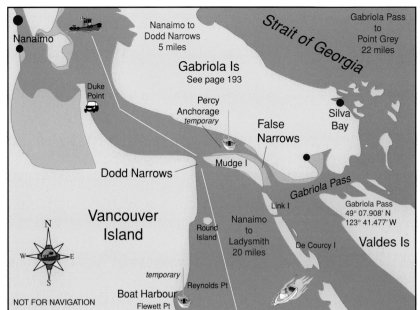

Left: As seen also in the photo below, the white line indicates passage through Dodd Narrows rather than False Narrows. Take the tide into consideration when transiting Dodd Narrows as currents can run up to 9 knots. Pass through at slack, or within one hour, in a slow boat and be very cautious about the faster currents in a fast boat. Wait in Percy Anchorage for slack or near slack water. Use False Narrows only on a medium, rising tide.

Opposite page: On the west side of Ladysmith Harbour, Ladysmith Marina offers some overnight moorage. The marina has adjacent marine service facilities.

moorage. Brief periods at anchor in this bay are possible. Several other indentations along the Vancouver Island coastline may also serve as brief temporary anchorages. **Boat Harbour** opens off Stuart Channel almost midway between Yellow Point and Dodd Narrows. The marina is private and offers no overnight moorage for visitors. Boat Harbour is the only place along this stretch of coastline that offers long term shelter. Possible anchorage may be found in about 4 metres over a mud bottom in the south nook of the harbour in the lee of Flewett Point, or opposite the docks to the south of Reynolds Point. Beware of the reef and rocks that extend well out from Flewett Point and others at the entrance.

Stuart Channel runs from Sansum Narrows past Ladysmith and continues along the Vancouver Island shoreline from the north tip of Thetis Island past Round Island to Mudge Island and Dodd Narrows with the De Courcy Group and Pylades Channel dividing it from Valdes Island. Cross Stuart Channel and take shelter at Ruxton Island or **Pirates Cove** on De Courcy Island (see page 186).

Approaching Dodd Narrows

Use Stuart Channel to approach Dodd Narrows. Pass either side of Round Island and head for the narrows west of Mudge Island. Passage through the notorious Dodd Narrows usually needs some planning, particularly if you have limited power resources in your vessel. Tidal currents can reach 9 knots. Hull speed vessels should exercise particular caution. A fast boat can skim through at most tides but it is always best to play it safe and navigate during slack.

The tidal exchanges and current speeds at Dodd Narrows are given in the official CHS tide tables with little if any calculations necessary. They are also available precisely in the tide tables book *Ports and Passes*.

Once through Dodd Narrows you are on your way to Nanaimo via Northumberland Channel. You will pass the large structure of the Harmac pulp mill and the Duke Point landing for the BC Ferries vessels from Tsawwassen.

Round Jack Point just after the ferries terminal and make a course for McKay Channel beyond the marker P4 off Gallows Point at the south tip of Protection Island to enter Nanaimo Harbour. Be mindful of Satellite Reef in the harbour and the shallow mud flats marked by P9 and P11 just beyond the commercial basin as well as P12 marking the reef off Bate Point on Newcastle Island.

Do not travel southwards after Jack Point as the water shallows out and dries across the entire expanse of the Nanaimo River delta.

Approaches to Nanaimo from the Gulf Islands. Although False Narrows looks wide and inviting, the passage is shallow. The best route is through Dodd Narrows west of Mudge Island (see page 194).

Above: A view of the anchorage at Mark Bay and the waters between Bate Point on Newcastle Island and Protection Island.

Below: Separated from Vancouver Island by Newcastle Passage, Newcastle Island provides shelter for the marinas along Nanaimo's waterfront.

Nanaimo

Marinas, a large Anchorage and Newcastle Island Marine Park

Charts 3313, 3447, 3458, 3475, 3443, 3463

The Bastion was built to protect the employees and families of the Hudson's Bay Company. It is the last freestanding building of its type in North America and the primary historical monument in Nanaimo. It now exists as a museum.

Nanaimo Bastion Museum Society
100 Cameron Road
Nanaimo BC V9R 2X1
Phone: 250-753-1821.

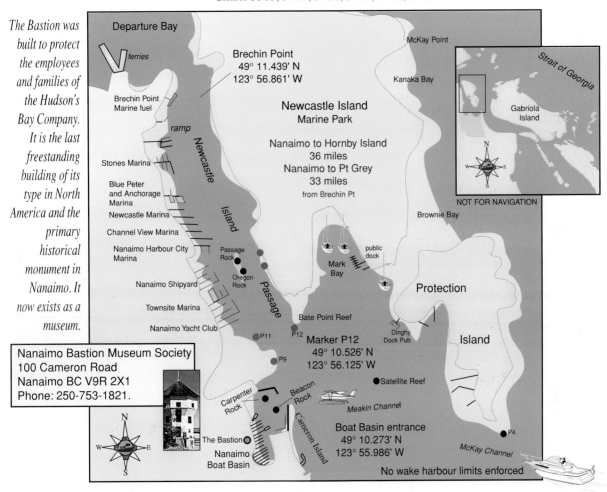

Departure Bay

ferries

Brechin Point
49° 11.439' N
123° 56.861' W

McKay Point

Kanaka Bay

Strait of Georgia

Brechin Point
Marine fuel

ramp

Newcastle Island
Marine Park

Nanaimo to Hornby Island
36 miles
Nanaimo to Pt Grey
33 miles
from Brechin Pt

Gabriola
Island

NOT FOR NAVIGATION

Stones Marina

Blue Peter
and Anchorage
Marina

Newcastle Marina

Channel View Marina

Nanaimo Harbour City
Marina

Nanaimo Shipyard

Townsite Marina

Nanaimo Yacht Club

Newcastle Island

Passage

Passage
Rock

Oregon
Rock

Bate Point Reef

P11

P12

P9

Brownie Bay

Mark
Bay

public
dock

Protection

Dinghy
Dock Pub

Island

Marker P12
49° 10.526' N
123° 56.125' W

Satellite Reef

Carpenter
Rock

Beacon
Rock

Meakin Channel

The Bastion

Nanaimo
Boat Basin

Cameron Island

Boat Basin entrance
49° 10.273' N
123° 55.986' W

P4

McKay Channel

No wake harbour limits enforced

N
W E S

If you are in Nanaimo, visit the floating Dinghy Dock Pub on Protection Island, then cruise across to the moorage at Newcastle Island or anchor off a short ways and go ashore at the Marine Park. The walk around Newcastle Island will work off the healthy sized meal you may have just enjoyed.

Enjoy the fascination of the various aspects of the island with its numerous views of the open Strait of Georgia or across the channel towards Nanaimo. The opportunity to put ashore children or guests who have come along with camping equipment helps break the trip and refresh the skipper for a pleasant cruise home.

Nanaimo and Newcastle Island have a lot to offer the mariner. The city is booming and progressive with lots of history, places of interest, services for the mariner and many festive annual events.

Development of the city of Nanaimo has been fast and furious in recent years. Private marinas and docks are plentiful with several having been upgraded substantially. The waterfront has undergone a massive facelift and new restaurants and public areas have evolved.

The Nanaimo public market is held on Fridays from 10:00 am to 2:00 pm at Pioneer Waterfront Plaza beside the Bastion.

Top: Nanaimo Boat Basin. This is the entrance to the visitor docks. They lie to the right of the blue vessel. The fuel dock can be seen to its left. Cameron Island docks are just inside the breakwater and the anchorage at Mark Bay can be seen in the distance.
Right: Farmers Market every Friday attracts locals and visitors alike.
Right, bottom: It is just a short run across Nanaimo Harbour to the anchorage.

This historic Hudson's Bay structure dates back to 1853. The Farmers Market is made up of farmers, bakers with breads, gourmet cookies and Nanaimo bars, and artisans with many one-of-a-kind items as well as people who prepare jams, pasta, cheese, meats and much more. Each day at noon from May to September sees a ceremony and the firing of one of the two canons that grace the upper level of the plaza.

There is a regular foot passenger ferry service between Nanaimo and Newcastle Island Marine Park in summer. The park's docks accommodate boats but space ashore is shared with the non-boating public. Another foot ferry serves the Dinghy Dock Pub on Protection Island.

Marinas and moorage abound in Nanaimo but space is at a premium and reservations for overnight moorage are highly recommended. Overnight anchorage is available in Mark Bay which extends well out from Newcastle Island towards Protection Island and can be quite crowded on a busy summer weekend. If you drop anchor there be wary of occasional potentially strong wind conditions. The most protected and available moorage is at the Port of Nanaimo Boat Basin in the lee of **Cameron Island**.

Nanaimo Harbour sees a great deal of waterborne recreational activity during the season. It is constantly busy with vessels plying between the large public dock basin, the

Nanaimo

49° 10.273' N
123° 55.986' W   VHF 66A
Charts 3313, 3447, 3458, 3443, 3475, 3463

Above: Nanaimo Boat Basin. Most visitor moorage is located to the left of the entrance and beyond the fuel dock. Cameron Island docks lie immediately beyond the breakwater. Be mindful of currents and wind at the Cameron Island dock. The open area of the basin is used primarily by float planes.

Nanaimo Boat Basin–Port of Nanaimo, BC.
Phone: 250-754-5053 Fax: 250-754-4186
Cameron Island Marina Phone: 250-755-1216.
Port Authority 250-753-4146 *www.npa.ca*
Moorage: Large civic marina with pleasure boat moorage in summer. All amenities include power on docks 15, 20, 30, 50 and 100 amp. Fuel dock has gas, diesel, mixed gas, ice.

Townsite Marina, 20 Townsite Rd
V9R 5T2 Phone: 250-716-8801
Boats 5.5 metres to 30 metres. Located adjacent to the Nanaimo Yacht Club. Washrooms, showers, laundry.

Moby Dick Oceanfront Lodge & Marina, 1000 Stewart Ave V9S 4C9 Phone: 250-753-7111
Vessels to 25 metres. *www.mobydicklodge.com*

Channel View Marina
566 Stewart Ave V9S 5T5 Phone: 250-741-0843
www.channelviewmarina.com

Nanaimo Shipyard Group, 1040 Stewart Ave
V9S 4C9 Ph: 250-753-1151   Chandlery 250-753-1244
www.nanaimoshipyard.com
Moorage, amenities, haulouts, repairs. Vessels to 60 metres.

Nanaimo Harbour City Marina, 1250 Stewart Ave
V9S 4C9 Ph: 250-754-2732 *www.harbourcitymarina.com*
Mostly permanent moorage. Washrooms, showers, laundry. Boatyard, travelift. Power and water. All amenities.

Newcastle Marina, 1300 Stewart Ave V9S 4E1
Phone: 250-753-1431 Guest moorage when available.

Stones Marina & RV Park, 1690 Stewart Ave
V9S 4E1 Phone: 250-753-4232 *www.stonesmarina.com*
Transient moorage available in summer. Washrooms, showers, laundry. Adjacent restaurant/pub on the property.

Anchorage Marina 1520 Stewart Ave V9S 4E1
Phone: 250-754-5585 Guest moorage when available.

Dinghy Dock Pub & Marina Phone: 250-753-2373
www.dinghydockpub.com

   BroadbandXpress is available in Nanaimo. Check with marinas. There is a fish market at the docks. Nanaimo has restaurants, pubs and theatres, arts and crafts exhibits, stores and galleries–all near most marinas. There are many festivities, the most famous being the Bathtub Race every July. Casino nearby. Visit the Dock Shop on the waterfront walkway.

   Walk-on ferries at Nanaimo Boat Basin depart for Newcastle Island and the Dinghy Dock Pub at Protection Island. Or anchor in Mark Bay and dinghy to this favourite floating restaurant/pub. The Newcastle Island Marine Park has docks, walking trails, camping and picnic sites.

Hazard: When proceeding past Oregon Rock use passage cautiously, proceeding between the gateway markers.

Blue Peter Boatyard (at Anchorage Marina) 250-754-7887
www.bluepeterboatyard.com
Petro Canada Marine fuel 250-754-7928, 250-754-7828
Brechin Esso Fuel 250-753-6122. Canada Customs.

Newcastle Island Marine Park–mooring buoys and dock *www.env.gov.bc.ca/bcparks/*

Dinghy Dock Pub on Protection Island and Newcastle Island Marine Park.

One of the biggest events of the summer is the annual sea festival and bathtub race which draws contestants from all parts of the world. While bathtub race speeds are fast, Nanaimo Harbour has strict speeding restrictions in the harbour, so proceed at no wake speeds at all times. Be wary also of floatplanes landing and taking off. Besides speed advisory markers there are other navigation aids to take note of–those marking Satellite Reef, Bate Point Reef, Oregon Rock and a shallow point off Shaft Point on Newcastle Island.

Newcastle Island Passage is a narrow passage with **Passage Rock** and **Oregon Rock** right in the middle, off Nanaimo Shipyard, and requires careful navigation with the best way being along the east side of the markers. Many an unwary mariner has spent time waiting for the tide to rise to float off the hull-ripping reef and the all-too-conveniently-located shipyard has been the beneficiary of those ignominious events. On the west side of Newcastle Island Passage the Nanaimo waterfront is crowded with marinas enjoying the protection of the large breakwater that is Newcastle Island. These are all private with most offering overnight moorage. A waterfront promenade lines the shore.

The **Royal Nanaimo Yacht Club** is located at the south end of the passage. It offers reciprocal overnight moorage to members of other yacht clubs.

Below: A big event in Nanaimo is the international bathtub race held during the city's Sea Festival every July. The bathtub race attracts participants from all over the world. The big bathtub carries race committee members and observers.

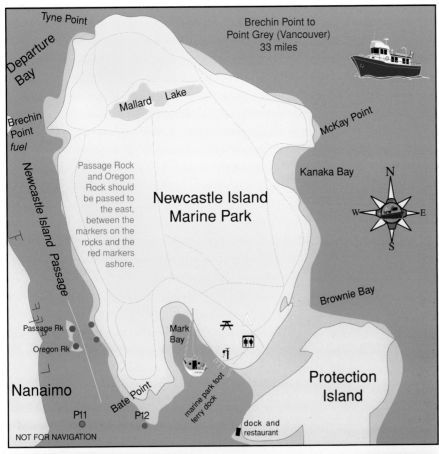

Tyne Point

Departure Bay

Brechin Point to
Point Grey (Vancouver)
33 miles

Brechin
Point
fuel

Mallard Lake

McKay Point

Newcastle Island Passage

Passage Rock
and Oregon
Rock should
be passed to
the east,
between the
markers on the
rocks and the
red markers
ashore.

Newcastle Island
Marine Park

Kanaka Bay

N

W   E

S

Brownie Bay

Passage Rk

Oregon Rk

Mark
Bay

Nanaimo

Bate Point

marine park foot
ferry dock

P11

P12

Protection
Island

dock and
restaurant

NOT FOR NAVIGATION

NOT FOR NAVIGATION

Visitor Centre

The pavilion on Newcastle Island was a focal point from 1931 until after World War ll when the Canadian Steamship Company operated a holiday resort on the island. Today the pavilion houses a visitor centre with static and audio-visual displays depicting the natural and cultural history of the island. The pavilion may be booked by groups and organizations.

Diagram left: Newcastle Island showing the location of the anchorage in Mark Bay as well as the Newcastle Island Passage waterway. Protection Island is separated from Newcastle Island by a drying shallows that can be used only by very small boats (dinghies, kayaks and canoes) at high tide.

Below: A ferry approaches Departure Bay with Nares Point on Newcastle Island to the left and Jesse Island to the right of the passage.

Opposite page top: The busy visitors' dock at the inner basin of Nanaimo's public docks. There is a casual dining facility and a fish and chips eatery on the docks. More restaurants, coffee shops and stores are located along the seawall and nearby in the city. Most visitors use these docks for overnight moorage.

The north end of the Newcastle Island Passage opens into Departure Bay beyond Brechin Point. This is the bay where the BC Ferries land after crossing Georgia Strait from Horseshoe Bay. There is a fuel dock at Brechin Point and another at the public dock in the harbour. In Departure Bay pass to the west of the marker at Shaft Point.

Newcastle Island Marine Park

Opposite Nanaimo and located in the harbour, Newcastle Island can be reached from across the harbour or by entrance to the harbour from the south or the north. Vessels arriving in Nanaimo Harbour from the Strait of Georgia may travel into Departure Bay where the BC Ferry terminal is located, and cruise slowly down Newcastle Island Passage via Brechin Point. They may enter also by way of Meakin Channel and McKay Channel around the south end of **Protection Island**.

Newcastle Island Marine Park is one of the busiest parks in or near the Gulf Islands. There are mooring buoys and a boat dock at the south end of the island for day and overnight use. Temporary anchoring is possible in Mark Bay to the

Anchorage in Mark Bay and Newcastle Passage beyond Bate Point on Newcastle Island. Marine park docks are on the north side of the bay.

northwest of the docks. Vessels also anchor in the shallows adjacent to **Mark Bay** off the drying passage between Newcastle and Protection Islands.

Facilities at Newcastle Island include a foot ferry landing, a boat and dinghy dock, a pavilion with dance floor, food concession, gift shop and snack bar. There are facilities for groups, a barbeque shelter, tables, fire pit, camping, showers, tenting and an adventure playground. Around the island there are picnic areas, toilets, beaches and playing fields and over 20 kilometers of trails for walking and some for bicycling.

Newcastle Island was once a significant coal mining site. A tunnel linking the island to Nanaimo was used for mining operations in the 1800s. Today it still exists but is not functioning, although at one time consideration was given to opening it as a pedestrian passage to the marine park.

Newcastle Island also saw an era of saltery and sandstone quarry operations. There are still remnants of these industries on the island. The San Francisco Mint was built from sandstone quarried on the island. Two columns recovered from the wreck of an early barque, the *Zephyr*, which sank off Mayne Island while delivering the columns to California are now standing near the Perriman quarry site. They were recovered in 1987 by members of the Underwater Archaeological Society of British Columbia and returned to Newcastle Island. The full story of Newcastle Island is told in the book *Newcastle Island, a Place of Discovery* by Bill Merilees. Herring salteries were operated on the island by Japanese fishermen prior to the second world war. It was used also as a shipyard at one time.

One of the attractions of marine parks is their developed campsites and walking trails for general use of the public, whether arriving by boat or by land via ferry. Newcastle Island's Garry oak, arbutus, red cedar and Douglas fir forest incorporates a small lake, campsites and extensive trails.

Other major marine parks in the Gulf Islands are at Sidney Spit, Montague Harbour and Bedwell Harbour which include developed campsites and picnic grounds, places where you can simply stroll or find a place to laze in the sun, on the beach or under the expanse of a large canopy of leafy trees. The substantial dock serving the island is in good repair. Most fingers accommodate smaller boats. There is usually good anchorage or mooring at the numerous mooring buoys placed and maintained by the parks branch, but a wind watch is still necessary.

Not far south of Nanaimo you are into the Gulf Islands and here the joy of sitting at anchor in or near places such as Ganges, Telegraph Harbour or Silva Bay can be rewarded with sightings of eagles or the occasional playful seal. To the north of Nanaimo lies the Northern Gulf Islands. These comprise Denman and Hornby Islands and Lasqueti and Sangster Islands plus a myriad smaller islands and islets.

Southern Gulf Islands

Sidney to Nanaimo

Charts 3313, 3441, 3442, 3443, 3473, 3475, 3476, 3477, 3458, 3478, 3462, 3463

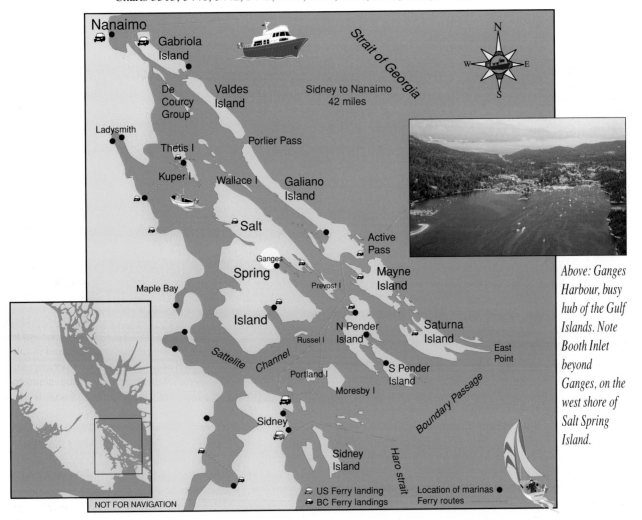

Above: Ganges Harbour, busy hub of the Gulf Islands. Note Booth Inlet beyond Ganges, on the west shore of Salt Spring Island.

There is an eclectic mix of people in the Gulf Islands and nowhere is this more evident than on Salt Spring Island. This centrally located island has a population of earlier settlers who relied on the low cost of living there and newcomers who have acquired lands and homes at increasingly high prices. There are artists, writers, sculptors, lawyers, doctors and actors. There are musicians, artisans, farmers, hoteliers, restaurateurs and numerous bakery, service industry and store assistants. Individuals on welfare sit side by side in the coffee shops with wealthy entrepreneurs, all apparently accepting one another as fellow islanders.

One of the most popular events in the Gulf Islands is the annual lamb roast on Saturna Island. It is held on July 1st (Canada Day), when hundreds of boats will be found at anchor in Winter Cove. A large dinghy dock is in place for the event but small boats can also be landed on the adjacent beaches. Anchorages abound in the Gulf Islands. There are numerous sheltered bays and coves but not all are totally protected from the wind. Nor do all offer ideal holding ground. Knowing the seabed composition helps enable the mariner to determine the right anchor, amount of scope and degree of holding to expect in a breeze. Sandstone cliffs in

The National Parks Island Reserve in the Gulf Islands is shown in green on the diagram to the right. Access to some of these, in particular the smaller islets and areas is restricted. Other parks, which do not fall under the National Island Reserve, are indicated throughout the guide.

Most campsites and trails located in the former provincial parks are now included in the National Park Reserve. These include Sidney Spit, Isle-de-Lis, D'Arcy Island, Portland Island (Princess Margaret Marine Park), Beaumont, Winter Cove and Cabbage Island.

Mooring buoys are located at Cabbage Island, Beaumont Marine Park on South Pender Island and at Sidney Spit. Buoys are subject to removal or change.

Cyclists are welcomed to use the roads on the Pender Islands, Mayne Island and Saturna Island. Note that when walking island roads it is important to be mindful of cars as the narrow pavement and sometimes lack of shoulders can be dangerous for both pedestrians and cyclists.

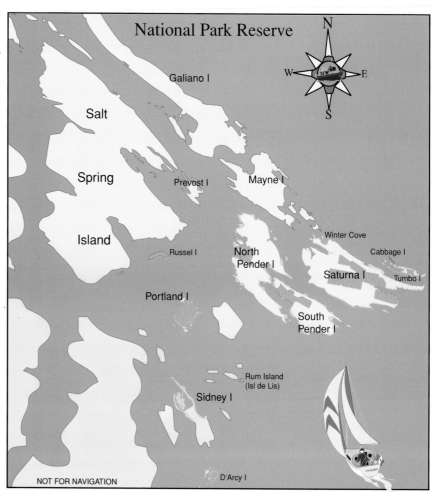

The Gulf Islands National Parks Reserve

The islands in the lower Strait of Georgia known as The Gulf Islands offer many anchoring and mooring alternatives. The diagram shows the main archipelago which makes up the group of islands that are most popular for overnight use. Note the cautions in the text and always be mindful of weather conditions and forecasts.

The Gulf Islands National Park Reserve, officially established in 2003, covers a substantial number of islands, reefs and islets throughout the archipelago. The larger islands and those with established facilities for mariners continue as such but with some improvements, while some of the smaller, lesser islets and reefs are protected and shore access is limited or restricted. Some of these smaller islets are seabird nesting sites or haulouts for marine mammals. Access is denied to the Isabella Islets, Imrie Island, Grieg Island and Reay Island, the Little Group, Sallas Rocks and Unit Rocks. Only kayakers may use the shoreline of Dock Islet. Access and camping is allowed on D'Arcy Island, Portland Island, Rum Island and Sidney Spit. The park areas include water protected zones up to 400 metres offshore of the controlled areas. For more information phone 250-654-4000 or go to *www.pc.gc.ca/gulf* on the Internet.

Please note that marinas in the Gulf Islands generally have very limited water supplies and restricted garbage disposal. They happily supply water, showers or laundry services to their paying moorage guests, on a limited conservation basis.

various parts of the Gulf Islands exemplify the geology of the archipelago. Almost all of the islands are composed of sandstone, shale and conglomerates. This sedimentary rock can be seen particularly on Saturna Island, Galiano Island, Valdes Island and Gabriola Island. Mixed with the conglomerate on these and other islands, there are various compositions of igneous rock, such as on the south end of Salt Spring Island and in the more northerly Gulf Islands (Lasqueti and Texada).

More volcanic (igneous) rock occurs on the south end of Vancouver Island. The composition of the shoreline adjacent to any anchorage helps provide information on the type of seabed in adjacent waters. Your detailed official charts provide information on the nature of the sea floor as well.

Top: Two ferries pass in Active Pass. This is the midway point for them between Swartz Bay in Sidney and Tsawwassen on the British Columbia Lower Mainland. Give them a wide berth and do not impede their headway in confined passages.
Left: Currents run to four knots in narrow passages such as the Pender Canal.

Tides, currents and geology

Tides and currents in the Gulf Islands are basically easy to understand. But do not underestimate them. Many an unwary mariner has run aground by not noting the height of the tides and the times of their lows. Tidal exchanges cover a wide range of height. The farther north the larger the fluctuation, so that at the south end of Vancouver Island you may experience a 2.5 metre tide while in the region of Denman and Hornby islands it could be as much as 5.2 metres.

Different phases of the moon, of course, affect the height of the tides making them larger or smaller at times. It is essential to understand that such fluctuations occur, so that you can allow for the amount of rode deployed when anchoring.

It is the tidal exchanges that determine also the flow of water into and out of the Strait of Georgia, the flow of the Fraser River into the Strait and the currents through the passages that provide entrance to the Gulf Islands.

Erosion renders a constant change to some islands. Sand and gravel deposits left by glacial action are found off the Saanich Peninsula with Sidney Spit a prime example of this phenomenon. Surrounding islands, shorelines and seabeds can be identified by eroding cliffs, light coloured sand and the accompanying good anchor holding grounds. These glacial drift deposits are also found off southern and southeastern Vancouver Island, and are readily identified by the resulting expansive sandy beaches and shallows.

Portland Island and Vicinity

Princess Margaret Marine Park, Russel Island, Moresby Island and BC Ferries Swartz Bay approaches.

Charts 3313, 3476, 3441, 3462

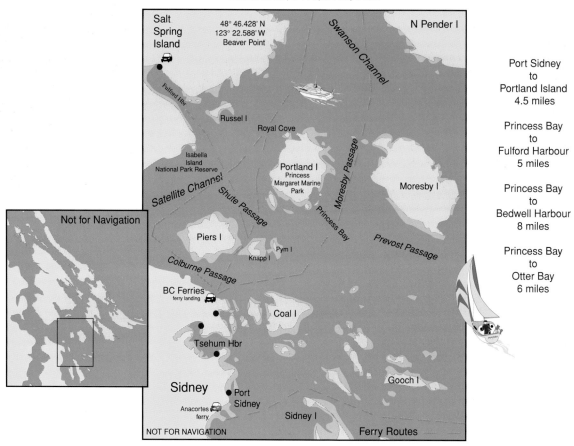

Port Sidney
to
Portland Island
4.5 miles

Princess Bay
to
Fulford Harbour
5 miles

Princess Bay
to
Bedwell Harbour
8 miles

Princess Bay
to
Otter Bay
6 miles

Princess Bay

Portland Island is southeast of Salt Spring Island off Satellite Channel and adjacent to Moresby Passage. It is only a few kilometres away from Sidney. Princess Margaret Marine Park encompasses all of the island and has been a popular day or overnight destination for southern Vancouver Island boat owners for a very long time.

The presence of shoals and reefs around the island, particularly on the east and northeast sides, requires a cautious approach. Use a large scale chart. The northwest and southwest shores have sandy beaches. Anchorage in fair weather conditions is best at Princess Bay and Royal Cove.

At low tide there is not much depth in Princess Bay near the shore. Check your depth before anchoring, especially during a receding tide.

Middens located near Kanaka Bluff reveal that the island was once used extensively by coastal First Nations people. The island was first settled in the 1880s by Hawaiian (Kanaka) immigrants. It was farmed until its transfer to the province. It became a marine park after being acquired by the province in 1967 from Princess Margaret who had received it as a gift commemorating her visit to British Columbia in 1958.

In 2003 Portland Island became part of the national park

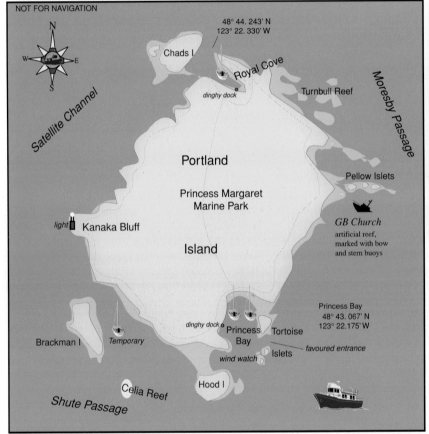

48° 44. 243' N
123° 22. 330' W

Chads I.

Royal Cove

dinghy dock

Turnbull Reef

Moresby Passage

Satellite Channel

Portland

Princess Margaret
Marine Park

Pellow Islets

light

Kanaka Bluff

GB Church
artificial reef,
marked with bow
and stern buoys

Island

Princess Bay
48° 43. 067' N
123° 22.175' W

dinghy dock

Princess
Bay

Tortoise

Temporary

Brackman I.

favoured entrance

wind watch

Islets

Celia Reef

Hood I.

Shute Passage

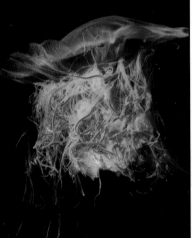

Top: Looking across Satellite Channel towards the Sidney ferry terminal. Portland Island at left and Piers Island to the right. The GB Church *artificial reef is a popular site for scuba diving. It has attracted lots of marine growth since its sinking in about 28 metres in 1989. Divers on the wreck and in other dive sites around BC will see a variety of passing marine creatures such as the large medusa pictured above.*

reserve. Through the park's marine host program, information is provided by volunteers from the Royal Victoria Yacht Club to visitors at a float in Princess Bay during the summer. A lovely trail crosses the island, starting at the apple and plum orchards in Princess Bay.

No access is allowed on nearby **Brackman Island**. It contains rare species of flora and old growth forest with some areas dating back 250 years. Temporary anchorage can be taken behind Brackman Island.

Up the east side of Portland Island Pellow Islets form a slight breakwater for mariners anchoring temporarily so that scuba divers can visit the *GB Church*. This was the first vessel sunk by the Artificial Reef Society of British Columbia. The point where the vessel was sunk off Portland Island is the closest to Moresby Island in Moresby Passage. The 56 metre *GB Church*, was sunk in 1989. Its location is well marked with fixed, permanent buoys for easy diving access.

Tortoise Islets just off Princess Bay also provide some promising scuba diving. Between the islets and Turnbull Reef a vast shallows with rocks and reefs actually attracts a few yachtsmen who know just how to avoid trouble and find their way into a cosy anchorage. This is only for the brave and when weather conditions permit.

If you have not stopped for a day or overnight at Princess Margaret Marine Park you have missed one of the prettiest islands in the area. Portland Island boasts one of the earliest

Above: Temporary anchorage at Princess Bay and Brackman Island (off Kanaka Bluff at far left). The shallow passage is navigable for small boats at high tide. Hood Island is in the left foreground and Tortoise Islets in the centre. Entrance is to their right. (Note: It is very shallow at the head of Princess Bay at low tide.)

Centre and bottom: At anchor in Princess Bay. Rocks off Tortoise Islets are in the foreground. The best entrance is to their north.

established marine parks. It is served by the anchorage in the south in Princess Bay which can be swept by southerly winds at times, so take note when monitoring the wind forecast before settling in for the night.

Park facilities on Portland Island include a dinghy dock, walk-in campsites, toilets, beach hiking and island trails. You are requested to keep dogs leashed.

Royal Cove

This small bay sheltered by Chads Islet in the northwest corner of Portland Island not only provides some anchoring space but also a small dinghy dock for getting ashore easily. A pathway leads through tall timbers and allows a comfortable stop on an expansive outcropping of rock where you can sit and watch the passing ferries, which, by the way, will rock the

Above and left: The anchorage in Royal Cove at the north end of Portland Island. It is quite protected, affected mostly by swells from passing ferries.

Below: Vessels lie at anchor in Princess Bay, one of the most popular anchorages and marine parks in the Gulf Islands. The anchorage is protected from all winds except southerlies and easterlies.

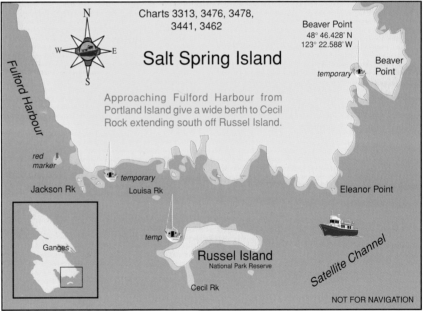

Charts 3313, 3476, 3478,
3441, 3462

Salt Spring Island

Fulford Harbour

Beaver Point
48° 46.428' N
123° 22.588' W

Beaver
temporary Point

Approaching Fulford Harbour from
Portland Island give a wide berth to Cecil
Rock extending south off Russel Island.

red
marker

temporary

Jackson Rk

Louisa Rk

Eleanor Point

Ganges

temp

Russel Island
National Park Reserve

Satellite Channel

Cecil Rk

NOT FOR NAVIGATION

Above: Photograph and diagram, right, show Russel Island. The temporary anchorage is seen at the west side of the island. It is also possible to find temporary anchorage in the lee of the Salt Spring Island shore near Jackson Rock. Some mariners choose to anchor at the head of Fulford Harbour. Do so only if there is no easterly wind in the forecast.

The museum (see page 105), of Bob Akerman, who is descended from the Salish and early settlers, depicts the history and culture of the area. It is located near Fulford Harbour.

vessels anchored in the cove. Enter Royal Cove from the north. Stern tying is recommended. The waterway southward out of the cove is obscured by a reef that protrudes from Chads Islet almost across the entire passage. At high water some adventurous souls will find their way through by keeping well over to the Portland Island shore. At this juncture you are not far from Fulford Harbour on Salt Spring Island where the locals gather at their favourite restaurant right at the ferry landing. Constant activity here creates a colourful aspect of life on the islands. Fulford Harbour is close to Sidney.

Russel Island

Like Portland Island, Russel Island was settled by Hawaiians in the late 19th century. The original house built by the immigrants still remains standing. A caretaker is resident on the island.

Overnight winds can blow towards the island or away from it and are not usually severe enough in summer to cause problems. A watch should be maintained if it blows down Fulford Harbour. Here there is limited but not recommended anchorage with some protection from southeasterlies. But northerlies and northwesterlies can disturb an overnight stay.

Watercolour by the author.

*Top: The Fulford ferry from Swartz Bay, Sidney, looms over the
adjacent public dock at Fulford Harbour.
Above: Bob Akerman in his cultural museum at Fulford.
Right, top: Impression of St Paul's church at Fulford Harbour.
Right: Bob Akerman's doll museum at Fulford.*

Going ashore you will find a trail on the island that wanders
through meadows and a forest of arbutus trees, Garry oak and
firs on the west side of the island. The east side is restricted.

Russel Island is one of several in the marine protected
areas of the Gulf Islands where shore access is allowed. Like
all accessible reserves, keep to the trail to help preserve the
fauna and flora of the area. A few tiny nooks between Eleanor
Point and Jackson Rock on the opposite shore provide
temporary anchorage. However, this shore is occupied by
private waterfront residences and care should be taken not to
obscure any private moorings or run aground on the protruding
reefs such as Louisa Rock, which is safe for most craft at more
than six feet below the surface at low water.

Fulford Harbour

Above: The classic yacht Taconite, *built for William and Bertha Boeing in 1930, cruises out of Ganges Harbour on an excursion through the Gulf Islands.*

Below: Looking across Swanson Channel from the coves south of Beaver Point towards Swartz Bay in the distance. Anchor temporarily only in the north cove. It is exposed to southeast winds.

Hawaiians

Hawaiian immigrant labourers, known as Kanakas, were brought into the Gulf Islands by the Hudson's Bay Company during the fur trade era. Many of them remained in the Gulf Islands rather than returning to their native Pacific islands, some settling on Salt Spring Island, Portland Island, Coal Island and Russel Island. The islands were originally inhabited by people of the Salish First Nations. Middens can be found on Russel Island and others in the archipelago.

Salt Spring Island

Ganges and favoured passages, islets and adjacent anchorages

Charts 3313, 3478, 3441, 3442, 3462, 3463

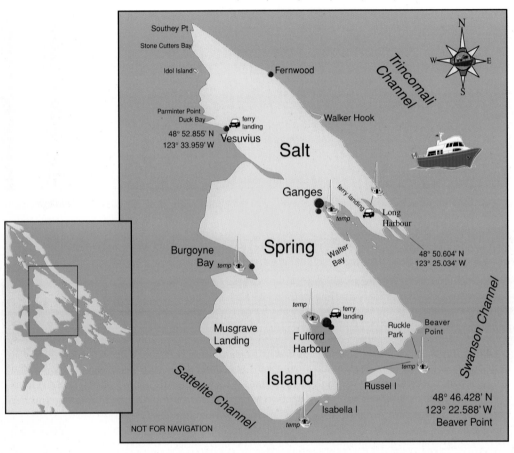

Ganges
to
Active Pass
7.5 miles

Ganges
to
Sidney
15.5 miles

Ganges
to
Fulford Harbour
12 miles

Ganges
to
Montague Harbour
7 miles

Salt Spring Island is the largest of the Gulf Islands and has facilities and amenities similar to mainland and Vancouver Island centres. The harbour at Ganges, the main centre of the island and of the Gulf Islands, is often fully occupied by boats at anchor and in marinas on busy summer weekends.

The earliest settlers on the island were African Americans who fled slavery in the United States in the mid 1800s seeking asylum in Canada. Today Salt Spring Island is the largest and most settled of all the islands in the archipelago. It enjoys some of the mildest weather conditions in Canada. This is one of the reasons people have discovered the island. Today it is populated by a mix of artists, musicians, farmers and craftspeople. There are art galleries and studios offering a choice of high quality arts and crafts from paintings and pottery to weaving, woodwork and sculptures.

Ganges holds an open air market every Saturday morning through the summer, April to October. The town is alive with vendors at the market and musicians in Centennial Park on the Ganges waterfront. Annual summertime events of interest to visiting mariners include the Round Salt Spring race in May, Sea Capers in June, Canada Day celebrations, an antique car show, Festival of the Arts and other cultural events in July, Fulford Day at Drummond Park in August and the Fall Fair at Ganges in September. There are two venues for golfing

Public docks:
Fulford Harbour–Inner dock. Fisheries & Oceans
Phone 250-537-5711
Phone 250-653-4728
The docks have a total float length of 36 metres. Amenities include a garbage drop, lights on the docks, power and a public phone ashore. Adjacent there is the ferry landing to Sidney and ashore there are restaurants and shops.

Fulford Harbour
Outside breakwater. Transport Canada dock Not recommended for overnight moorage. The float length is 16 metres. A public phone is located ashore. Chamber of Commerce Phone: 250-537-4223

The marina, public docks, ferry landing and shallows at the head of Fulford Harbour. Anchor in the shallows in calm conditions.

enthusiasts–the Salt Spring Island Golf and Country Club and the Blackburn Meadows Golf Course. Birdwatching is also popular on Salt Spring Island with over 100 species to be viewed. Visit the island visitor's bureau in Ganges.

Besides Ganges, other settlements of interest to mariners range from little more than a dock at **Fernwood** to the busy ferry landing at Fulford. Oddly the number of marinas that cater to visiting boats outnumber the anchorages along the shores of the island. However there are more anchorages at nearby islands. See the sections on Prevost Island, Portland Island, Wallace Island and Galiano Island.

Travelling north across Satellite Channel after departing Saanich Inlet or Sidney on the Saanich Peninsula a mere five miles will take you to Fulford Harbour. En route it is possible to stop briefly in the cosy nook formed by **Isabella Island** off Isabella Point. Look for an alternative if a southwest wind picks up. We spent the night there once rafted two boats together. The wind came up and we began to drag anchor at about 2 am. We were forced to leave and chose to cruise across Sattelite Channel to the marina at Canoe Cove.

Move on to more protected facilities, perhaps in Fulford Harbour. There is also temporary anchorage where you can stop for a while in the lee of Russel Island.

Fulford Harbour

Fulford Harbour opens into Salt Spring Island off the east end of Satellite Channel and southwest of Swanson Channel. First Nations land occupies the shore adjacent to Jackson Rock and the marked reef that protrudes into Fulford Harbour just beyond.

Farther up Fulford Harbour is the BC Ferry landing, a public dock and Fulford Harbour Marina. Pass Cecil Rock off Russel Island, Jackson Rock to your starboard and the red beacon just beyond it. Enter Fulford Marina just beyond the ferry landing, minding the propwash from a ferry if there is one at the dock at the time. This wash also surges into the marina so wait for the ferry to leave if you are entering a tight space, and tie up securely once you have landed. Easy moorage is on the outside of A Float but check for space with the marina manager. A public dock farther inside the protection of the breakwater is usually full of permanent resident boats. Alongside the marina is **Roamers Landing** fuel dock.

In summer months the long inlet with its shallow head provides temporary anchorage. Monitor wind and weather forecasts before settling in for the night. Winds can cause some discomfort and you may be better off tied up at the nearby marina.

Fulford Harbour Marina

Fulford Marina, to the left, and the public docks in the shelter of the ferry landing to the right. The small facility between the marinas is the Roamers Landing fuel dock.

5–2810 Fulford-Ganges Rd
Salt Spring Island BC V8K 1Z2   VHF 66A
Phone: 250-653-4467 Fax: 250-653-4457
www.saltspring.com/fulfordmarina

48° 46.119' N
123° 27.161' W

Charts 3313, 3478, 3441, 3442, 3462, 3463

Moorage and Services:

Guest and permanent moorage is available in the protection of a large breakwater float. Fuel is available seasonally next door at Roamers Landing. There is water and power at the dock and showers and washrooms on land. Enjoy waterfront gazebos and the barbecue area. A laundry is located off premises. The Fulford Inn, about a kilometre away, has a pub as well as a beer and wine store.

Otters and seals and many species of birds including eagles and herons, can be seen on nearby beaches. Places of interest include nearby historic churches. At the Fulford settlement find funky stores, arts and crafts, bakery, groceries and restaurants.

Drummond Park is located near the inn. Nearby there is Bob Akerman's private museum of native art and local memorabilia and his wife's classic doll collection.

Salmon charters are available. Winery tours: arrangements can be made at Fulford Harbour.

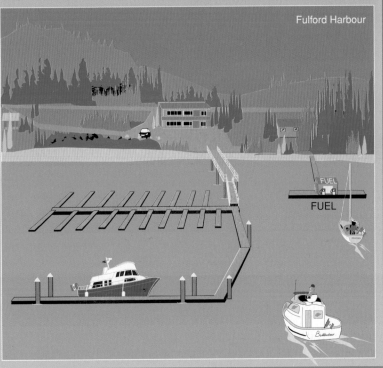

Fulford Harbour

Above: A ferry travels along Swanson Channel towards Swartz Bay at Sidney from the direction of Active Pass.
Campers crowd the Ruckle Provincial Park grounds at Beaver Point on Salt Spring Island.

Left: Boats take temporary anchorage in the cove between Beaver Point and Eleanor Point. See aerial photo on page 100.

If you spend time at the marina or public dock, or if you choose anchoring out and going ashore by dinghy be sure to visit the historic St Paul's Church a short distance along the road. The church once stood at Cowichan Bay but was moved and rebuilt on the present site at Fulford Harbour. The various components of the church were hauled in canoes by people of the First Nations from Cowichan Bay to Salt Spring Island. Walk beyond the church to the old Fulford Pub and Inn for a good pub lunch at its restaurant.

For many years local resident Bob Akerman has run an interesting museum he established a short way along the Fulford Ganges road. It is worthwhile visiting the museum, which is filled with local history and artifacts. Ask him to also show you the massive display of collectible dolls. Returning to the landing at Fulford Harbour, mix in with the local community and enjoy the ambience of the rural atmosphere. In the settlement there are arts and crafts shops, restaurants, a post office and the ferry landing. Fulford comes alive with the arrival of every ferry throughout the year, and particularly with its Fulford Days every August.

Leaving Fulford Harbour for Ganges pass inside of Russel Island keeping clear of Louisa Rock and continue past Eleanor Point towards Beaver Point. It is possible to stop in the snug cove immediately south of **Beaver Point** and anchor in fair weather. Here you will have a magnificent view of passing

Above: Ganges, the popular Gulf Islands destination where every Saturday morning the farmers market attracts a large crowd of visiting mariners. Photo shows part of Madrona Bay and the Chain Islands to the right.

ferries, Ruckle Provincial Park at Beaver Point and Mount Baker lying to the east, looming over the near and distant islands.

Following Satellite Channel into Swanson Channel around Beaver Point enter Captain Passage and pass either side of or between the Channel Islands as you approach Ganges Harbour. Deep Ridge, a long shallow bar, projects southeastwards off the northern of the two islands. It is marked by a green flashing light. Prevost Island on the north side of the passage has good anchorage. (See page 119)

Continue into Ganges Harbour passing Batt Rock either side of its marker. Watch for numerous crab trap floats as you progress towards Ganges.

Ganges

When coming from points such as Porlier Pass or Active Pass (or from Montague Harbour), Ganges Harbour can be entered via Captain Passage from Trincomali Channel between Salt Spring Island and Prevost Island. The harbour entrance faces North Pender Island across Swanson Channel.

Ganges Marina

161 Lower Ganges Road
Ganges BC V8K 2T2   **VHF 66A**
Phone: 250-537-5242 Fax: 250-538-1719
www.gangesmarina.com

Charts 3313, 3478, 3442, 3462, 3463

48° 51.257' N
123° 29.835' W

Ganges Marina is a very busy place in summer. Reservations are recommended, particularly for long holiday weekends.

Moorage and Services: Guest moorage. Reservations taken. Fuel: Gas, diesel, oils and other services are available. There is water at all slips, and power: 15, 30, and 50 amps. The marina offers laundry, showers and washrooms. The marina store has some supplies, including ice, t-shirts and books. BroadbandXpress wireless internet.

Daily, weekly and monthly rental of private rooms or suites.

Coffee and muffins are served in the mornings. Ask about complimentary bikes and baby strollers. Nearby are bakeries, fresh produce, groceries (Thrifty Foods 250-537-1522), restaurants, arts and crafts, hotels, B&Bs, bistros and pubs. Winery tours and golfing nearby. Walk and cycle on the hilly island roads.

Chamber of Commerce Ph: 250-537-4223.

Ganges Marina

Above: Ganges Marina (also opposite) with many boats anchored out in Ganges Harbour on a busy summer weekend. Note the public breakwater outer dock and the L-shaped dock beyond it. This latter dock, known as Kanaka Wharf, has since been extended with additional fingers. The dinghy dock is in the basin between Kanaka Wharf and Ganges Marina. It is adjacent to the downtown shopping centre. Inset: The fuel dock at Ganges Marina.

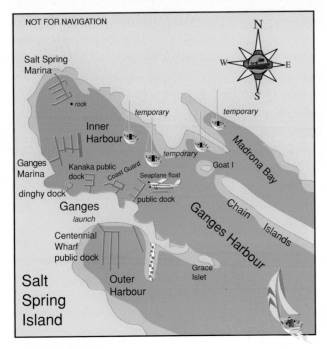

Ganges Harbour can be a windy piece of water and although many vessels moor there it is a place to anchor only temporarily. Monitor the weather for the wind prediction and if you have a comfortable boat with good ground tackle stay at anchor in the harbour overnight, but be mindful of the potential for a disturbed sleep. During summer there can be many tranquil nights anchored in the harbour, but just as many windy nights, with the breeze picking up in the afternoons. It is advisable to arrive early to find space at a marina or stay at a nearby sheltered cove for the night and visit Ganges in the morning. The marinas are busy in summer and it is best to make reservations if you plan to dock for a night or more.

Moorage is available at the outer public docks in the main harbour or, if space permits, at those on the south side of town. Privately operated Ganges Marina and Salt Spring Marina provide overnight and extended mooring with most facilities needed by mariners.

In addition to overnight moorage, Salt Spring Marina provides access to Harbours End Marine and Equipment, an authorized dealership for several brands of engines and other equipment. A licenced restaurant is located alongside.

Above: The popular summertime Ganges Saturday morning market.
Inset: Artwork at Pegasus Gallery.
Left: A group of musicians entertains the crowds in Centennial Park.
Note: Caution should be exercised when walking on roads due to the sometimes heavy traffic and narrow shoulders.

Ganges Marina sells fuel and has many services for mariners. It is located just beyond the breakwater and public docks and has a breakwater dock of its own with protected moorage at its numerous slips.

Ganges is the business centre and hub of the Gulf Islands. It is not only located on the largest of the Gulf Islands but also it has the largest population of all communities in the archipelago. Salt Spring Island residents and visitors by boat

or by road via the BC Ferries system use Ganges as a shopping and cultural centre. The town is alive with weekend shoppers and visitors and it is a most worthwhile place to visit. Things to do include the Ganges Saturday public market, crafts and art galleries, restaurants, coffee shops, bistros and other food establishments, walking and cycling on island roads and some nearby waterfront and beachfront access. Public docks are located nearby with ready access to the town shops.

Activities on Salt Spring Island as well as its renowned arts and crafts attract many visitors. The farmers' market is held on the waterfront on Saturdays and has become a very colourful attraction. It is regarded as one of the best of its kind in Canada. The work of local artists can be seen at the market and also at the art shops and galleries in Ganges. A favourite is Pegasus Gallery. See *www.pegasusgalleryca.com.* Visit also Mahon Hall on the opposite side of the roadway above Ganges Marina. It is the venue for ArtCraft which exhibits the works of over 200 Gulf Islands artists and artisans. Check *www.artcraftgallery.ca* Uptown, the large ArtSpring hall, which is a fascinating building, holds stage events, art exhibits, concerts and theatre performances. Check *www.artspring.ca.*

Shopping at Mouat's historic store provides opportunity to stock up on the items you need for your boating comfort,

Looking south over the anchorage and marinas at the head of Ganges Harbour. The nearest docks seen in the photo are those of Salt Spring Marina. Beyond it lies Ganges Marina with the outer public docks abutting the downtown waterfront. A long, narrow breakwater extends from the small peninsula as protection for the inner public docks, which are mostly occupied by commercial boats.

safety and convenience. The many other speciality, souvenir and book stores in the town will provide hours of pleasurable shopping or window shopping. Check out places such as Mouat's Old Salty Shop, several well-stocked book stores, Thrifty Foods and an eclectic mix of restaurants.

The restaurants are of a variety that will enable you to select from a wide range of menus. Hastings House, one of the top restaurants in Canada, is located in Ganges. The restaurant will take reservations and collect you at your boat for a meal. It is expensive but will provide you a memorable gourmet experience that is hard to match. A favourite casual diner is Barb's Buns where you will find a wide variety of breads, pastries and light meals.

Most of the Salt Spring Island events are focused around Ganges. The more popular of these for mariners include a free

Salt Spring Marina

48° 51.354' N
123° 29.882' W

Chamber of Commerce
Phone: 250-537-4223

Chart 3313, 3478, 3442, 3462, 3463,   VHF 66A

124 Upper Ganges Rd,
Salt Spring Island BC V8K 2S2
Phone 250-537-5810

Moorage and Services: BroadbandXpress wireless internet.
Guest moorage and Seattle Yacht Club station. Water and 15 and 30 amp power at the docks. Showers, washrooms, laundry, plus souvenirs, coffee, ice, bait and fishing gear are available on site. Car, scooter, kayak and boat rentals are available. Moby's Pub serves meals. Hastings House restaurant nearby. Walking on island roads, some nearby waterfront and beachfront access. Adjacent and nearby are restaurants, stores, the Ganges Saturday farmers' market, arts, galleries, groceries, hotels and B&Bs.
An adjacent full service marine business has a chandlery and marine service including haulouts, towing and repairs. Avoid Money Makers Rock off the end of the docks, marked by inflatable buoys.

Harbours End Marine & Equipment Ltd

122 Upper Ganges Rd, Salt Spring Island BC V8K 2S2
Phone 250-537-4202 Fax 250-537-4029
Marine sales and service, chandlery. Located at Salt Spring Marina.

Public docks Phone/Fax: 250-537-5711

Ganges Boat Harbour (Inner Harbour)
Salt Spring Island Harbour Authority
Located behind the breakwater there is 326 metres of dock. Facilities include launch ramp, garbage and oil disposal, water, power, washroom and showers (serves local public docks). Adjacent to restaurants and shops. *Public docks office located here.*

Kanaka Public Visitors Wharf–alongside Coast Guard
Floating breakwater dock with several fingers. Facilities and water and power are available. Adjacent to restaurants and shops. Fuel is available at Ganges Marina.

Ganges Boat Harbour (Outer Harbour)
Breakwater dock with several slips and aircraft landing. Garbage disposal, pumpout, water and power. *Public docks. Check in at office in Inner Harbour for stays over two hours.*

Above: The anchorage and Ganges marinas. Note the reef in the passage between Madrona Bay and Ganges Harbour.

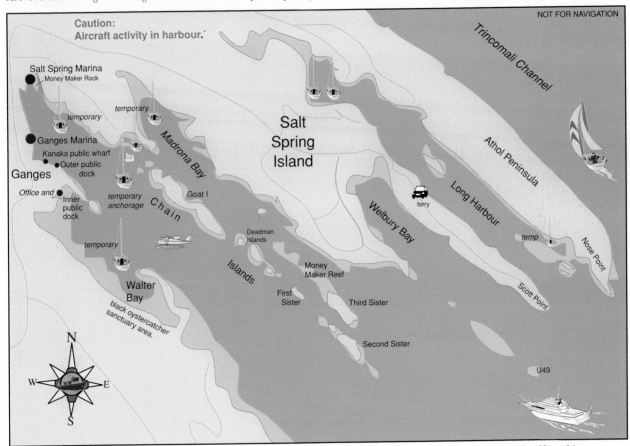

There are temporary anchorages at Walter Bay and Madrona Bay that are not protected from all winds. Ganges Harbour itself is subject to occasional severe wind conditions and when they come in from the southeast you could be in for a night of anchor watch duty.
There is good anchorage nearby at Prevost Island in Annette Inlet or at Glenthorne Passage.

Right: The Inner Harbour behind the breakwater on the south side of Ganges has limited moorage, mostly for permanent customers.

concert and the antique, classic and collectible automobile show on Canada Day and the Fall Fair in September.

If you cannot find moorage at a suitable marina on Salt Spring Island you may want to anchor out in the harbour, or for more protection, around the corner in **Madrona Bay**. This bay lies in the lee of the Chain Islands and is entered from Ganges Harbour by passing either end of Goat Island carefully avoiding the rocks in the passage. Access can be gained also between the rocks off the Deadman Islands and First Sister Island. Keep well clear of the shoals off First Sister Island and pass to the southwest of a beacon marking several tiny rocky islets opposite the Deadman Islands.

The best entrance to Madrona Bay, however, is between Welbury Point and Third Sister Island, when arriving from Captain Passage. When entering Madrona Bay travelling from that direction, stay close to Scott Point and Welbury Point to avoid the shallows marked by green buoy U49 off Welbury Bay. Travel clear of the marker on Horda Shoals when navigating from Captain Passage into Ganges Harbour.

Above centre left and right: Open air businesses give Ganges a Caribbean flavour. The flower shop is located on the waterfront. There are restaurant patios with music and entertainment in summer and arts and crafts, book stores, ice cream vendors, a large supermarket, art galleries and souvenir stores.
Above: Tranquil early morning in Ganges Harbour.

Biggest of the Islands

The population of Salt Spring Island is about 10,000. The island is 185 square kilometres in size. It has 135 kilometres of shoreline and 650 kilometres of roads.

The annual rainfall is 84 centimetres. There are numerous parks including Ruckle Park at Beaver Point and 589 metre high Mount Maxwell.

Above: Three views of Long Harbour with its ferry landing, the Royal Vancouver Yacht Club station and the anchorage at its head.

On the southwest shore of Ganges Harbour **Walter Bay** offers limited anchorage sheltered from southeast winds. The bay is mostly occupied by a private yacht club marina.

If you plan to leave Ganges Harbour by way of Madrona Bay you will have to pass through the narrow opening at the northwest end of Goat Island and take passage along the north shore of the island. Shallow water extends off Deadman Island so navigate closer to the reef marked with the red beacon and then turn to port staying close to the Salt Spring Island shore to avoid the reefs and rocks off the northwest end of Third Sister Island. Pass between Welbury Point and the green marker U 49, remaining closer to the point to avoid the extensive reef that the buoy indicates. Or, you can pass

Salt Spring Island Annual Events

Year round artists studio tours, Around Salt Spring Sailing race in May, Artcraft show and sale June to September, Canada Day Celebrations–Festival of the Arts July 1st, Fulford Days in August, The Fall Fair in September.

midway between Third Sister Island and Welbury Point straight out towards Captain Passage and cruise around the east side of the U49 marker. Welbury Bay offers temporary anchorage in ideal conditions. Round Scott Point to enter Long Harbour and Nose Point to continue into Trincomali Channel, or cross Captain Passage to visit Prevost Island.

Long Harbour

Opening into the southeast end of Salt Spring Island this harbour accommodates a ferry terminal as well as a Royal Vancouver Yacht Club outstation facility. Temporary anchorage may be taken in the lee of the islets at the entrance, beyond Nose Point. The buoy U50 marks a rock off the northwest tip of the islets. The yacht club station is to port as you continue into the harbour. Farther up is a widening bay with a good protected anchorage in shallow water. It is 2.7 metres deep with a mud bottom.

When cruising close to shore, consideration should be given to the boats and homes of local waterfront residents.

The other side of Salt Spring Island

The north shore of Salt Spring Island has little protection for mariners. In Trincomali Channel temporary anchorage in the lee of **Walker Hook** is possible. There is a beach on the southeast side of the promontory that is favoured by locals. Beyond that is **Fernwood** with a small exposed dock. If you were to tie up here with a small boat, try the local restaurant. It comes very highly recommended.

Enter Houston Passage around Southey Point. There is

Right: Walker Hook on the Trincomali Channel side of Salt Spring Island. It affords some protection for a temporary stop to visit the beach.

The dock at Fernwood on the Trincomali side of Salt Spring Island. It is located well to the north along an exposed shore and has limited use due to passing traffic and sea conditions during inclement weather.

Fernwood

Public dock. Walker Hook, Salt Spring Island
Charts 3313, 3442, 3462
Float length 12 metres.
There is little to find at this dock other than a nearby store and restaurant. The dock is exposed to the open waters of Trincomali Channel.

Vesuvius Bay

Capital Regional District public dock. Salt Spring Island.
Phone: 250-537-1638
Ferry landing from Crofton.
Float length 12 metres.
There are two restaurants adjacent to the ferry landing. One has a dock of its own.

temporary anchorage in Southey Bay. Pass Grappler Rock, Stone Cutters Bay and Idol Island heading for points along the south and southwest shore of Salt Spring Island. Round Parminter Point, Duck Bay and Dock Point to enter **Vesuvius Bay**. A public dock adjacent to the Vesuvius ferry landing is relatively sheltered and can accommodate a few small boats. Stop here or at the nearby private dock on the other side of the ferry landing to enjoy a lunch at the waterfront restaurant.

Beyond Vesuvius Bay is **Booth Bay**. If it is calm it is possible to anchor and explore Booth Inlet that opens off this wide bay and extends to within less than two kilometres of Ganges. It can only be done in a dinghy at high tide. There is less than one metre of water in the inlet at low tide and a drying bar seals it off from the bay.

Burgoyne Bay is a deep indentation into the south shore of Salt Spring Island. It opens off Sansum Narrows opposite Maple Bay and has a small public dock at its north end. Towering along the south side of Salt Spring Island Bruce Peak, Mount Maxwell and Mount Sullivan cast their long shadows across the shoreline of Sansum Narrows as well as the Fulford Valley to the east. The shallow end of Burgoyne Bay is a known swimming area in summer. Anchor nearby but

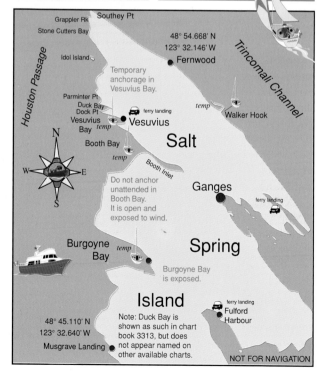

restaurant dock
ferry dock
public dock

Above and left: Vesuvius docks. The top aerial photo shows the landing facing onto Stuart Channel with Houston Passage and Tent and Kuper islands beyond.

Below and bottom: The public dock and the restaurant dock flank the ferry landing.

keep a weather watch for winds from the southeast and the northwest. The latter will also bring a buildup of seas.

Sansum Narrows sees a fair amount of wind. Not necessarily strong, but often when it's not blowing elsewhere. This wind is caused by the hot air off either shore and the tunneling effect of the narrows. Sometimes the wind in Satellite Channel carries into the narrows from the south. Tidal currents in Sansum Narrows run up to three knots and there are frequently rips and swirls, but these are generally not dangerous. Beware of the rock off Sansum Point and steer wide of it. It is possible to travel either side of Burial Islet and Musgrave Rock.

At **Musgrave Landing** there is a dock popular among a group of regular visitors. Take a spot at the dock if you find one. The regulars will make you feel welcome. Do not use the bigger dock on the opposite side of the cove as this is private. The famous round-the-world sailor Miles Smeeton and his family pioneer farmed the adjacent land for many years.

Nearby anchorage and marina facilities can be found at Maple Bay, Genoa Bay and Cowichan Bay (see page 63).

Leaving Salt Spring Island by way of Ganges you

The pub building seen here was closed pending site development.

115

Musgrave Landing with its limited space is a popular weekend spot near Sansum Narrows. Docks in the background are private.

Burgoyne Bay

Salt Spring Island public dock.
Phone: 250-537-5711 Charts 3313, 3478
Float length 10 metres.

Musgrave Landing

Salt Spring Island public dock. Charts
3313, 3478 Float length 12 metres.

may want to travel no farther than Prevost Island. For that unspoiled gem in the Gulf Islands is one of the finest of the lot and once you stop there you may be very disinclined to continue for a while. The island forms a natural breakwater to the outer reaches of Ganges Harbour. Part of the island's appeal is that its land is protected by being incorporated in the National Parks Reserve.

Burgoyne Bay

Eagles, herons and peregrine falcons may be seen in the Burgoyne Valley estuary. The shoreline is their nesting place. Burgoyne Bay lies in a deep fjord beneath Mount Maxwell. It is the largest undeveloped bay in the islands with an expansive shallow area abutting the shoreline. A public dock is located on the approaches to the head of the bay, at the end of a road from the interior of Salt Spring Island. Like several other islands and areas of Salt Spring Island, Burgoyne Bay has a large protected grove of Garry oak.

Top: Maple Bay from Burgoyne Bay.
Right: Running through the south end of Sansum Narrows into Satellite Channel.

Below, left: Looking south along Sansum Narrows from Maple Bay.
Below right: Burgoyne Bay, showing fog rolling in at Sansum Narrows to the right and the exposed public dock at left.

Top: The 1895 light at Portlock Point on Prevost Island is seen after passing through Active Pass into Swanson Channel.
Right: Tranquil Ganges Marina from the outer public dock.
Below: Looking south, Prevost Island, centre, with Montague Harbour on Galiano Island to the left and Nose Point on Salt Spring Island to the right.

Prevost Island

Anchorages and ambience near Ganges, Salt Spring Island

Charts 3313, 3478, 3442, 3462, 3463

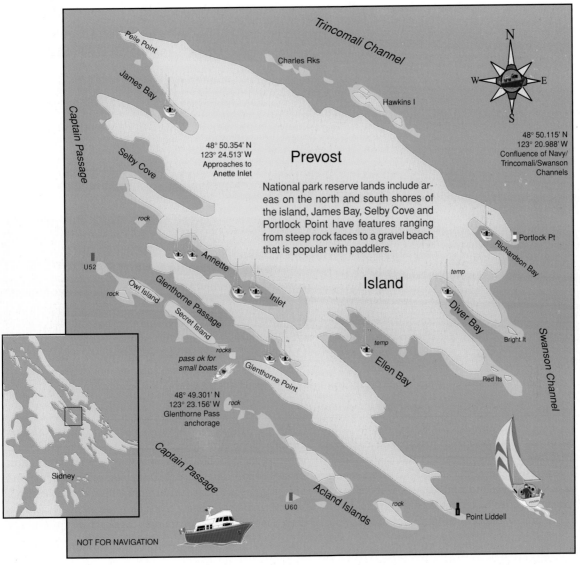

National park reserve lands include areas on the north and south shores of the island, James Bay, Selby Cove and Portlock Point have features ranging from steep rock faces to a gravel beach that is popular with paddlers.

Prevost Island lies directly across Trincomali Channel from the south end of Active Pass. Mariners crossing the Strait of Georgia to enter the Gulf Islands use Active Pass for direct access to Salt Spring Island, the Penders and other popular destinations in adjacent waters, including Prevost Island. Captain Passage, adjoining Ganges Harbour gives access to the west side of Prevost Island and to the protected anchorages of Annette Inlet and Glenthorne Passage. They are among the most protected anchorages in the Gulf Islands. If you moor in Annette Inlet or Glenthorne Passage you can watch amazing sunsets that could have you quickly reaching for your camera. Early on a Saturday morning you may be

Above: Prevost Island's south shore looking northwest from Point Liddell. The Acland Islands are to the left of Prevost Island and entrance to Glenthorne Passage just beyond.
Right: A narrow passage south of Secret Island allows small boats to enter the pass. The favoured anchorage is to the right. Annette Inlet lies beyond.
Below: At anchor in Annette Inlet and Glenthorne Passage.

Prevost Parkland

National parks reserves are located at the north and south ends of Prevost Island. The island is covered in large groves of arbutus and cedar. Most of the island is still private, belonging to the family of Digby De Burgh, who settled there in 1920. The family farm still raises sheep.

The park land at James Bay and Selby Cove forms a narrow point adjacent to a deep cove with a shoreline facing partially onto Trincomali Channel.

making for a convenient landing at Ganges. Preferably go by adequately powered dinghy, to visit the colourful morning market with its bright array of speciality items, arts, crafts, souvenirs, foods and novelties.

Peile Point at the north end of Prevost Island faces up Trincomali Channel. The point and adjacent property is mostly parkland that includes **James Bay** and **Selby Cove**.

Although these anchorages are exposed to winds from the northwest they offer mostly good holding and it is worthwhile stopping for short periods in fair conditions to go ashore. Trails lead to viewpoints and there are some toilets and campsites. If you enjoy strolling along the shoreline visit O'Reilly Beach in James Bay. The favoured anchorages are

not in the parkland area. On the Trincomali side of the island navigate with care either side of Hawkins Island and Charles Rocks. If you are arriving from active pass go west to enter Captain Passage past Peile Point or east to enter Swanson Channel past Portlock Point.

Annette Inlet

Leaving Trincomali Channel and entering Captain Passage, pass Selby Point, Selby Cove and Annette Point to reach this anchorage. The opening to Annette Inlet anchorage is guarded by an unmarked drying rock at the entrance. Take care and use a chart when entering or leaving. Mild winds blow through Annette Inlet sometimes and it is most comfortable to anchor

Left: Annette Inlet. The anchorage is protected from most wind conditions. Centre: Entrances to Annette Inlet and Glenthorne Passage. Bottom: Captain Passage divides Prevost Island from Salt Spring Island. Note the Acland Islands passage at bottom left of the photograph.

Glenthorne Passage

Glenthorne Passage is a long thin inlet formed by Secret Island and an extended broken reef that divides it from Ganges Harbour. The inlet ends in a wide, shallow basin with a narrow opening off Glenthorne Point onto Captain Passage at the neck. This is what makes it a passage.

Enter Glenthorne Passage after passing the point to the south of the Annette Inlet entrance. Travel into the passage from the northwest of Owl Island. Another entrance is via the opening between Owl Island and Secret Island. An alternative for reaching the east cove is by squeezing between Glenthorne Point and the rock just west of it. This is passable at high or low tides but it is best only for small boats and during slack water. Those who know the opening use it, mostly in smaller boats. Anchoring anywhere in the inlet will not impede the passage of boats as it is not actually a through route for boat traffic. Watch for private mooring buoys and floats through the passage. This popular overnight anchorage has good holding ground in about 4.6 metres over muddy shallows in its eastern cove. Anchoring is also possible between Prevost Island and Secret Island. Occasionally windy conditions in Glenthorne Passage have been known to keep anchored boat crews up at night.

Owl and Secret Islands serve as a breakwater from Captain passage. Along the south shore of Prevost Island passage is best taken on the outside of the Acland Islands, carefully keeping clear of the reef that stretches northwest of the larger of the two islands.

in the lee of the land where possible. There is a drying bay at the far eastern end of Annette Inlet. It is calm in most conditions and secure for a good overnight stay just beyond the narrows at the entrance. Annette Inlet has some of the warmest water for swimming in the Gulf Islands.

Above: Captain Passage overlooking the Channel Islands towards the north end of Prevost Island and Trincomali Channel beyond Nose Point, Salt Spring Island. The Channel Islands were used by First Nations for harvesting shellfish, sea urchins and other seafood.
Right: Captain Passage with Prevost Island at left.
Below: Sunset in Glenthorne Passage.

Above: Away from the crowds, at sunset in the Gulf Islands. This was taken while lying at anchor at Prevost Island looking west towards Ganges Harbour.
Right: A local boat leaves the anchorage at Glenthorne Passage. Just beyond the stern of the vessel and the dinghy the small opening that allows smaller craft to enter or leave the anchorage can be seen. It is deep enough for most small to medium sized boats. Beware of currents during tide changes.

On the outside of Prevost Island Red Islets, Hawkins Islet and Bright Islet are wooded with Garry oak and arbutus (madrona).

A red channel marker U60 keeps larger vessels well offshore beyond the shallows on the southwest side. It is possible to navigate smaller craft on the inside of the Acland Islands but be mindful of a rock that is less than 6 feet below the surface at low tide off the smaller island. On the southeast side of Prevost Island temporary anchorage can be taken in **Ellen Bay** or **Diver Bay**. Continuing along the rugged east shore there is room in the lee of Portlock Point at **Richardson**

Bay for a couple of small boats to anchor in shelter from northeasterlies. Here you could row ashore and find a position to view the ferries passing as they enter and leave Active Pass.

Rounding Prevost Island, Hawkins Island dominates a small group of islands off the north shore. Shallows and rocks continue beyond this island towards Peile Point. Caution should be exercised when passing inside or near them. Cross Swanson Channel and explore the Pender Islands.

Pender Islands

North Pender, South Pender and the picturesque Pender Canal

Charts 3313, 3477, 3441, 3442, 3462

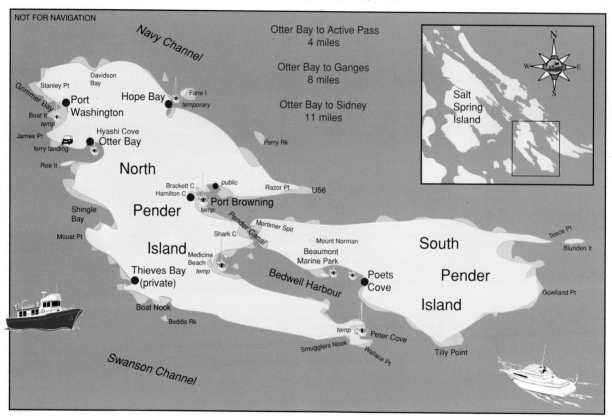

The Pender Islands are blessed with beautiful, unspoilt and charming features providing moorage, anchorage and safe stops for all boat operators. They are centrally located between Plumper Sound and Saturna Island to the east, Navy Channel and Mayne Island to the north, Boundary Pass to the south and Swanson Channel to the west separating them from Salt Spring Island and Prevost Island. They can be approached in a southeasterly direction out of Active Pass or southwestward from East Point on Saturna Island.

The Penders are among the most popular islands to visit in the archipelago, having their fair share of boating destinations and lots of variety in facilities and a few fair to good anchorages. Bedwell Harbour, separating them in the south, has long been a major destination of choice as well as a Border Information Service point (customs). There are marine parklands and national reserve areas on the Pender Islands, with Beaumont Marine Park having the most substantial facilities for beachfront recreational usage.

Pender Canal, separating South from North Pender, is a narrow passage which curves its way under a low bridge connecting the two islands.

Port Washington

From Active Pass travel south down Swanson Channel leaving Stanley Point to port. Pass Willey Point and enter **Grimmer Bay** to reach Port Washingtron. From Salt Spring Island or points south cross Swanson Channel, pass James Point and continue to the west of Boat Islet.

The 80 metre dock for accessing land is located in the bay. It is a good spot for launching small paddle craft. This landing and the bay took their name from Washington Grimmer, an early settler at Pender Island. The dock is exposed to

Port Washington

North Pender Island Capital Regional District.
Charts 3313, 3441, 3442, 3462.
The public dock is managed by wharfinger. Phone: 250-539-3036. The dock is a designated aircraft float, used also as a water taxi landing. Nearby arts and crafts and walking on the island roads. This is fair weather moorage. Boats may anchor temporarily in the southeast corner of the bay, avoiding a rock at the edge of the shallows. There is wave action from the wake of passing ferries.

Top: The Port Washington floats will accommodate several small to medium sized boats.
Above, left: Port Washington general store, located at the head of the dock, which closed down in the past decade after serving passing vessels since the early 1900s became an art gallery and coffee shop, but there were plans to restore it to its old status as a general store.
Above right: Approaching the landing at Port Washington. It is possible to anchor in Grimmer Bay for short durations. The bay is exposed to the wash from passing ferries and is open to winds from the northwest.

wash from passing traffic. It is not a large dock but will accommodate a few boats tied up either side. At one time it was a landing for cargo and mail steamers. Temporary anchorage may be taken in the bay between the dock and Boat Islet. It is not advisable to leave a boat unattended while lying at anchor in such open bays.

This is an historic spot on North Pender Island. The old 1910 Port Washington general store served the community and passing vessels for decades. After closing down in the 1980s it later reopened and became a popular community coffee shop and arts and crafts store. In 2005 there was talk of it being redeveloped to its former historic status as a general store. Marine supplies and home hardware were avail-

able at the original store. Washington Grimmer's historic Old Orchard farm is located a short distance along the road. For more information on homesteads and island touring refer to *The Southern Gulf Islands* by Spalding/Altitude Publishers.

Continue out of Port Washington, rounding Boat Islet and passing James Point, to enter Otter Bay.

Otter Bay

Otter Bay opens off Swanson Channel, the route taken by the BC Ferries between Sidney and Tsawwassen via Active Pass. The ferry landing at the outer north shore of Otter Bay serves the Pender Islands. It is located on the approaches to the

protected marina in the northwestern bight of the bay. The only disturbance is the regular swell from passing vessels, that wash into the cove.

This wide open bay with its **Hyashi Cove,** more commonly referred to as Otter Cove, lies about midway between Mouat Point to the south and Stanley Point to the north. Vessels arriving from the direction of Active Passage will pass the small landing at Port Washinton in Grimmer Bay.

National Park Reserve land includes Roe Lake and **Roesland**, a small tract of waterfront in Otter Bay. This is the site of a resort that closed down in the 1990s leaving a beautiful piece of land that includes abandoned cabins and a tidal trail leading to Roe Islet which protrudes into the bay. It is worth visiting for the view over Otter Bay and Shingle Bay.

Otter Bay Marina is a popular, busy marina at Hyashi Cove. A store and swimming pool are among the attractions at this destination. The store has groceries, snacks, cappuccino, local crafts, paintings, clothing, books, some fresh produce, canned goods and frozen foods among other items. The marina office can provide information on local island services such as mechanical, towing, bed & breakfast and ferries schedules. A large lawn is a playing field for the children and several picnic tables have been placed along the waterfront.

Take your golfing equipment for a day on the nearby course. If you want a catered meal go to the golf club. The golf course has a restaurant that many visiting boaters walk to for breakfast or other meals. Also nearby, just beyond the ferry landing is a highly recommended restaurant and several bed and breakfast establishments.

The weekend and extended period destination at Otter Bay is busy during summer as well as off season. There is

Above: Otter Bay Marina is located to the left. Anchorage is possible in summer, although the bay is exposed to some wind and ferry wash. The marine park reserve area includes Roesland on the far side of the bay.

good anchorage in the bay and shelter from most conditions. You can drop the hook in depths from 12 to 18 metres. During busy weekends this anchorage can be packed and if you are there early enough select a place to drop anchor as far out of reach as possible of the incoming swells from passing ferries. Most of the swell is dissipated by the time it rounds the curve of the bay and reaches the anchorage. Make sure you allow a reasonable amount of scope in your anchor line to avoid swinging into a neighbouring boat. Keep the rise and fall of the tide in mind when anchoring.

When the marina is full with moorage customers mariners anchored off are welcome to go ashore by dinghy and visit the facility. If there is space, check into the marina and enjoy all of its facilities, including the pool. A small fee may be charged for brief stops or docking a dinghy at the marina during busy weekends or summer holiday times.

On the island there are many interesting places from craft stores to fine restaurants, overnight accommodations and services for the many permanent and holiday residents.

For many years the Otter Bay Marina operated with minimal dock space and limited service. When Chuck Spence took over running the facility he and his late wife, Kay, set about enlarging the docks, replacing the buildings on shore and adding amenities to make a visit a more enjoyable experience. They achieved this and more with the provision of a swimming pool, coffee bar and store. The pool has hours set aside for adult and family use.

Top: Otter Bay Marina docks. Above: The marina store.
Left: A lookout and flags mark the marina entrance.

Left: Anchor out in the bay when the marina is full. Check in for moorage when there is space available. Brief stops at the marina during busy summer periods when the docks are busy is acceptable. Call first as boats with reservations could arrive at any time.

Otter Bay was not always the laid back cruising destination it is today. At one time it flourished as a fishing centre featuring such establishments as cannery, saltery and reduction plant. In 1963 it took on a new life as a marina and by 1972 it had moved to the ownership of Bob and Karen Melville. After nearly 20 years they moved to the BC interior when David Bromley bought the marina and the Spences took over managing it.

The Melvilles left a legacy at Otter Bay Marina in the way of Karen's flower and vegetable garden as well as the fruit trees that can be found on the property. Kay Spence passed away in 2002. In 2005 it was being managed by Chuck Spence with Lori Threlfall running the store.

Chuck and Kay created their own legacy with the additions they made to the property. Their arts and crafts selection, the covered barbecue area and their friendly welcome to moored guests became their trademark. New buildings added to the property and completed in 2005 are part of the *Currents* timeshare development.

From Otter Bay travel along Swanson Channel past Shingle Bay, Mouat Point and Thieves Bay in the direction of Bedwell Harbour. Thieves Bay is a private marina belonging to residents of adjacent Magic Lake Estates and no moorage is available for transient vessels unless invited by a member. This cosy nook is easily identified by its rock breakwater.

Above: Hyashi Cove, Otter Bay and Shingle Bay on the west shore of North Pender Island. Moresby Island lies beyond. Gooch and Rum Island are to the left behind Moresby Island. Otter Bay Marina is located in Hyashi Cove (photo opposite page).

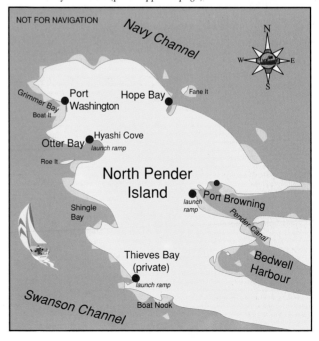

48° 47.876' N
123° 18.762' W
Charts 3313, 3441, 3442, 3462   VHF 66A

Otter Bay Marina

2311 MacKinnon Rd RR1
Pender Island BC V0N 2M1
Phone: 250-629-3579 Fax: 250-629-3589
Hazard: Keep to starboard of green spar U 57.
Marina services: Launch ramp (small craft).
Moorage. Large marina with permanent and transient
moorage. Reservations advised in summertime. There
is water at the dock. Use sparingly please. Power at the
docks is 15 and 30 amp service. Laundry, showers,
washrooms. Garbage disposal for marina customers.
Swimming pool with family and adult hours.
The store has some groceries, gifts, bait, ice, books,
charts, fishing tackle and licences. Road access adjacent
to the marina property for walking or cycling. Take
care walking the narrow island road. View eagles,
herons, otters and seals. Cabin sleeps 4–5 people.
Private cottages at the *Currents* development.
Bicycle, boat and kayak rentals. Picnic tables, barbecue
area. Gazebo. Deck on breakwater at marina. 10 minute
walk to the golf course and club coffee shop/restaurant.
The Islander Restaurant and BC Ferries dock are
located nearby.

Hyashi Cove/Otter Bay Marina

Beyond Thieves Bay steer clear of Beddis Rock. It serves as a protective breakwater for Boat Nook, a shallow indentation in the shoreline protected somewhat by Beddis Rock that shows significantly on approaches. This tiny cove is inadequate for mooring and serves local residents using small boats. The passage from here to Bedwell Bay is clear along Oaks Bluff and around Wallace Point.

There are significant tide rips at this point. Steer wide to avoid the worst of them and enter Bedwell Harbour passing clear of the rock off **Peter Cove**. This cove offers tempiorary anchorage. Slow down as you approach Hay Point. Just beyond is Poets Cove Resort and Spa with its expansive marina docks. The wash your power boat causes as you approach can do a lot of damage to the docks and boats at the marina.

Bedwell Harbour

This is one of the main American entrances to Canadian waters in British Columbia. It is a busy phone-in Border Information Service port throughout the summer months June through September. It is essential that visiting vessels clear customs and be prepared to stop at an official entry port before proceeding elsewhere in Canada. Bedwell is one of the most used entry ports for vessels arriving, including returning Canadians, out of the San Juan Islands or Puget Sound.

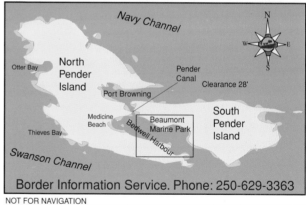

Border Information Service. Phone: 250-629-3363

NOT FOR NAVIGATION

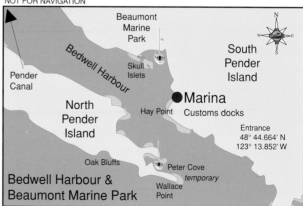

Bedwell Harbour & Beaumont Marine Park

130

Left: The anchorage and vessels on mooring buoys in Bedwell Harbour. The marina at Poets Cove Resort and Spa can be seen in the curve of the bay.

Inset: Boat Nook between Thieves Bay and Bedwell Harbour. Note Beddis Rock offshore and take a course clear of it.

Centre: Looking west over Bedwell Harbour.

Opposite page: Sunset at Poets Cove marina. Diagrams showing the location of Beaumont Marine Park and its proximity to the Pender Canal which cuts between North and South Pender Islands linking Bedwell Harbour with Port Browning.

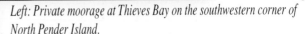

Left: Private moorage at Thieves Bay on the southwestern corner of North Pender Island.

Bedwell Harbour was named for a senior officer of the *Plumper*, an auxiliary steam sloop that served in surveying BC waters between 1857 and 1860. The harbour can be entered via the **Pender Canal** north of the park or from Swanson Channel to the south. The canal separating the two Pender islands was constructed in 1902. The bridge was built in 1955.

Bedwell Harbour is a popular anchorage with many mooring buoys provided by the Parks Service. **Beaumont Marine Park** on South Pender Island abuts the harbour. The 34 hectare park is situated on South Pender Island with its

Charts 3313, 3477, 3441, 3462
48° 44.886' N
123° 13.737' W

Poets Cove Resort and Spa

9801 Spalding Rd, South Pender Island BC V0N 2M3
Phone: 250-629-2111 Fax: 250-629-2105   VHF 66A
Toll Free 1-866-888-2683
www.poetscove.com

Moorage and Service. Customs–phone: 250-629-3363. Gas and diesel fuel available. This is quite a large marina with mostly transient moorage. There is water at the dock–but a limited supply. Power at docks: 15 and 30 amp service. Laundry, showers, washrooms and tackle.

Hotel lodging with swimming pool. Pool and hot tub included with moorage. There is a full service spa on premises. Fitness centre, cycling, golf, kayaking and scuba diving. The property has a licensed lounge and a restaurant in the Aurora Room. Breakfast, lunch and dinner are served. Also patio service and meals at the poolside. There is a small general store offering fresh baked goods, gifts and groceries. There is also a beer and wine store. Bicycle rentals. Road access walking or cycling. Nearby hiking trails. Live music at weekends in summer. Play area and pet area nearby or adjacent.

The cove is adjacent to Beaumont Marine Park. Camping and hiking are popular at the park. Nearby Mount Norman is accessible by trail. Mooring buoys are located nearby in Bedwell Harbour.

Above: Poets Cove Resort and Spa and its large marina.
Below: Facilities at Poets Cove include a luxury hotel and amenities for mooring and hotel guests.

Above and left: Pender Canal, the man-made passage that connects Bedwell Harbour with Port Browning.

Far left: Marina manager, Tara Hodgins, pumping gas at the fuel dock at Poets Cove.

west facing location providing long daylight hours.

In the park there are camping and daytime facilities with picnic tables, toilets, drinking water and scenic trails to walk to points of interest (see *Hiking the Gulf Islands* by Charles Kahn–Harbour House Publishing).

An expansive beach and launching ramp provides good access for small boats and kayakers. Immediately adjacent to Beaumont Marine Park is 274 metre Mount Norman (Regional Park) where hiking opportunities are excellent and panoramic vistas are abundant.

Mooring buoys are located off the south end of the park southeast of Skull Islets. They provide safe overnight mooring for vessels of all types and most sizes and anchoring is comfortable in almost all weather conditions. Large yachts should anchor in the bay. The park enjoys protection from the open waters of Boundary Pass by the southern tip of North Pender Island which protrudes beyond the southern shore of South Pender Island to form a natural breakwater for the bay. However, sometimes southeasterly winds can cause discomfort to boats anchored or moored in parts of the bay. Additional anchoring is available off **Medicine Beach** in the far west end of Bedwell Harbour.

Right: looking west over Port Browning and North Pender Island. The marina lies at the head of the port and the canal opens off to the left beyond the hills rising to the south. Razor Point is seen in the centre with the coast of North Pender Island leading off to the right. Round marker U58 to the east of it when travelling into or out of Port Browning.

Right: Passage through Pender Canal between the Pender Islands. The clearance is 8.3 metres (28 feet) at low tide and the width between the main piers under the bridge is 12.3 metres (40 feet). Depths can be as low as 1.2 metres (about 4 feet). Tidal currents run up to four knots.

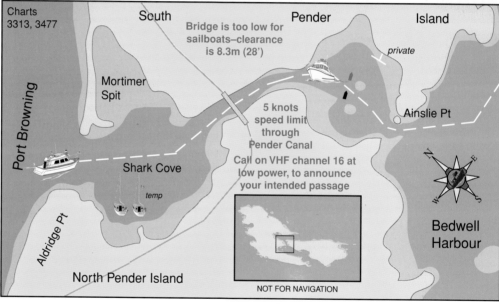

Charts
3313, 3477

South   Pender   Island

Bridge is too low for
sailboats—clearance
is 8.3m (28')

private

Mortimer
Spit

Port Browning

5 knots
speed limit
through
Pender Canal

Ainslie Pt

Call on VHF channel 16 at
low power, to announce
your intended passage

Shark Cove

temp

Aldridge Pt

Bedwell
Harbour

North Pender Island

NOT FOR NAVIGATION

Bedwell Harbour is a busy place in summer. Not only is it an entry point for visitors and returning Canadians from the waters of Washington State but also it is one of the most popular anchorages in the Gulf Islands. To the south of the anchorage, the marina at Poets Cove provides a broad range of facilities and services. They include a spa, swimming pool, showers, laundry, a small general store and snack kiosk and a restaurant in the hotel. The hotel is popular among visitors arriving by boat or by road via ferries from Sidney or the mainland. The docks are extensive and power and water are available. The water is in limited supply due to the relative short supply from its on-island source. The fuel dock serves gas and diesel and other marine products.

The Border Information Service dock is situated adjacent to the marina. Mariners entering Canada or returning from the USA can stop at this dock to phone in for customs clearance. Some vessels will be asked to proceed to Sidney for inspection. It is essential that visiting vessels clear customs before stopping elsewhere in Canada.

Boat access between Bedwell Harbour and Port Browning via the canal is a scenic 12 metre wide waterway that separates the two Penders. It is narrow and has some reefs but the channel is quite well marked. The canal passes from Bedwell Harbour beneath a road bridge (clearance under the bridge is 8.3 metres or 28 feet) that has been featured in many photographs of the area. Its northern entrance is in **Shark Cove** and

Left: Tilly Point at the south tip of South Pender Island. Beyond the point, in Boundary Pass, is Blunden Islet and Saturna Island. Blunden Islet is part of the national park reserve. Inset: Underwater on a clear day at Tilly Point.

Bottom: Port Browning Marina. This is the nearest marina to the North Pender Island shopping centre. Docks and facilities include pub, liquor store and restaurant. A large expanse of lawn is used frequently in summer for yacht club or group gatherings.

a white sandy beach on **Mortimer Spit** where you will usually see people sunbathing or children fishing from shore.

Leaving Bedwell Harbour, navigate past Ainslie Point and pass between the red and green spar buoys U53 and U54. After passing under the bridge navigate past Shark Cove. The large scale chart 3477 or chart book 3313 with an enlarged section of the passage should be referred to when transiting Pender Canal. Adhere to the strictly enforced 5 knot speed limit through the canal. The restriction has been imposed not only for the safety of vessels meeting in the constricted waterway but also to help control erosion of the banks. Pass through the Pender Canal slowly to minimize wash as there are private docks along the shore. Travelling south, larger craft should not venture too far across the head of Bedwell Harbour as there is a rock nearby that is less than two metres below the surface at low tide.

Port Browning

Access to Port Browning from Bedwell Harbour is via the Pender Canal. Travelling into Port Browning through the canal Shark Cove opens as a small bay with the white sandy beach at Mortimer Spit. This passage and the adjacent shoreline makes a most picturesque and scenic side trip. Consider your timing if you plan to use the canal as tidal currents can run up to four knots. Remember to use the large scale chart when transiting the passage.

If you do anchor nearby and visit **Mortimer Spit** on South Pender Island by dinghy there is a cairn near the bridge that indicates an archaeological site discovered in 1903 and designated a heritage site in 1957. First Nations artifacts dating over 5,000 years have been uncovered in a dig on the banks of Shark Cove on North Pender Island since the 1980s.

Anchorage is fair in Port Browning. Southeast winds can blow in summer time giving some discomfort to anchored boats. Many boaters headed for Port Browning make their way to the marina. Those who anchor out choose the shallows along the shore off Hamilton Beach at the head of the bay.

On the north side of the bay, near Port Browning Marina, there is a 50-metre public float which is usually full of local boats. A reef protrudes into the bay off **Bracket Cove** between the marina and the public dock. Care should be taken to navigate according to the chart and steer clear of the marker on the reef, keeping it to starboard as you approach the docks in the marina. The public dock is a small float adjoining the

The head of Port Browning. Anchorage is taken off Hamilton Beach in good weather. The marina is in the centre at Hamilton Cove. There is a small public dock to the right, beyond Brackett Cove. Stay east of the red reef marker when going between the public dock and the marina.

Charts 3313, 3477, 3441, 3442, 3462

Port Browning Marina

4605 Oak Rd, North Pender Island
BC V0N 2M0   **VHF 66A**
Phone: 250-629-3493 Fax: 250-629-3495
www.portbrowning.com
Moorage and Service.
Clear customs by phoning 250-629-3363. Moorage. Large marina with mostly transient moorage. Water at dock. Power at docks 30 amps. Laundry, showers, washrooms.
On site restaurant and licenced pub with patio service serves breakfast, lunch and dinner. Summer music/entertainment. Swimming pool. Tennis. Road access walking or cycling. One kilometre to the general store. Float plane service. Wireless Internet service.

Browning Harbour

North Pender Island Public dock
Phone: 250-629-3423
Manager • Float length 27 metres. Store and shopping complex nearby. Port Browning Marina is located almost directly opposite.

Entrance to harbour:
48° 46.191' N
123° 13.963' W

Marina:
48° 46.579' N
123° 16.249' W

Port Browning Marina

PUB Restaurant

Hamilton Cove

Market

Every Saturday morning May to October, a farmers' market is held 10 am to 1 pm at the Community Hall. The hall is located about two kilometres from the Driftwood Centre.
Community Hall, Pender Island BC
Phone: 629-3669.

Yacht race

The Round-the-Penders yacht race is held every year in August. It starts at Port Browning.

Left: A fire destroyed the Hope Bay store in 1999. It was rebuilt and reopened complete with restaurant and other facilities in 2005.

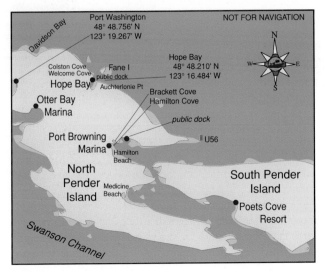

Hope Bay

Hope Bay is located on the north shore of North Pender Island. A lot has happened there in recent years. The historic Corbett family store built, in 1912, was destroyed by fire in 1998. The building also housed the Hope Bay post office. In 2000 a start was made on rebuilding it, but this ended with a shortage of funds. In 2003 a group of 27 local residents banded together and formed a cooperative to finish the job. They improved on the original rebuilding plan and finished with a new structure in 2005. The new building, which resembles the original, is greatly improved and accommodates an array of businesses as well as a restaurant and an art gallery.

The bay was an important centre in the early 20th century. It saw the coming and going of steamships landing their passengers and cargo. Famous, historic coastal vessels such as the *Iroquois*, the *Princess Mary* and the *Lady Rose*, stopped at the landing regularly. The ships served the needs of local settlers and the Corbett General Store, which was also known as The Little Store with the Big Stock.

Hope Bay is exposed to wind from the east and northeast. The bay cannot provide safe moorage at all times and the small 90 metre dock marina is battered by uncomfortable sea conditions when it is windy, especially with winds blowing from the east, predominantly in the winter months. The marina is located on the outside of a small drying inlet that opens onto Plumper Sound at Auchterlonie Point.

While east winds can sweep into the bay some protection is afforded from northerlies by Fane Island. There are shallows

northern shore of the bay and if space is available it affords a possible stop with the option of walking along the adjacent road up to the Driftwood shopping centre. At the shopping centre you will find a grocery store, post office, book store, bakery, liquor store, restaurant, craft and gift shops and a variety of other businesses that tend to change from time to time. An automotive service station is located adjacent to the main shopping centre. A farmers' market is held at the community hall every Saturday morning during summer.

off **Colston Cove** and **Welcome Cove** as well as in the passage between them and Fane Island. Entrance to Hope Bay can be made either side of the island keeping clear of the exposed reef in the middle.

Temporary anchorage is possible in Hope Bay in the shallows that drop to about one-and-a-half metres of water at low tide. If there is no room at the dock, anchoring and going ashore by dinghy to visit the store and restaurant is worthwhile.

Sitting at anchor or at the dock you will have good views across Plumper Sound of Saturna, Samuel and Mayne Islands. Sometimes freighters awaiting access to coastal ports use the Sound as a roadstead.

When cruising Plumper Sound as a route between Navy Channel (Hope Bay) and Port Browning steer well clear of the shallows indicated by the presence on your chart of Perry Rock. Also round Razor Point clear of the reef marked by the red buoy U56.

If you proceed around South Pender Island it is possible to take passage between Teece Point and Blunden Islet (see diagram page 134) although currents in this narrow passage suggest a preferred passage around the islet. Temporary anchorage in **Camp Bay** is possible, avoiding easterly winds. Beyond Camp Bay pass clear of the rock at Higgs Point and the light at Gowlland Point and head for **Tilly Point** at the south tip of the islands. This prominent point has a tiny shallow cove that small boats have been known to use as a temporary stop. A small islet protrudes off shore with a drying reef extending from it. This islet is the site of a popular scuba diving location. Strong tidal currents wash through the cove making it essential to maintain an anchor watch at all times.

Hope Bay

North Pender Island
Phone: 250-629-9990
Managed by harbourmaster. The float length totals 69 metres. There are lights on the docks and a public phone ashore. Stores, arts and crafts and a restaurant with a magnificent view overlook the small marina.

The docks are exposed to southeasterly winds which are mostly prevalent in winter. In summer a low swell or the diminished wash of vessels passing offshore sometimes roll into the exposed marina.

Pender Island Launching

If you have arrived by ferry, you will be able to launch trailer boats at Otter Bay or Thieves Bay. Launch by hand at Hope Bay or Shark Cove's sandy Mortimer Spit beach at the Pender Canal.

Top: Navy Channel showing Hope Bay and approaches.

Left, centre: Anchored in Hope Bay. Depth drops to less then one metre at low tide. Anchor in line with the docks. The cove is open to easterly and southeasterly winds. The dock can accommodate a few small boats.

Left: A way to see all parts of the islands is by scooter, seen here at the Otter Bay Marina waterfront. A small moped or electric bike can be carried on many boats and taken ashore at marinas.

Opposite page: Ceremony at the new Hope Bay store building in 2005. The last postmaster at the former store, Stuart Corbett, addresses the audience.

Saturna Island

Tumbo and Cabbage Islands, Winter Cove, Lyall Harbour, Boot Cove and Boat Pass

Charts 3313, 3477, 3441, 3442, 3462

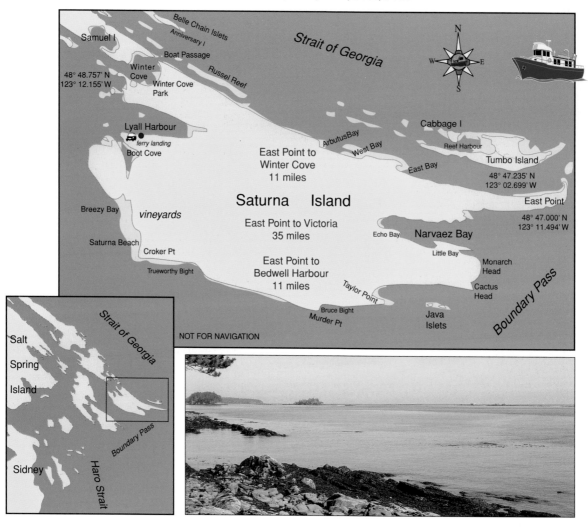

Saturna Island is one of the larger Gulf Islands. It serves as a breakwater from the Strait of Georgia to the archipelago. Its southern tip at East Point protrudes into Boundary Pass which, with Haro Strait, divides the US San Juan Islands from Canada. This point is one of the entrances to the Gulf Islands. The passage sees a lot of heavy marine traffic.

Just off East Point, in the Strait, lies Cabbage Island and Tumbo Island. These islands are a well-known and popular destination which includes the anchorage in **Reef Harbour**

and is part of the Gulf Islands National Park Reserve system.

Cabbage and Tumbo Islands

Cabbage Island is located off Tumbo Island to the north of East Point on Saturna Island. Entrance to the anchorage in Reef Harbour is from the Strait of Georgia or Tumbo Channel. Regular visitors use Tumbo Channel and cut between the two kelp patches at the northwest tip of Tumbo Island to reach the anchorage. Use the large scale chart. A white sandy

140

Top: Cabbage Island lies off Tumbo Island and East Point on Saturna Island. The marine park has facilities for camping and picnicking. Bald eagles and black oystercatchers use it as a nesting site. The island was used at one time for fox fur farming, timber harvesting and coal mining. Its name is derived from the word tombolo, a land shape in which a sandbar extends to an island from an adjacent shoreline.

Bottom: Sandstone cliffs on the south shore of Saturna Island.

Opposite page: The entrance to Boat Passage from the Strait of Georgia. Note the reefs, clearly seen in the photo. Use local knowledge and a large scale chart to navigate the narrow, current-swept waterway.

Whales

As you travel in this area you may come across a pod of orcas (killer whales). A lot of whale watching is conducted in adjacent passages and sightings of these large marine mammals is quite possible. Mariners are cautioned to not approach them or in any way encroach on their territory. Regulations require that mariners keep at least 100 metres away from them and not chase after them to get closer. If you happen to be in their path and there is confined space in which to manouvre safely, simply stop and wait until they have passed if it is safe to do so.

beach lines the shore of Cabbage Island, which is exposed to northwesterly and easterly winds.

It is safe to stop at this park in fair weather, using the anchorage off Cabbage Island.

The sandy beaches, swimming and sunbathing makes this park a popular one. There are mooring buoys, camp sites, picnic tables and toilets. It is a popular place for kayaking.

Tumbo Island was incorporated into the National Parks Reserve in 1997 after a history of attempted coal mining and fox raising. There is still private property on Tumbo Island. Tie up to a mooring buoy or anchor in Reef Harbour.

Boundary Passage to Lyall Harbour

Boundary Passage washes the southern Saturna Island shore. Currents swirl and tumble off East Point with streams

Above: Tumbo Island, off East Point, Saturna Island. The San Juan Islands lie beyond. Cabbage Island and Tumbo Island are part of the Gulf Islands National Park Reserve. Tumbo Island can be explored using the short trail network. There is a house on Tumbo Island that is private. Kids will enjoy the tidal pools and sandy beaches in Reef Harbour.
Clear the reefs at the northwest end of Tumbo Island when entering the marine park waters to reach the anchorage in the lee of Cabbage Island. Anchor in two to five metres (low tide).

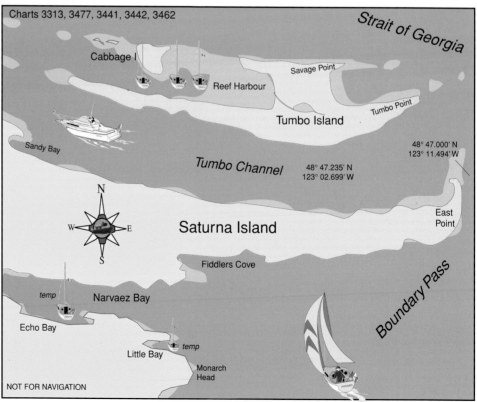

Charts 3313, 3477, 3441, 3442, 3462

Strait of Georgia

Cabbage I

Savage Point

Reef Harbour

Tumbo Point

Tumbo Island

Sandy Bay

Tumbo Channel

48° 47.235' N
123° 02.699' W

48° 47.000' N
123° 11.494' W

N
W E
S

Saturna Island

East Point

Fiddlers Cove

Boundary Pass

temp

Narvaez Bay

Echo Bay

Little Bay

temp

Monarch Head

NOT FOR NAVIGATION

142

The patio at the winery affords a magnificent ocean view. Visitors stop to taste wine, order a meal and enjoy the ambiance of the establishment. A classic vehicle seen on the property.

Saturna Beach
The first store and post office on Saturna Island was opened at Saturna Beach in 1896. The area was part of a sheep farm whose co-owner Warburton Pike gave the nearby 401 metre mountain its name. For many years the annual lamb barbecue was held at Saturna Beach until it was moved to Winter Cove.

up to 5 knots. Stay clear of Boiling Reef. Along the southern shoreline of Saturna Island, anchorage is possible at Narvaez Bay where majestic scenery includes a view of Mount Baker to the east. **Little Bay** and **Echo Bay** are tiny nooks in the south shore of **Narvaez Bay** and are part of the national parks reserve land in the Gulf Islands. A hiking trail across the centre of the island begins on the headland between these two tiny coves. Anchor according to depth and wind. A temporary stop is recommended. Avoid southeasterlies if you want to remain at anchor in the bay overnight.

Continue northwest in Plumper Sound passing Java Islets either side taking temporary anchorage in **Bruce Bight** or continue along the shore past Taylor Point and Murder Point and on to Coker Point with Mount Warburton Pike looming above Brown Ridge.

Moor at **Breezy Bay** if you wish to visit the Saturna Island Family Estate Winery and the Bistro. They are located about a kilometre from the bay, up a hill that rises gently on the lower slopes of Mount Warburton Pike. If the ten minute walk appears too strenuous for some members of your group call

Opposite page: The community dock at Breezy Bay providing access to the Saturna Vineyards.
Left: The landing at Saturna in Lyall Harbour. This is a small dock with minimal space. The inside of the finger is close to a steep cliff on shore. There is fuel at the dock and a general store ashore. It is adjacent to the BC Ferries Saturna Island landing. A pub/restaurant overlooks the waterfront adjacent to the ferry landing.
Below: Another view of the dock and landing at Saturna.

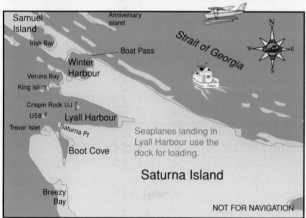

Seaplanes landing in Lyall Harbour use the dock for loading.

NOT FOR NAVIGATION

the vineyards at 250-539-3521. They will send a vehicle to pick you up. Stopping is permitted for up to two hours at the dock, preferably by dinghy while your larger boat is tied to a mooring buoy or anchored out. It is a very shallow bay and larger vessels should anchor in deeper water and use their dinghies to reach the dock. Do not leave an anchored boat unattended. This can be an enjoyable stop to do some wine tasting and spend lunchtime on the restaurant patio. No overnight moorage is available at the dock.

Just beyond Breezy Bay towering sandstone cliffs reach up sheer from the water's edge at Elliot Bluff. As you continue the circumnavigation of Saturna Island you will reach Saturna Point, Boot Cove, Lyall Harbour and Winter Cove. Round Payne Point and steer clear of the shallows marked by the red buoy U58 as you approach the settlement of Saturna at Saturna Point. Adjacent, there is a ferry landing, a dock and

very limited moorage. It also is a fuel stop and there is a post office, a pub/restaurant and a general store. Talk to the staff at these places about visiting the winery if you have not already done so. It is a fair walk from the landing to the winery but this is an alternative way to get there. Or go back to the vineyards' dock at Breezy Bay by way of Plumper Sound.

The island has many bed and breakfast establishments, numerous art studios and some home based businesses. There is no pharmacy and no bank on the island.

Lyall Harbour

The anchorage in this open bay is preferably for larger vessels. It is exposed to most winds and although the harbour lies in the lee of a southeast shore, even southeasterlies blow down the Lyall Valley into the harbour causing discomfort and concern. Temporary anchorage can be found in Irish Bay

145

Above: The east side of Winter Cove. Reefs that are covered at high tide run into the anchorage here and on the opposite shore. Be cautious when anchoring.
Right: Boot Cove. The entrance is in lower centre of the photo.

Lyall Harbour Public Wharf

& Fuel Dock, 102 East Point Rd,
Saturna Island BC V0N 2Y0
Phone/Fax: 250-539-5725
Harbour Master 250-539-2229
Marina services:
Government dock at Saturna Landing. Limited space– mostly drop off/pick up. Not intended for overnight. Fuel: gas, diesel, outboard mix, oil. General store–fishing tackle, hardware, licences, ice, bait, groceries, supplies. Propane available nearby. Restaurant–Lighthouse Pub. Post office and liquor store nearby–about 2 kilometres. Look for typical island tranquility. View eagles, herons, otters and seals. A local quarry supplied sandstone to Victoria. Visit the stone house ruins at Taylor Point. Adjacent facilities: BC Ferries at Lyall Harbour. Use caution manouvering when ferry operating. Winter Cove anchorage. Saturna Lodge and restaurant at Boot Cove and Vineyards on the island–enquire at store.

Annual lamb barbecue every July 1st, Canada Day, at Winter Cove. Arrive early, anchor and use dinghy dock.

but protection from wind is somewhat better in Winter Cove.

Between Lyall Harbour and Winter Cove note that a reef extends beyond King Islets and Veruna Bay that should be avoided. A buoy marks another hazard at Crispin Rock marked by a red-green-red buoy, flashing red, in the middle of Lyall

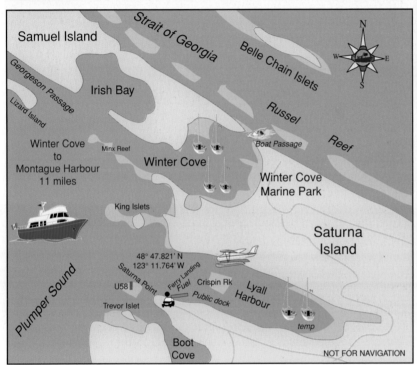

The map shows:

Samuel Island
Strait of Georgia
Belle Chain Islets
Georgeson Passage
Irish Bay
Russel
Lizard Island
Reef
Winter Cove
to
Montague Harbour
11 miles
Minx Reef
Winter Cove
Boat Passage
Winter Cove
Marine Park
King Islets
Saturna
Island
Plumper Sound
48° 47.821' N
123° 11.764' W
Saturna Point
U58
Trevor Islet
Ferry Landing
Fuel
Crispin Rk
Public dock
Lyall
Harbour
temp
Boot
Cove
NOT FOR NAVIGATION

Top right: Boats anchored in Winter Cove.
Top left: Boat Passage is a short cut for small
boats to and from the Strait of Georgia.
Above: Boat Passage from the Strait.

Harbour. If you anchor here do so deep inside the harbour to avoid submerged cables across the entrance. Saturna landing in Lyall Harbour has a small dock with limited space. It is adjacent to the BC Ferries Saturna Island landing so be mindful of ferry activities. There is fuel at the dock and ashore you will find a general store, and a pub/restaurant that overlooks Lyall Harbour and the ferry landing.

Boot Cove

Anchorage is not recommended in this cove. There is not much space to anchor in its protected lee shore which is lined with numerous private floats. There is no public moorage in Boot Cove. The cove sees a lot of wind. Best bet for fair to good nearby overnight anchorage is in Winter Cove or Horton Bay on Mayne Island. Trevor Islet at the entrance to Boot Cove is privately owned.

Winter Cove

Easiest access is from inside the Gulf Islands rather than from the Strait of Georgia. When entering from the Strait, vessels cruising to Winter Cove are advised to use Active Pass or other waterways into the islands rather than Boat Pass.

The entrance from the **Belle Chain Islets** at **Boat Passage** is tricky and intimidating, especially to new mariners. The large scale chart should be referred to when transiting the passage. On a word of caution, this is not a passage to be taken lightly. It runs at up to 7 knots, is suitable for small craft only and navigation should be done in keeping with the right chart and tidal and current information. Enter Winter Cove from Plumper Sound by steering clear of Minx Reef opposite the south end of Samuel Island (See page 154).

Anchorage in Winter Cove is quite protected with minimal wind disturbance in summer. But the occasional blow may cause a little discomfort. Anchor clear of a reef that pro-

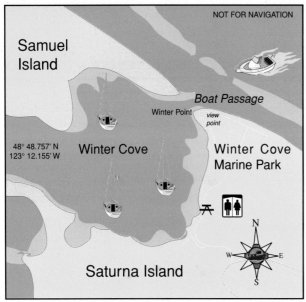

Above and opposite top: Winter Cove with the entrance to Boat Passage from the Strait of Georgia. Use local knowledge and a large scale chart to navigate this waterway. Lyall Harbour lies to the left. Irish Bay on Samuel Island, is seen beyond Winter Cove. Farther northwest along the Saturna shore is the Belle Chain Islets (right in top photo).

Above: Cabbage Island, Tumbo Island and East Point on Saturna Island lie to the south of Boat Passage.

trudes from the southeast shore and another, smaller one on the northwest shore.

Although Winter Cove is exposed to winds from the northwest, and is extremely shallow at places, it affords protected anchorage for limited periods. Open grassy stretches and shady adjacent woods provide a picturesque setting for this park. It is used frequently as a picnic spot by ferry passengers, cyclists and kayakers. There are picnic tables, toilets, shoreline or forest walking trails and a dinghy dock–in the summer only.

Overnight anchoring should be planned carefully according to wind forecasts. No camping is permitted but Winter Cove park, part of the Gulf Islands National Park Reserve,

makes a spendid place for picnics and hiking. There are pleasant waterfront trails and viewpoints, particularly overlooking Boat Pass and the Belle Chain Islets.

One of the most popular events in the Gulf Islands is the annual lamb barbecue on Saturna Island. It is held on July 1st (Canada Day), when hundreds of boats can be found at anchor in sheltered coves from Horton Bay to Winter Cove. A large dinghy dock is in place in Winter Cove for the event. Dinghies can also be landed on the adjacent beach. A shuttle is available for going ashore. Other summer events on Saturna Island include the Saturna Vineyard harvest celebration in September, an artists' studio tour in July and August and a market at the community hall every Saturday.

Anniversary Island in the Belle Chain Islets off Samuel Island.

NOT FOR NAVIGATION

Saturna Island

Top: On a busy Canada Day boats from far and wide descend on the landing in Winter Cove.
Above left and right: It makes one's mouth water just looking at the pictures of the barbecue. Arrive early to ensure tickets for the event.
Right: Boats take over the cove for the annual Canada Day celebrations at Winter Cove on Saturna Island.

Above and left: Boat Passage is not to be taken lightly but is passable by a powerful small boat even when the current is strong. It is used mostly by those familiar with it. Below: Arts and crafts are on sale at the Canada Day event. There are waterfront trails in the park.

Tea & Coffee

Mayne Island

Active Pass to Georgeson Passage, Horton Bay, Samuel Island

Charts 3313, 3473, 3477, 3442, 3462

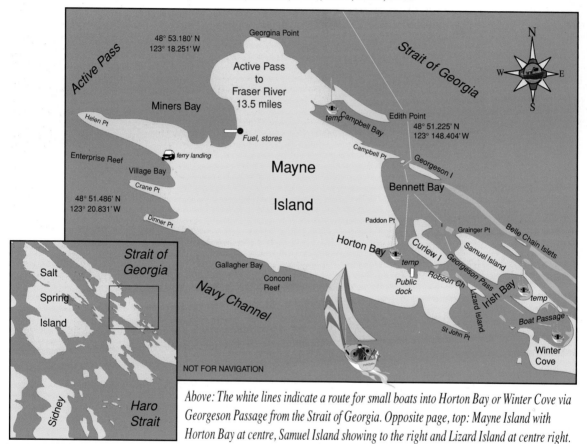

Above: The white lines indicate a route for small boats into Horton Bay or Winter Cove via Georgeson Passage from the Strait of Georgia. Opposite page, top: Mayne Island with Horton Bay at centre, Samuel Island showing to the right and Lizard Island at centre right.

Horton Bay

Access to Horton Bay is through Bennett Bay from the Strait of Georgia. Careful passage should be taken wide of Edith Point when arriving from the north or northeast. Pass carefully between Campbell Point on Mayne Island and the north end of **Georgeson Island**. It is necessary to angle through the passage and turn west after passing the reef on your starboard side at the entrance. Continue across Bennett Bay and enter Horton Bay between Paddon Point and Curlew Island in mid channel. Use the other side of the island to enter Georgeson Passage for a route to Winter Cove. Passage can be taken either side of the islets and rocks in the passage off Grainger Point but the west side close to the rocks is deepest. At the entrance to the islands, temporary anchorage may be taken in **Campbell Bay**. It is exposed to southeast winds.

Horton Bay is entered via Georgeson Passage past Lizard Island from the south. Alternatively, use Robson Channel with care noting the current and a reef marked by kelp at the entrance. There is a public dock in Horton Bay which is often quite busy, but there's a good chance of finding a spot to raft up. If you want to go ashore and access the island this is a good point to do so, although there are no facilities at the head of the dock. Anchorage in the bay is safe but be mindful of the currents, especially during the off slack periods and near the passages approaching the anchorage. The best anchorage away from the currents is to the northwest in the shallows. Use a large scale chart for safe passage into the bay.

Georgeson Island

Horton Bay

Bennett Bay

Georgeson Island

Campbell Bay

Campbell Bay

Minx Reef

Horton Bay

Robson Passage or Georgeson Pass can be used by small boats going into Horton Bay past Lizard Island. From the Strait of Georgia cross the Campbell Bay entrance and pass to the north of Georgeson Island, avoiding the reef off Campbell Point. White lines in the photos indicate approximate course. Use a large scale chart. The photo at left shows the entrance to Horton Bay from Georgeson Passage. Above: Minx Reef at Irish Bay.

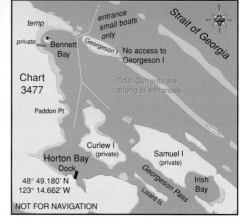

Top: Horton Bay with Bennett Bay and Georgeson Island beyond. Horton Bay is a Canpass check-in station. Above: Sandstone cliffs in Campbell Bay.

Samuel Island

Lying between Mayne Island and Saturna Island is privately owned Samuel Island. This small island forms a breakwater from the Strait of Georgia for Plumper Sound. It also abuts Winter Cove, forming its northwest shore. Georgeson Passage, which runs between the island and Lizard Island, is used to access Horton Bay or en route from Winter Cove or Irish Bay to the Strait of Georgia by way of **Bennett Bay** and through the small gap between Georgeson Island and Campbell Point. Samuel Island provides shelter to Irish Bay, Horton Bay and Winter Cove. Samuel Island and a point on Mayne Island are landmarks for aircraft flying between Victoria and Vancouver. Winter Cove is formed by the curve of the south end of Samuel Island and the bight at the north end of Saturna Island.

Irish Bay

Irish Bay forms a major indentation into Samuel Island. It is an open anchorage exposed to southerly winds. Anchorage

Bennett Bay National Park Reserve

Campbell Point between Campbell Bay and Bennett Bay is national park reserve land that affords a magnificent view across the Strait of Georgia and of the Belle Chain Islands. These and Georgeson Island have old growth forest of Garry oak, Douglas fir and arbutus. They support a very sensitive ecosystem and are marine mammal haulout sites and nesting areas for oystercatchers, gulls and guillemot. Anchor temporarily near the private jetty on the west shore.

is temporary in the southeast section with the northwestern portion providing daytime stopping only. It is fairly deep in most of Irish Bay with shallows only around the edges. Most mariners anchor in about 3 metres behind the south side of the entrance. The anchorage is not recommended for overnight or prolonged stays. Adjacent Lyall Harbour is also subject to strong winds at times. See Saturna Island section page 140.

As mentioned earlier, Minx Reef off Irish Bay must be avoided when travelling into or out of the bay or to and from Winter Cove. The reef extends to almost parallel with the tip of the southeastern point of land at the entrance to Irish Bay.

Horton Bay with Robson Channel beyond the moored boats. These are private moorings.

Above: On the right, a ferry approaches the Mayne Island landing in Village Bay. Another makes a wide sweep around Enterprise Reef. Left: Views showing Active Pass, Miners Bay and Village Bay.

Active Pass and Miners Bay

The passage from the south end of Mayne Island to Active Pass takes the mariner past St John Point opposite Lyall Harbour. Follow Plumper Sound through Navy Channel, avoiding Conconi Reef (see diagram on page 152) and the shallows to the southeast of it. Passing between Davidson Bay (see diagram on page 137) on North Pender Island and Dinner Point on Mayne Island, emerge into Swanson Channel.

Follow a course inside Enterprise Reef by keeping buoy U51 to your port and enter **Village Bay**. There is temporary anchorage here, preferably day only as the bay is wide open and exposed to northwest winds and the wash of passing vessels. Continue around Helen Point into Active Pass.

Enter Active Pass from the north by keeping the Gossip Shoals buoy well to your starboard. In the centre of the northern entrance, off Georgina Point lighthouse is Fairway Bank. Tidal rips and waves can be very short and steep here and small boats will be bounced around severely. Avoid this spot by passing closer to either shore. I usually favour the Galiano side of Active Pass, keeping clear of the few shallows between Burril Point and Mary Anne Point.

Passing ferries and large vessels cause washes that roll into Miners Bay and disturb boats tied up at the small dock. This is a fuel stop and the small marina is suitable only for brief duration stops. It is used largely to serve the local community. At the head of the wharf there is a hotel with pub and lounge, a general store, a book store and some gift shops.

Currents run up to 8 knots off Helen Point at the south end of Active Pass and 5 knots off **Sturdies Bay**.

Mayne Island
The island has a small population. Less than 1,000 people inhabit the 21 square kilometre island but it sees its fair share of visitors in summer. Georgina Point Lighthouse and the Japanese Gardens are heritage sites worth visiting. Mayne Island is popular among bird watchers, paddlers and cyclists.

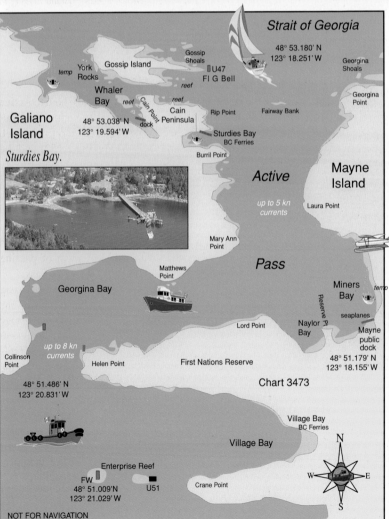

Sturdies Bay.

Galiano Island

Strait of Georgia

48° 53.180' N
123° 18.251' W

Gossip Island
Gossip Shoals
Gossip Shoals
temp
York Rocks
Whaler Bay
Cain Point
reef
reef
reef
dock
Cain Peninsula
48° 53.038' N
123° 19.594' W
Rip Point
Fairway Bank

Georgina Shoals
Georgina Point

Sturdies Bay
BC Ferries
Burril Point

U47
Fl G Bell

Active

Mayne Island

up to 5 kn currents

Laura Point

Mary Ann Point

Pass

Matthews Point

Georgina Bay

Miners Bay
temp
seaplanes

Reserve Pl

Lord Point
Naylor Bay
Mayne public dock

Collinson Point
up to 8 kn currents
Helen Point
First Nations Reserve
48° 51.179' N
123° 18.155' W

48° 51.486' N
123° 20.831' W

Chart 3473

Village Bay
BC Ferries

Village Bay

N
W   E
S

Enterprise Reef
FW
48° 51.009'N
123° 21.029' W
U51
Crane Point

NOT FOR NAVIGATION

Above: Active Pass. Ferry traffic necessitates careful navigation while transiting this major gateway to the Gulf Islands. Strong currents to eight knots require careful planning. Ferries pass each other regularly, meeting in the centre and creating the need for even greater care.
Below and bottom: The fuel dock at Miners Bay in Active Pass. It is a Canpass check-in station. Nearby temporary anchorage, near the shore, is subject to wash from passing ferries.

Galiano Island

Active Pass to Porlier Pass
Montague Harbour

Charts 3313, 3473, 3442, 3443, 3462, 3463

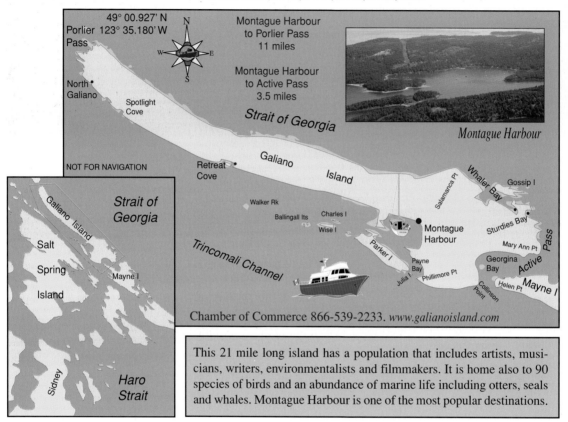

49° 00.927' N
Porlier 123° 35.180' W
Pass

Montague Harbour
to Porlier Pass
11 miles

Montague Harbour
to Active Pass
3.5 miles

Strait of Georgia

North Galiano

Spotlight Cove

NOT FOR NAVIGATION

Galiano Island

Retreat Cove

Walker Rk

Ballingall Its

Charles I

Wise I

Trincomali Channel

Parker I

Payne Bay

Julia I

Phillimore Pt

Salamanca Pt

Whaler Bay

Gossip I

Montague Harbour

Sturdies Bay

Mary Ann Pt

Georgina Bay

Active Pass

Collinson Point

Helen Pt

Mayne I

Montague Harbour

Chamber of Commerce 866-539-2233. *www.galianoisland.com*

Strait of Georgia

Galiano Island

Salt Spring Island

Mayne I

Sidney

Haro Strait

This 21 mile long island has a population that includes artists, musicians, writers, environmentalists and filmmakers. It is home also to 90 species of birds and an abundance of marine life including otters, seals and whales. Montague Harbour is one of the most popular destinations.

Two important waterways wash the shores of Galiano Island, Active Pass at the south end and Porlier Pass at the north. These busy passages are major gateways to the Gulf Islands. Active Pass sees a constant stream of traffic from small pleasaure boats crossing the Strait of Georgia from mainland marinas, to the ships of the BC Ferries fleet. BC Ferries operates a regular stop at Sturdies Bay on Galiano Island, a short way into the Strait of Georgia side of Active Pass. Ferries run to and from Swartz Bay on Vancouver Island and from Mayne, North Pender and Saturna Islands as well as Tsawwassen south of Vancouver. Exercise caution in the path of ferries as they have limited manouevering capability, especially in the confines of the passage. Active Pass currents run at up to 8 knots with swirls and overfalls. Be cautious,

especially at Fairway Bank between **Georgina Point** and Rip Point. Short, high standing waves can bounce a small boat right out of the water and dip the bow right under. Navigate either side of the bank.

Porlier Pass at the north end has no ferry traffic but small, slow boats and sometimes tugs pulling tows converge on the passage during slack tides. Porlier can run at speeds up to 9 knots during flood tides and 8 knots at ebb tides.

Other than the very substantial Montague Harbour, the only place to anchor in adequate overnight protection against wind and weather in the vicinity of Galiano Island is at the southeast end. Here it is possible to lie in the shallows of Whaler Bay or stop at the public dock as space permits.

There is very limited anchorage in Sturdies Bay where the

Above: Sturdies Bay ferry landing in Active Pass. Gossip Island serves as a breakwater for Whaler Bay which opens off the Strait of Georgia.
Below: The dock at Whaler Bay accommodates small local craft as well as several fish boats. There is sometimes space for another boat or two.

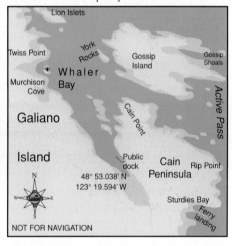

ferry lands to disembark arriving passengers and vehicles and to take on its outgoing load. This bay is subject to some movement of water washed in by passing ferries and other craft, but it can provide fair overnight anchoring for a few boats. Beware of a long reef extending down the middle of the bay in front of a large resort hotel. Anchor on the far side away from the ferry dock and small craft landing. Stopping at the small craft landing is permitted, subject to space and leaving free the space designated for commercial traffic.

Whaler Bay

If you are trying to cross the Strait of Georgia from Active Pass but are delayed due to sea conditions you have several choices: Go back through Active Pass to Montague Harbour, Prevost Island, Pender Island or Salt Spring Island. Or remain on the Strait of Georgia side of the pass and linger at Whaler Bay on Galiano Island. Entrance off the Strait of Georgia is between **Gossip Island** and Lion Islets just northwest of Active Pass. It can be entered also from Active Pass between Gossip Island and Cain Peninsula.

Whaler Bay has a small public dock which is often fully occupied by commercial vessels as well as those belonging to local residents. There is an anchorage off **Murchison Cove** that is fairly protected from westerlies by Galiano Island and from easterlies by Gossip Island. It is in the lee of Twiss Point on the Galiano shore opposite the north end of Cain Peninsula. There are reefs and rocks throughout the bay and a large scale chart is necessary for safe passage and for finding suitable mooring. Be wary particularly of York Rocks off the north end of Gossip Island and the reef off Cain Point.

Above: If you have time while in Whaler Bay walk across to Sturdies Bay (left) in Active Pass and visit the local bakery and deli. There are more stores, a service station, hotel and the ferry landing in the vicinity.

Parker Island, which forms a massive natural breakwater to Montague Harbour. It is possible also for small vessels to navigate mid channel through the small passage between Julia Island and Parker Island.

Gray Peninsula protrudes from Galiano Island creating a bight in which marine park mooring buoys have been set. In summer these buoys fill up quickly early in the day and many boats arriving later anchor all around the harbour.

Montague Harbour Marine Park is one of the most popular anchorages in the Gulf Islands. In addition to the many mooring buoys, the harbour has moorage and anchoring in a generally well protected bay and a dock for small boats and dinghy access to shore. A marine interpretive centre is located on the water with summer viewing of marine life and with park staff on hand at weekends in July and August. Sunbathing and swimming are ideal at the sandy beaches in the harbour and on the north side of Gray Peninsula. This latter promontory is a fairly heavily forested piece of land connected to Galiano Island by a narrow isthmus.

The park is extensive with recreational vehicle and tent camping, a launching ramp, tables, picnic areas and toilets. There are trails to the beaches and other scenic locations. For campsite reservations call 1-800-689-9025.

Space is sometimes available at the public dock. A walk along the local roadway will take you to Sturdies Bay ferry landing and the island's south end business centre where you will find a variety of services including a book store, art galleries, a restaurant, grocery store, bakeries and gifts, arts and crafts stores. There are numerous lodges and bed and breakfast establishments on the island.

Montague Harbour

The harbour is located on the west side of southern Galiano Island. Entrance is from Trincomali Channel from the south through the passage between Julia Island and Phillimore Point, or from the north on the Galiano side of

Above: There are mooring buoys, a marine park and a dinghy dock at the northwest end of Montague Harbour. The marina on the east side caters to overnight and extended stays. The south entrance at top of photo opens off Trincomali Channel near Active Pass. Right: A floating bakery caters to boaters in Montague Harbour anchorage.

A full service marina is located a short distance across the harbour from the park. It is a busy place in summer, catering to visitors and local residents at the coffee shop and cafe with a patio overlooking the marina. This is also a popular fuel stop in the Gulf Islands.

Good scuba diving is possible in Active Pass and at nearby Enterprise Reef. Diving by charter boat is recommended.

The lee shore of Galiano Island extends along Trincomali Channel. Northwest of Montague Harbour and Parker Island a string of islands and islets includes Sphinx Island, Wise Island, Charles Island and Ballingall Islets. Passage is possible through them into Trincomali Channel. Use a good chart to avoid the rocks, especially around Wise Island and Ballingall Islets. Look for sandstone cliffs along the Galiano Island shore.

Trincomali Channel is wide and subject to wind. Navi-gate clear of Walker Rock, Governor Rock and Victoria Shoal. If you are travelling along the Salt Spring Island shore steer clear of Atkins Reef. These are all marked with navigational aids. Governor Rock requires a wider berth than the others due to a reef that extends west of the channel marker U45.

A short distance beyond Walker Rock on Galiano Island is **Retreat Cove** (see page 164). This tiny sheltered nook is protected from northwesterlies by Retreat Island. The shallows between the island and Galiano Island dries at low tide.

Montague Harbour Marina

Above: The docks at Montague Harbour Marina.

3451 Montague Rd   **VHF 66A**
RR 1 S-17 C-57
Galiano Island BC V0N 1P0
Phone: 250-539-5733 Fax: 250-539-3593

48° 53.465' N
123° 23.545' W

Charts 3313, 3473,
3442, 3462, 3463

www.nwboat.com/montague

Moorage and Services: Gas and diesel fuels and water are available at the dock with transient and permanent moorage. Power is 15 and 30 amps at some slips.

The general store has groceries, ice cream, gifts, island arts and crafts, books, charts, fishing licences, ice, bait and tackle.

The marina's Harbour Grill is a licensed restaurant with a sundeck. Light meals and draft beer are available. No off-sales.

A bus is available in summer for trips to the Hummingbird Pub located mid island, to Sturdies Bay or the golf course.

Kayak and moped rental services and boat tours are available. Adjacent facilities include the marine park at Montague Harbour where you will find mooring buoys and a small dock. The park has extensive walks and a campground, beaches and picnic facilities.
Tourism information–Phone 250-539-2233
www.galianoisland.com

162

Left: The store overlooking the docks at Montague Harbour Marina.
Below: Marina owner Marilyn Breeze takes a moment from her busy summer schedule. The marina can be seen at the far left in the aerial photo of the harbour. Note the beach on the north side of Gray Peninsula.

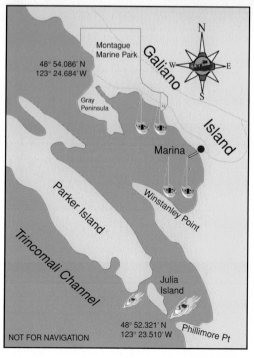

Montague Marine Park
48° 54.086' N
123° 24.684' W

Gray Peninsula

Galiano Island

N
W E
S

Marina

Winstanley Point

Parker Island

Trincomali Channel

Julia Island

48° 52.321' N
123° 23.510' W

Phillimore Pt

NOT FOR NAVIGATION

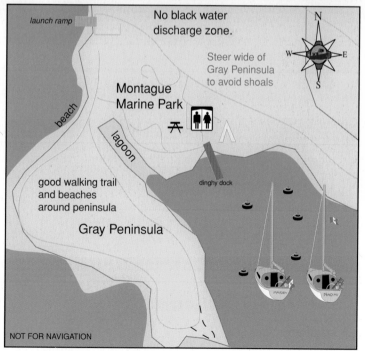

launch ramp

No black water discharge zone.

N
W E
S

Steer wide of Gray Peninsula to avoid shoals

Montague Marine Park

beach

lagoon

good walking trail and beaches around peninsula

Gray Peninsula

dinghy dock

NOT FOR NAVIGATION

Above: Montague Harbour with Parker Island in the foreground. Julia Island, seen to the right, can be passed either side. The passage to the left is much narrower and shallower than the main entrance, to the right of the island.
Below: Retreat Cove. This basin is located midway along the southwest shore of Galiano Island. The cove itself dries partially. It has a small dock, the one nearest to the entrance. There is space for a boat to anchor in the middle of the cove. The north side of the cove dries at low tide and is not a passage.

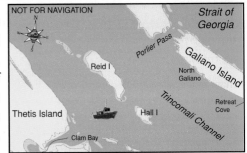

Above: Temporary anchorage may be taken at Dionisio Point in Porlier Pass.

There is a dock on the southeast side of Retreat Cove that can accommodate a couple of boats but it becomes very shallow at the inner end at low tide. The north part of the cove is not suitable for navigation.

Farther along the Galiano Island shore is **Spotlight Cove** that affords little protection from wind and another, deeper inlet that is occupied by private docks.

North Galiano, also known as **Spanish Hills**, has a small temporary dock with a store at its head. This is an exposed nook that is subject to lots of wave action from passing vessels and winds that come out of several directions. Brief stops at the dock are okay in calm weather.

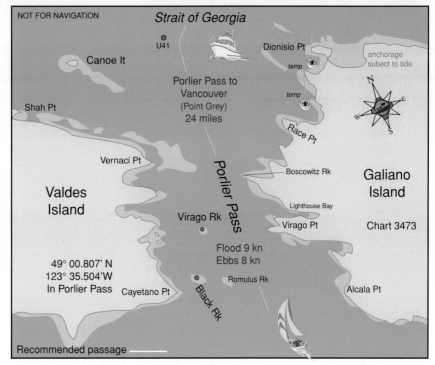

NOT FOR NAVIGATION

Strait of Georgia

Canoe It

U41

Dionisio Pt

anchorage subject to tide

Porlier Pass to Vancouver (Point Grey) 24 miles

temp

temp

Shah Pt

Race Pt

Vernaci Pt

Boscowitz Rk

Galiano Island

Lighthouse Bay

Valdes Island

Virago Rk

Virago Pt

Chart 3473

49° 00.807' N
123° 35.504'W
In Porlier Pass

Flood 9 kn
Ebbs 8 kn

Cayetano Pt

Black Rk

Romulus Rk

Alcala Pt

Recommended passage ———

Porlier Pass

Porlier Pass separates the northwest end of Galiano Island from Valdes Island. The pass has a series of nooks and coves. Some of them are slightly out of the current that floods up to 9 knots and ebbs up to 8 knots, especially off Race Point. It is best to forego anchoring in these in preference for the bight at **Dionisio Point Park**.

Leaving Porlier Pass for the Strait of Georgia, Dionisio Point forms a low bight of land with a well defined beach

Park and playground

Montague Harbour Marine Park is one of the finest on the coast, competing strongly with Prideaux Haven in Desolation Sound. It draws visitors by land and sea in large numbers in summer to enjoy the beaches, shoreline and mountain views, hike its Douglas fir forests and to walk through the rare Garry oak woodlands. Mount Galiano and the tall bluffs of Bluff Park at Georgeson Bay in Active Pass command magnificent panoramic vistas of the Gulf Islands. Galiano's shoreline includes some of the more prominent sandstone cliffs in the Gulf Islands. They can be viewed during a slow cruise along the southwestern shore between Montague Harbour and Retreat Cove.

The island was named for the Spanish explorer Dionisio Alcalá Galiano who explored the area aboard the schooner *Sutil* in 1792.

facing northwest. It is shallow but with enough water for temporary anchorage in calm weather. Beware of the reefs that protrude northward in line with either side of the beach. The park is intended for day use and has no facilities. The bay on the Strait of Georgia side of Dioniso Point dries at low tide and although possible, is not suitable for anchoring.

Mariners from all parts of the British Columbia lower mainland use Porlier Pass to reach the Gulf Islands. Their objective is usually Thetis Island or other destinations nearby, such as Wallace Island or the De Courcy Group. Sailboats and slow motor yachts will avoid Porlier Pass when the currents are at their strongest. It is best at high tide during or near slack. Refer to the tide tables for timing your passage.

Boats travelling from the Strait of Georgia through Porlier Pass from a north or northeasterly direction pass to port of Canoe Islet (the islet to your starboard) and its extensive reef marked at its south end by marker U41. Keep well off Dionisio Point to avoid the shallows previously mentioned. Pass well clear of Race Point and its nearby Boscowitz Rock to your

Top: Galiano Island occupies 57 square kilometres along the outer edge of the Gulf Islands, its east shore facing the open Strait of Georgia. Retreat Cove is the only suitable place to find shelter on the west side between Montague Harbour and Porlier Pass.
Above: Tied up at a float in Whaler Bay.

port and keep Virago Rock to your starboard.

If you are heading north or south in Trincomali Channel adjust your course once clear of Porlier Pass. You may prefer to head for the gap between Reid Island and Hall Island for continuation to Thetis Island. If so, continue straight towards the south side of **Reid Island** passing abeam of Romulus Rock. Pass between the islands, keeping a good distance off the Reid Island reefs. Go well beyond this passage, heading for the south end of Norway Island then turn on a course towards Clam Bay to avoid Centre reef.

The Strait of Georgia side of Galiano Island from Whaler Bay to Porlier Pass is exposed with no shelter or anchorage.

Top: A sailboat struggles against the Porlier Pass current off Race Point while a fast powerboat scoots past Canoe Islet in the Strait of Georgia. Note Reid Island, the tip of Hall Island and Norway Island with Clam Bay and The Cut to Telegraph Harbour in the distance (page 174).

Centre: Temporary anchorage may be taken in the north cove of Dionisio Point (north side of isthmus). Some vessels find their way through the shallows into the Strait of Georgia-facing cove. This is protected to some extent by the islets and reefs but should be considered temporary shelter and hazardous to enter. It makes a pleasant stop for those with small, shallow draft boats, willing to take the time and trouble to navigate the shallow water.

Left: Heading through Porlier Pass into the Strait of Georgia. Race Point is most prominent, to the right.

Panther Point and the adjacent temporary anchorage at the south end of Wallace Island. The anchorage in the centre of the island is at Conover Cove and to its north is Princess Cove. Beware of reefs extending beyond the entrance of Princess Cove and also in Houston Passage off the openings to the anchorages. Note the Secretary Islands and Kuper and Thetis islands beyond Wallace Island. There is a dinghy dock in Princess Cove and a dock for several boats in Conover Cove with an extended finger that serves as a dinghy dock.

Wallace Island

Passages, Islets and the Secretary Islands near Porlier Passage

Charts 3313, 3442, 3443, 3462, 3463

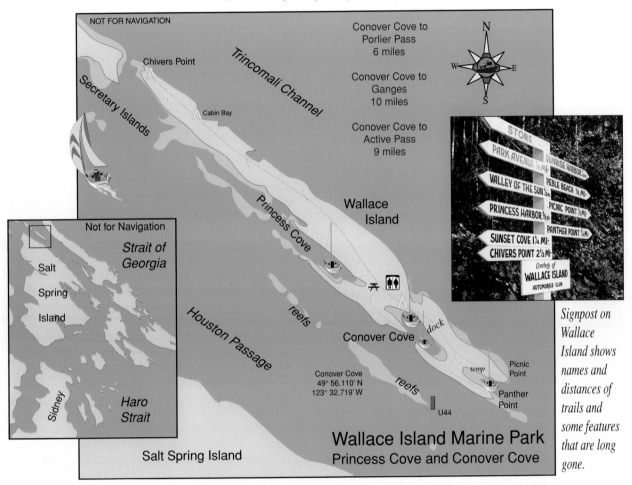

NOT FOR NAVIGATION

Chivers Point

Trincomali Channel

Secretary Islands

Cabin Bay

Conover Cove to
Porlier Pass
6 miles

Conover Cove to
Ganges
10 miles

Conover Cove to
Active Pass
9 miles

Princess Cove

Wallace
Island

Not for Navigation

Strait of Georgia

Salt

Spring

Island

Houston Passage

Sidney

Haro Strait

reefs

Conover Cove

dock

Conover Cove
49° 56.110' N
123° 32.719' W

reefs

temp

Picnic
Point

Panther
Point

U44

Salt Spring Island

Wallace Island Marine Park
Princess Cove and Conover Cove

STORE
PARK AVENUE ⅛ MI.   SUNRISE HARBOR
VALLEY OF THE SUN ½ MI.   PEBLE BEACH ¼ MI.
PICNIC POINT ½ MI.
PRINCESS HARBOR ⅜ MI.
PANTHER POINT ¾ MI.
SUNSET COVE 1¼ MI.
CHIVERS POINT 2½ MI.
Courtesy of
WALLACE ISLAND
AUTOMOBILE CLUB

Signpost on Wallace Island shows names and distances of trails and some features that are long gone.

From Porlier Pass you may travel south between Reid and Hall Islands, between Norway and Mowgli Islands off the north end of the Secretary Islands and down Houston Passage past Jackscrew Island. There are rocks and reefs in the vicinity and use of a large scale chart is essential. Temporary anchorage is possible in the indents of the **Secretary Islands**, but take precautions to avoid the rocks as charted.

Cruise to the Secretary Islands from Porlier Pass as described on page 166 or from Active Pass by way of Trincomali Channel. Wallace Island lies between Galiano Island and Salt Spring Island just south of the Secretary Islands.

Travelling from Telegraph Harbour by way of The Cut,

pass Penelakut Spit taking a heading for the north end of Norway Island to clear the shallow area in the middle of the passage. Small boats generally need not be concerned about this rock as it is more than six feet beneath the surface at low tide. Larger boats elect not to use The Cut. From Norway Island follow Houston Passage minding the marked reefs and pass around the south side of Jackscrew Island. Reefs running parallel to Wallace Island form a breakwater to the entrances of **Princess Cove** and **Conover Cove**. Use caution entering these coves, minding the drying reefs at the entrance to Princess Cove. Good anchorage for a fair number of boats can be found at Princess Cove or for a few at Conover Cove.

"There are several cabins on Wallace Island. The Conover Cabin has the most historical significance. It was begun in 1889 by settler Jeremiah Chivers and enlarged in 1946 by David Conover. A picnic shelter, was built in the 1930's. A 'fad' began in 1996 with driftwood art being hung in the shelter. Another cabin, known as the upper cabin, was built around 1950 and is an example of the vacation cabins that were rented out when the Conovers had a summer resort on Wallace Island."
—*Ellen and Cees den Holder, K2 Park Services*

Views of Princess Cove and Conover Cove.
Top left, top right and above: Anchored in Princess Cove. Centre left: Aerial photo shows the extent of Conover Cove. Deepest water is north of the dock. Left and below: At Conover Cove.

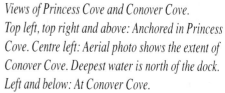

Wallace Island is an extremely popular and desirable stop in the Gulf Islands. This marine park is a superb place for those wanting to go ashore and walk. Trails run the length of the island and provide good walking and exercise. Along the pathway that transects the island there is a manual water pump that produces fresh water that should be boiled before use. The pathways wind through the woods to either end of the island with magnificent views out over Trincomali Passage and Houston Passage. There are tiny beaches or rocky coves to stop at and some spectacular views along the way. Grassy landings, camping and picnic sites are prominent features of this idyllic island. No fires are allowed on shore and some private waterfront property is located near or adjacent to the landings. The grounds, historic cabins and docks are maintained regularly by the park services staff.

The park includes facilities at Chivers Point, Cabin Bay and Conover Cove such as toilets, picnic tables and a shelter for group events. Camping and mooring fees are in effect.

Conover Cove with its historic landing and walking paths was once the private home of writer David Conover whose novels *Once Upon an Island* and *One Man's Island* have intrigued readers for decades. Conover, a wartime photographer, met and photographed Marilyn Monroe before her debut into fame and helped launch her career.

The shallows occupy most of the basin near the shoreline,

Top and above: Anchorage is taken in the north end of Conover Cove. The docks are usually busy but an early arrival may be rewarded with space. If anchored out go ashore by dinghy and walk the trails on the island. The dock is located immediately inside the entrance.

especially in the south side of Conover Cove. Drop anchor in the deeper water to the north. Anchorage in 10 to 11 metres is possible in Sunrise Bay at **Panther Point.** It is sheltered from all but southeast winds. In Princess Cove, stern tying to the shore leaves room for other vessels to drop anchor. Stern ties on shore are marked. Dinghy docks in both coves assure access to the island for mariners lying at anchor.

Above: Trincomali Channel lies in the foreground with Reid Island to the right and Hall Island to the left. Beyond them lies Norway Island near Penelakut Spit at the south side of the entrance to Clam Bay. The Cut can be seen between Thetis and Kuper islands in the centre of Clam Bay. The Secretary Islands begin at far left.

Left: Forlorn, the remains of an early model Jeep rests alongside a path on Wallace Island.

Opposite page: Arbutus trees hang over the water's edge in Conover Cove on Wallace Island and the public dock is a convenient place to stop for boats visiting the marine park. Limited space at the dock usually has most boats anchored nearby in the cove during summer.

Dinghy docks have been placed in Conover Cove and Princess Cove for access to the marine park. Overnight moorage fees are in effect at the dock in Conover Cove but there is no charge for use of the dinghy docks.

Left: The Secretary Islands with Jackscrew Island in the foreground. There is space for a few boats to anchor in the cove facing Porlier Pass, seen in the distance. The cove is part of the opening between the islands. The narrow section dries at low tide. Anchor also in the nook at Mowgli Island at the northwest side of the islands (see page 174).

Thetis Island

Telegraph Harbour, Kuper Island, Clam Bay and Preedy Harbour

Charts 3313, 3477, 3442, 3443, 3463

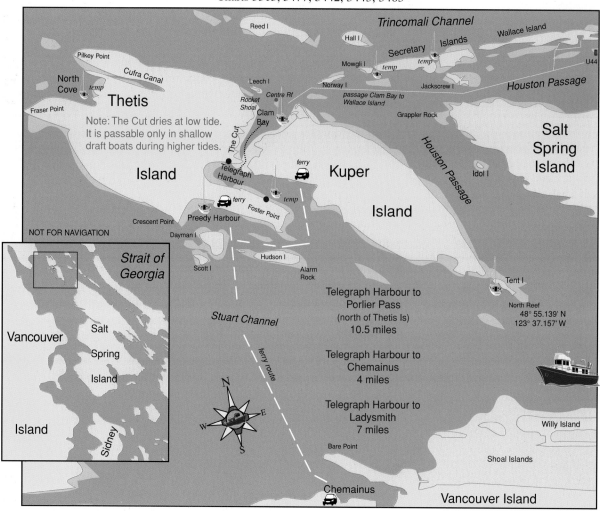

Arriving at Clam Bay from Porlier Pass, you can stay there during calm conditions or continue into Telegraph Harbour where you will find overnight moorage at one of the two marinas. This is a popular and busy harbour.

The shallow, narrow passage that separates Thetis Island from Kuper Island is the eastern entrance to one of the most centrally located and popular anchorages in the Gulf Islands. The boat passage (known as **The Cut**) lets shallow draft boats through at medium to high tides and denies passage to all but the tiniest of craft at low tides. It dries at a one foot tide.

Despite the quirks and whims of the famous passage, it is the waterway that experienced cruising yachtsmen associate with Telegraph Harbour. Explore the area. Take a dinghy ride from Clam Bay through The Cut and see the shallows for yourself before taking your boat through.

The alternative and safest route into Telegraph Harbour is around the south end of Kuper Island or to the north around Thetis Island. If you are coming from a Vancouver Island base and returning to Vancouver Island after a stay at Telegraph Harbour, the shallow passage between Thetis and Kuper is not

Thetis Island facts of interest

The 4,000 acre island's average rainfall is a paltry 115 cm. Its population is about 350. The island was named for the 36-gun frigate *Thetis*. It is divided in half by the 49th Parallel.

A favourite destination

At Thetis Island you can choose to stop in Telegraph Harbour for a hearty lunch at one marina or a light meal and milkshake at another . You could anchor out or find overnight moorage and walk the roads of the island. Along the road following the canal which separates Thetis Island from Kuper Island you will find yourself in a rural setting where it is common to see domesticated geese and other varieties of waterfowl. Or, once safely tied up at the dock you can walk down to the ferry landing and board a ferry for Chemainus, a town that needs no introduction to local residents as well as many foreign visitors. Often Chemainus and its famous murals are high on their list of priorities.

The Gulf Islands are inhabited by large numbers of talented and renowned artists. Their works can be seen, admired and purchased at many local art and craft centres.

Originally there was a bridge that connected Thetis and Kuper islands because the school and post office were located on Kuper Island. The bridge was removed in the 1950s and plans were set for the canal between the two islands to be dredged to allow passage of larger vessels. However it was not dredged and now it dries at low tide.

Top: The view south over Telegraph Harbour and Kuper Island shows also Trincomali Channel and the Secretary Islands at left and Stuart Channel to the right.
Centre: Telegraph Harbour from the southwest.
Above: Porlier Pass from Houston Passage with the Secretary Islands in the centre. Mowgli Island is at the far left with Hall Island beyond.

Above: Clam Bay and Telegraph Harbour. To the left, Kuper Island is home to the Penelakut First Nations. Stuart Channel lies in the background.
Below: The Cut, from the west. Note the bight at Penelakut Spit which affords some protection for the anchorage in Clam Bay.

Above: The Cut is clearly seen between Thetis and Kuper islands.
Left: The passage becomes shallow and almost dries at low tide.

an issue. But if you are crossing the Strait of Georgia and entering the Gulf Islands through Porlier Pass in a small boat then consider The Cut as a passage. Choose a high tide to approach this shallow waterway or plan the longer, but safer and pleasant, detour around either Thetis or Kuper Island.

Clam Bay

Some vessels will stop and anchor in Clam Bay while waiting for the tide to rise to enable safe passage through The Cut to Telegraph Harbour. Many use Clam Bay as a destination. It is subject to some wind conditions but summertime breezes rarely cause difficulty for boats at anchor. Favour the southeast shore of the bay where you can take anchorage in calm conditions in the lee of **Penelakut Spit**. It is shallow with a

sandy bottom adjacent to Kuper Island. I have seen small vessels beached on Kuper, but it is a First Nations reserve of the Penelakut tribe and should be respected as private.

The south route from Porlier Pass around Kuper Island to Telegraph Harbour is followed by passing between Norway Island and Mowgli Island. Steer west of the marked rock and islets beyond them and continue along the south leg of Houston Passage to enter Stuart Channel. Pass well clear of the shallows off Tent Island and Sandstone Rocks then take a course past the south side of Tent Island and follow the Kuper Island shoreline past Augustus Point and Active Point. The anchorage at **Tent Island** off Kuper Island is shallow and boats should anchor not too close to the beach. It is generally well protected in summer and only westerly winds and the occasional large boat passing may cause a disturbance. Continuing to Telegraph Harbour, stay north of North Reef and Escape Reef but steer wide around the shallows at Active Point and Donkele Point.

When rounding Thetis Island from the north the western entrance to Telegraph Harbour is via Preedy Harbour where seals can be seen sometimes sunning themselves on the rocks

Above: Telegraph Harbour and the ferry landing at Kuper Island.
Right: The cove at Tent Island off Kuper Island is shallow and boats should not anchor too close to the beach.
Bottom: North Cove at the north end of Thetis Island has some reefs protruding from shore but anchorage is possible in appropriate depths when there is no northerly or northwesterly wind.

just off Foster Point. Thetis Island Marina juts out into the main passage and posted signs call on boats entering Telegraph Harbour to slow down.

The anchoring area in the curve of the harbour is separated to some extent by the placement of private local residential mooring buoys. Take care not to run afoul of them.

The two local marinas offer all weather moorage with services and extensive facilities. These are available to guests mooring overnight at the marinas. Mariners anchored out may access the marinas by dinghy in order to visit the stores and post office. Places of interest include the island winery.

At Thetis Island Marina look for the post office, liquor store, pub and restaurant. At Telegraph Harbour Marina you will want to head up the dock for the delicious old-fashioned milkshakes for which the 50s style marina store has become famous, or a cafe style light meal.

The regular clientele at the two marinas can be quite different. Naturally, the pub is more of a social centre and congregating place for those who enjoy the pub atmosphere.

Above: South view of Preedy Harbour showing Dayman Island and Scott Island. False Reef can be seen to the right. Anchoring is best between Telegraph Harbour Marina and Thetis Island Marina.
Left: The marked reef at the south end of Preedy Harbour.
Bottom: A boat motors up to the fuel dock at Telegraph Harbour Marina. Entrance to The Cut is beyond the depth marker at right.

Thetis Island Marina's pub serves meals from a varied menu. Paul Deacon and his staff cater to moorage customers with fuel and marina service as well as operate the busy pub, off sales, restaurant, store and post office.

Telegraph Harbour Marina, farther into the harbour, is suitable for families and family activities. They serve a hot breakfast and light lunches. Owners Ron and Barbara Williamson promise a warm welcome to all mariners. Many visitors to these marinas have found themselves cancelling their continuation plans in favour of just staying around longer than planned. The harbour is very protected from winds and weather and moorage is usually available with reservations preferred in the busy summer period.

Not far from Telegraph Harbour Marina is a well-known supplier of fresh roasted coffee, open at most times to sell their rich aromatic beans or freshly ground coffee to islanders and visitors alike. Just stroll up to the entrance of their property and make your purchases at the gate stall.

Preedy Harbour is a fairly exposed anchorage but larger vessels have little problem from the occasional summer winds. Most anchor near the shallows in the north end of the bay near the floats of the large Bible school and summer camp on the waterfront.

Thetis Island is known for its arts and crafts. Crafts on sale on the island represent the works of various islanders and prices are generally more favourable than those for similar items in the cities. Enquire about their wares and location details at the two marinas.

If you enjoy strolling, a walk along any of the Thetis Island roads is relaxing and easy without any significant hills or traffic. At low tide you can don your boating boots and go beachcombing along the dry but marshy flats of The Cut and watch your fellow boat owners trying their luck getting through.

Like most of the Gulf Islands water is in short supply on Thetis and visitors are asked to use only what they need. Garbage is a problem for marinas but they do allow disposal of garbage by moorage customers. The convenience stores at both marinas carry some souvenirs, charts and books as well as a selection of items for replenishment of boating supplies. Other than these stores at the two marinas there are no shops or shopping centres on the island. However, Chemainus on Vancouver Island, which is nearby or a short ferry ride away, has a wide selection of stores and restaurants to please everyone. It is worth the ferry ride to stroll around this artistic Vancouver Island centre. The passenger ferry leaves Thetis Island for the run across Stuart Channel eight times a day.

Preedy Harbour

Often overlooked due to the better known shelter of Telegraph Harbour, Preedy Harbour is where the ferry from Chemainus lands. This lovely bay, surrounded by spectacular scenery, also offers some quiet and semi-protected anchoring

A sailboat slips through Preedy Harbour. Beyond, a powerboat lies at anchor for a temporary stop at the beach off Hudson Island.

Map labels:

To Porlier Pass

Norway I

Centre Reef

To Wallace Island

Leech I

Penelakut Spit

Rocket Shoal

Clam Bay

Kuper Island

Thetis Island

The Cut

Use The Cut at your own risk. It's best at high tide. Use the markers as a guide and stay centre of the trench in the channel. All anchorages indicated are affected by wind. It is safest to stay at a marina. Do not anchor so as to restrict vessel movement at local marinas. Kuper Island is the private property of the Penelakut First Nations.

Telegraph Harbour Marina

Telegraph Harbour

ferry dock

Thetis Island Marina

temp

ferry dock

dinghy dock

temp

Beacons

FIR

Preedy Harbour

temp

Dayman I

Hudson I

ferry route

Scott I

Alarm Rk

N 48° 58' 083"
W 123° 40' 952"

False Reef

Pleasure boat passages

NOT FOR NAVIGATION

in favourable weather. The best anchorage is located in the north end of Preedy Harbour. Be cautious, especially in other parts of the harbour. Read the signs for submarine cables.

Preedy Harbour is protected by **Hudson Island** and Dayman Island, both privately owned. A passage between them is used as the Chemainus ferry route to Thetis Island. The ferries pass nearby so expect the occasional but mild wash from them. A small craft dock is located alongside the ferry dock that can be used for dinghies from vessels anchored in Preedy Harbour. There are some hazards to be mindful of when entering Preedy Harbour so consult a large scale chart.

When entering Telegraph Harbour by way of Preedy Harbour from the north pass near Crescent Point and follow a mid channel course between Thetis and Dayman Islands. Pass southwest of the beacons marking rocks and reefs opposite Hudson Island.

At the north end of Thetis Island **North Cove** is protected from all but northwesterly winds. Drop the hook in the south corner of the cove, avoiding the reef extending off shore. Do not anchor in **Cufra Canal** (page 174) which opens into the island at the east side of the cove, as it dries at low tide. The adjacent land is private property.

Telegraph Harbour Marina

48°58.890' N
123° 40.224 W

Charts 3313, 3477, 3442, 3443, 3463

Thetis Island, BC, V0R 2Y0 VHF 66A
Phone: 250-246-9511 Fax: 250-246-2668
Toll Free 1-800-246-6011
www.telegraphharbour.com

Moorage and Services: 3000 feet of moorage. The marina offers gas and diesel fuels, oils, marine supplies, fishing gear, charts, bait, ice, laundry, showers and washrooms. There is limited water–use sparingly. Power at the docks is 15 and 30 amps. The store/coffee shop has groceries, milkshakes, ice cream, baked goods, snacks, frozen foods, books, gifts, arts and crafts. Light breakfasts and pizza, salad and sandwiches are available in the Burgee by the Bay coffee shop. Tables inside or on the patio. There is a recreation building, a playground and facilities for volleyball, shuffleboard, horseshoes and picnic/barbecues. Groups may book events. Nearby there is parkland, beach trails and road access for walking or cycling. The marina is near the ferry to Chemainus with its shops and famous murals. Farmers' market on Saturdays.

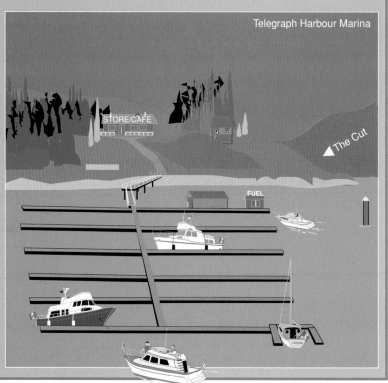

Telegraph Harbour Marina

Left and below: The store at the marina is busy in summer offering refreshments and light meals.

Telegraph Harbour Marina is seen from the air on the opposite page. Note the boat passage (The Cut) and the shallows.

Left: Shallow anchorage. Many of the boats moored in the bay are on private buoys.

Bottom: The docks are a popular place for mariners to meet.

Thetis Island Marina and Pub

48° 58.661' N
123° 40.135' W

Charts 3313, 3477, 3442, 3443, 3463

Thetis Island BC V0R 2Y0
Ph: 250-246-3464 Fax: 250-246-1433
Web: www.thetisisland.com
VHF 66A
Moorage and services:

Transient moorage. The fuel dock sells gas, diesel and propane. Desalinated water–in very limited supply–guests are asked to use it sparingly. Power at the docks is 15 and 30 amps. Laundry, showers and washrooms are available to guests. There is a liquor store, post office and store with groceries, dairy treats, bakery products, frozen foods, gifts, arts and crafts, books and snacks. Marine supplies are available including tackle, bait, charts, tide tables and ice. The restaurant/pub serves meals inside or on the large sunny patio. Catering to yacht clubs–pig roasts, barbecue pit, covered pavilion. Float plane service to marina. The facility is located near the ferry landing for Chemainus.

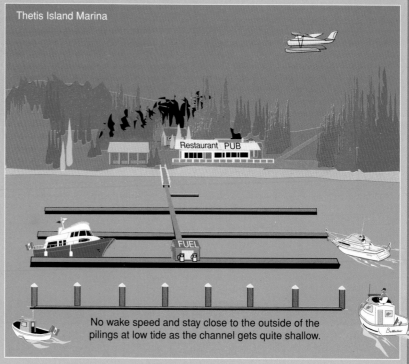

Thetis Island Marina

Restaurant PUB

FUEL

No wake speed and stay close to the outside of the pilings at low tide as the channel gets quite shallow.

Opposite and top this page: Thetis Island Marina from the air clearly shows the layout of the docks.

Above: The fuel dock at Thetis Island Marina and boat owners taking part in a game at an annual Rendezvous.

Centre: Restaurant service at the marina pub is extended to the patio.

Bottom: The pub is part of a complex with store, liquor agency and post office.

De Courcy Group

Ruxton, Whaleboat, Mudge and Link Islands
Plus Valdes Island to Gabriola Passage

Charts 3313, 3475, 3443, 3463

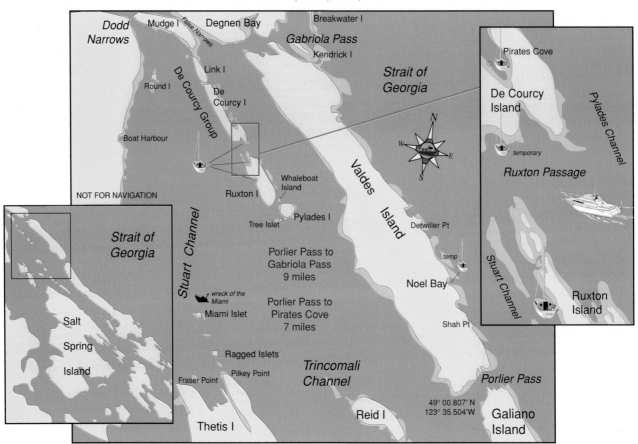

Whaleboat Island

This group of islands lies between Stuart Channel and Pylades Channel directly north of Fraser Point at the tip of Thetis Island. Leaving Preedy Harbour travel past the shallows off Fraser Point and take a course past the Ragged Islets. Small craft run past the beacon on the Ragged Islets or between them and Pilkey Point. In so doing exercise care finding the deepest passage. The wreck of the *Miami* lies in shallow water off Miami Islet. Travel around the red buoy U40 to your starboard and proceed well clear of Danger Reefs, passing Tree Islet also off to your starboard. Enter Whaleboat Passage or take a heading on Ruxton Passage and the beacon marking the reef at the north end of Ruxton Island.

If you elect to visit Whaleboat Island you will find it tucked in behind the south end of Ruxton Island. It is in the northern section of Whaleboat Passage and is shown as a marine park on recent editions of charts. If approaching Whaleboat Passage from the direction of Porlier Pass keep well off the north end of Pylades Island to avoid its reefs and shallows. There is limited anchorage in the shelter of Whaleboat Island and a fair number of boats use the passage to travel between Pylades and Stuart Channels. The location is a short distance north from Porlier Pass or south from Gabriola Passage. This is an undeveloped marine park but has been maintained in its pristine condition representing the

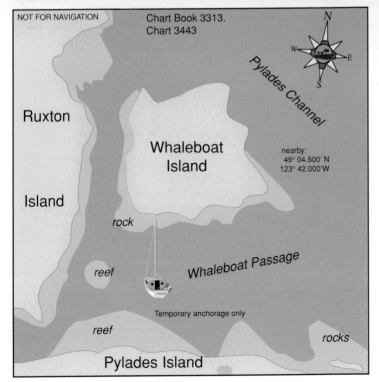

Above: Whaleboat Island, seen clearly also in the photo to the left, blends with Ruxton Island. Pylades Island is separated from Ruxton Island by Whaleboat Passage. There is a reef and a rock to be aware of as shown in the adjoining diagram. Use your large scale charts 3313 and 3443 for accurate navigation and safe anchoring.

NOT FOR NAVIGATION

Chart Book 3313.
Chart 3443

N
W   E
S

Pylades Channel

Ruxton

Island

Whaleboat
Island

nearby:
49° 04.500' N
123° 42.000'W

rock

reef

Whaleboat Passage

Temporary anchorage only

reef

rocks

Pylades Island

best of the natural state of the Gulf Islands. There are no park facilities. Some mariners use the narrow pass between Ruxton Island and Whaleboat Island for anchorage while others prefer the more open area south of the shallow reef nearby. The anchorage is temporary and care should be taken to avoid the indicated rocks.

Ruxton Island

Anchor in **Herring Bay** at the north end of Ruxton Island. It faces onto Ruxton Passage south of De Courcy Island and can be reached from Stuart Channel or Pylades Channel. Entrance to the bay is best by passing between the islets off the north end of Ruxton Island and the beacon on the reef opposite them. At less than high tide this reef has large drying rocks with a white sandy beach. The bay is exposed to northerly winds, known to cause serious problems in stormy weather.

There is a small, shallow cove on the west side of Ruxton Island that also affords temporary, fair weather anchorage. It is exposed to wind and sea conditions from the southwest.

Above: Kayakers love the area when it is calm. The red beacon marks the reef at Herring Bay, Ruxton Island. The beacon is also seen in the inset. Herring Bay at the north end of Ruxton Island is not only a popular anchorage but also it is considered overflow anchorage for the nearby Pirates Cove. Weathered sandstone ridges form the inner shore. The entrance faces northwest from Ruxton Passage. The temporary anchorage shown on the east side of Herring Bay should be used only for a short duration.
Inset below: Sandy beach areas among the exposed reefs at low tide mark the entrance to Herring Bay.

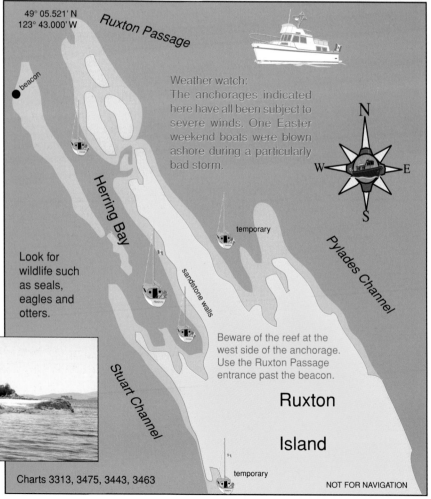

49° 05.521' N
123° 43.000' W

Ruxton Passage

beacon

Weather watch:
The anchorages indicated here have all been subject to severe winds. One Easter weekend boats were blown ashore during a particularly bad storm.

N
W — E
S

Herring Bay

Look for wildlife such as seals, eagles and otters.

temporary

sandstone walls

Pylades Channel

Beware of the reef at the west side of the anchorage. Use the Ruxton Passage entrance past the beacon.

Stuart Channel

Ruxton

Island

temporary

Charts 3313, 3475, 3443, 3463

NOT FOR NAVIGATION

Top: Herring Bay anchorage on the northwest side of Ruxton Island.

Left: The anchorage at Ruxton Island's north end is protected in most conditions in summer. Beware of northerly and northwesterly winds. The white sandy beaches and exposed reefs make for popular sunbathing spots, easily accessible by dinghy from moored boats. Entrance is from the north past a beacon (not shown in photo) to your starboard.

Below: The anchorage on the west side, centre of Ruxton Island. It has a very shallow entrance and a small basin within the cove that has enough water for small craft to anchor. Enter with care at lower tides.

Left upper and bottom: Noel Bay on the exposed side of Valdes Island near Porlier Pass. It is a temporary stop good for viewing the Strait of Georgia. Noel Bay is the favoured temporary anchorage of the two coves seen in the lower photograph. Another cove, close north of Detwiller Point which lies farther along the Valdes Strait of Georgia shoreline, is more exposed and not favoured although there are mooring buoys placed there.

Note: Squalls frequently blow into Pirate's Cove abeam of those stern tied on the east side of the anchorage. In these circumstances boats have been known to blow together. Keep a wind watch when warnings are issued.

Stern tying is strongly recommended. Look for tie-up rings in the shoreline. There is a white arrow on the shore at the entrance and an X on a tree that shows alignment with the passage into Pirates Cove.

NOTE: Private markers may not always remain in position.

Entrance to Pirates Cove is around a reef extending beyond the beacon to opposite a point marked on the shore. Watch your depth and keep an eye on the submerged reefs as you enter.

Visitors are fascinated to learn of the dubious recent history of De Courcy Island. There is a lot more to the story than told in this guide. See the bibliography and suggested reading on page 247.

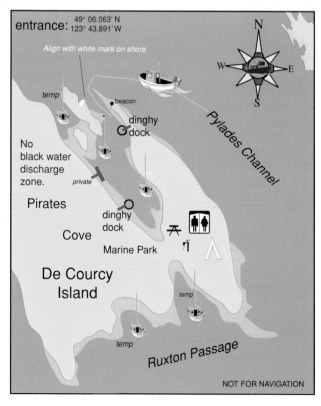

entrance: 49° 06.063' N
123° 43.891' W

Align with white mark on shore

temp

beacon

dinghy dock

Pylades Channel

No black water discharge zone.

private

Pirates

dinghy dock

Cove

Marine Park

De Courcy Island

temp

temp

Ruxton Passage

NOT FOR NAVIGATION

190

Left: From the south looking into Pirates Cove.
Above: Pass between the reef and the red marker.
Spar buoy U 38 marks the outer edge of the
exposed reef.

Anchorages are available also nearby at Pirates Cove Marine Park on De Courcy Island, or Degnen Bay off Gabriola Passage to the north of Pylades Channel. Just beyond Degnen Bay and through Gabriola Pass is Silva Bay where facilities are available for fuel, moorage and supplies.

Pirates Cove Marine Park is a short distance north and beyond Ruxton Island on De Courcy Island. This is a popular anchorage and a good preferred alternative to Whaleboat Marine Park. There is also good anchorage at Herring Bay in fair weather at the north tip of Ruxton Island.

Pirates Cove Marine Park

The cove is located at the southeast end of De Courcy Island facing onto Pylades Channel. Care should be taken at the point of entry into the cove, as there is a reef extending beyond the natural rocky breakwater. In summer this usually has a telltale covering of kelp. A white marker on shore also reveals where the reef ends. In the entrance as the narrow passage widens there is another reef to starboard. Ensure that you pass this submerged rock before turning into the cove keeping slightly east of centre channel. Directly ahead is a dinghy dock. Another is on the opposite shore. There are also private docks in the cove. Use a large scale chart (3475) and watch the depth of the waters ahead of you as you navigate.

The anchorage has depths of up to 3 metres. It is deeper in the east side of the cove. If you anchor at high tide you may wind up touching bottom at low water. Northwesterly winds can affect boats anchored along the east side of the cove. The small dinghy docks should not be used for moorage other than for dinghies. If the anchorage becomes crowded additional anchorage is available at Herring Bay.

Pirates Cove Marine Park is extensive and includes walking trails, toilets, campsites, picnic tables and a park host during summer.

There is a trail to a beach and anchorage facing Ruxton Passage and a view point of some interest. There are fasci-

nating sandstone formations lining the shore around Pirates Cove. Explore the tidepools and walk the island trails. Walk the beach and note the abundance of arbutus (madrona) trees.

Pirates Cove has been a popular marine park for a long time. The cove's checkered history includes the settlement on the island of the infamous Brother XII who was known to have coerced crew, and especially wives, to remain on the island leaving their vessels to sail off without them.

Beyond Pirates Cove one can easily reach Degnen Bay or Silva Bay on Gabriola Island with its many facilities. After leaving Pirates Cove Marine Park your northbound choices are Dodd Narrows and the city of Nanaimo or Gabriola Passage and the community of Silva Bay.

Some mariners choose to stop at unnamed coves. Do so with caution and watch tidal action and wind forecasts. Be prepared to maintain an anchor watch if you decide to stay overnight.

A popular anchorage

Pirates Cove Marine Park on De Courcy Island is one of the most popular anchorages in the Gulf Islands. The park has two anchoring areas, the most popular with recreation boaters being the one that faces the northwest. Mooring rings for stern tying are located along the shoreline. The quieter south-facing corner is generally preferred by kayakers as a haulout and campsite. Two day-use-only dinghy docks allow access to picnic and camping areas in the park.

Several middens in the park indicate use of the land for over 3000 years. The rich intertidal area is abundant with clams, oysters and sand dollars. Mooring fees are in effect.

De Courcy Island was named after Michael de Courcy, captain of the H.M.S *Pylades*, a vessel that charted these waters from 1859 to 1861.

The De Courcy Group and Pylades Channel with the mountains and foreshore of Vancouver Island in the background can be seen beyond Gabriola Pass. Kendrick Island and Dogfish Bay are in the foreground. Degnen Bay is to the right, midway through the passage.

Brother XII at the De Courcy Islands

Island folklore has it that Brother XII, resident on De Courcy Island, would lure wives away from their husbands aboard visiting boats at Pirates Cove. There are many versions of the story of Brother XII or Albert Edward Wilson, an Englishman who had travelled to British Columbia and worked in Victoria in the lowly capacity of baggage clerk. These tales of the strangely alluring cult leader have been told in several books including *The Brother XII: The Devil of De Courcy Island* by Ron MacIsaac, Don Clark and Charles Lillard, and *The Promise of Paradise* by Andrew Scott.

In 1927 Wilson convinced some people in his home country that a solar collision was imminent that would affect life on earth. He adopted the title of Brother XII and, using a yacht he received from a wealthy woman, he embarked on a voyage to BC. He had influenced many to join him in a new found existence in this far off land as part of an organization he established and called the Aquarian Foundation.

Wilson was described as a slim figured man with a pointy nose and pale eyes. His slouch and the wart at the tip of his nose characterised him as almost fictional. How he impressed people, and especially some of the more wealthy of the community, is beyond reason. This he did before he left Britain and again when he was settled in the Gulf Islands. He ended up with property not only on De Courcy but also on Vancouver Island and Valdez. Among those to join his group were professional people and socialites, barons, and business executives from back home as well as from across North America. Some came to join him, others sent money to support the "cause." And amazingly, they put up with abusive treatment from their erstwhile leader.

On the newly settled lands the Foundation set about establishing new communities. Houses were built to replace tents in which they had been living. Work was onerus and some of the cult abandoned the community. *The Vancouver Sun* carried a story at the time about one woman who was left abandoned on a remote beach on Vancouver Island after her relatives reported to police that she had run away from her new husband to join the cult. She was but one of about 700 who escaped Wilson and his dictatorship.

Wilson ended up in court, sued by some members for embezzlement of large sums of their money. Staunch supporters stood by him and the trial was a fiasco. However, in 1930, local authorities eventually shut him down, forcing the society to be dissolved. He returned to England but returned later and built fortifications on his land.

Brother XII was not only brutal but also a sadist. He beat followers who disagreed with him, threatened them with a "peaceful new life" and made other suggestions of terminating their miserable existence under his rule. He claimed to have visions and mystical powers. He pursuaded yet another wealthy woman to part with some of her wealth and she donated $25,000 to the Foundation. He met another woman whom he convinced to marry him, sent his present wife back home and then drove the new one insane when she produced a girl instead of a boy child who he had claimed would be the new leader of his people. He went back to England with yet another wife called, Madame Zee.

Perhaps this is where the tales of his luring wives from their husbands originated. Another bit of folklore was that he left gold buried on De Coucy Island when he and one of his staunch women followers fled under death threats against him. Wilson ended up in Switzerland where he died under the name of Julian Skottowe. Not his first alias. He changed his name to Amiel de Valdez when the society was dissolved in the 1930s.

His land was eventually divided up among some remaining members but monies granted to them in a court hearing were never paid. He had been a master of skulduggery, a charmer of women, and a very false prophet.

Gabriola Island

Gabriola Passage, Degnen Bay, Silva Bay
Dodd Narrows and the way to Nanaimo

Charts 3313, 3475, 3458, 3443, 3463

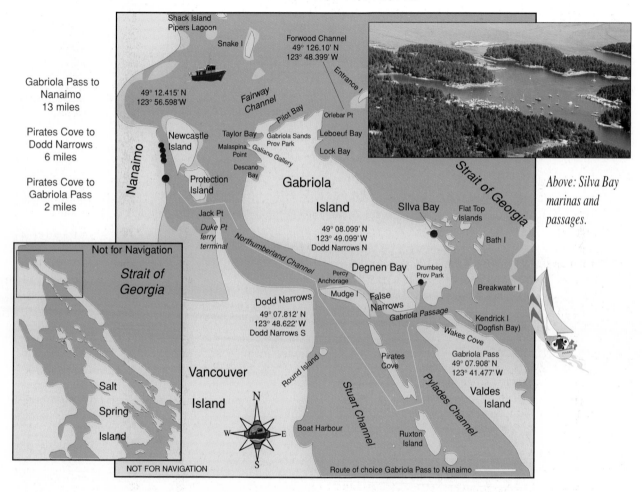

Gabriola Pass to
Nanaimo
13 miles

Pirates Cove to
Dodd Narrows
6 miles

Pirates Cove to
Gabriola Pass
2 miles

Above: Silva Bay marinas and passages.

NOT FOR NAVIGATION

Route of choice Gabriola Pass to Nanaimo

The shortest distance from Vancouver to the Gulf Islands is by way of Gabriola Island. A popular destination is Silva Bay with its marinas and spacious, albeit sometimes windswept, anchorage. Entrance to the sheltered passages and islands in the lee of Gabriola Island is either past the north end of Gabriola via Entrance Island or through Gabriola Pass at the south. The north entrance is usually used as a route to Nanaimo from across the Strait or for venturing southwards into the Gulf Islands when coming from northern waters.

Views of the swift waters of Gabriola Passage are possible from **Drumbeg Park**. Here too one can find sandstone formations. This park is known for its Garry oak ecosystem and excellent swimming conditions.

Gabriola Island is home to many artists and their work can be seen and purchased throughout the island. A short walk from any of the marinas will take you past homes offering crafts and art. Many of these works are available also at stores on the island.

If you find yourself at Gabriola Island in October take in the Thanksgiving Gallery tour of island artists' studios. *www.festivalgabriola.ca*. And if you find your way to the village not far from **Descano Bay** you will find coffee bars, a large grocery store, pharmacy and a variety of smaller but surprisingly delightful stores and galleries.

Top: Dodd Narrows looking north into Northumberland Channel from Stuart Channel.
Above: False Narrows, separating Mudge Island from Gabriola Island.

False Narrows

This waterway, wedged between Gabriola and Mudge islands, is navigable only for small boats. Reefs protrude right into the passage and at low tide it becomes impassable for anything but paddle boats. There are range markers in the channel that should be strictly monitored at all times when taking passage through this possible alternative route to Cumberland Channel. Currents run at up to 4.5 knots, a lot less than Dodd Narrows. Larger boats should avoid False Narrows. To the northwest of False Narrows is **Percy Anchorage**, used frequently by vessels waiting to pass southward through Dodd Narrows at slack tide. To reach this anchorage, approach from Northumberland Channel when travelling into the Gulf Islands from Nanaimo or by way of Dodd Narrows when leaving Stuart Channel northbound.

Top: Dodd Narrows. Use chart 3457. Vessels often congregate in Percy Anchorage at the east end of Northumberland Channel to await slack tide. The currents run to eight knots in the passage.

Left:The shallow passage between Link Island and Mudge Island (left) is not navigable. Some boats have taken anchorage in the basin formed by the indent between the two islands and the reefs either side. This is not a recommended overnight anchorage. Careful use of the large scale chart should be made when approaching places like this.

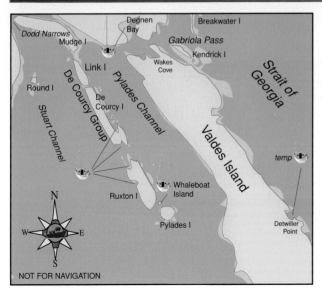

Dodd Narrows

When leaving Pirates Cove, or travelling to Nanaimo by way of the protected inside passage, head for Dodd Narrows. If you are travelling along the Vancouver Island shoreline from Ladysmith and Yellow Point avoid the reef that protrudes well off shore at Flewett Point just before **Boat Harbour** (see page 83). Pass either side of Round Island and through Dodd Narrows at or near slack tide.

From Silva Bay and Degnen Bay, Pirates Cove or Ruxton Island enter Stuart Channel by way of Ruxton Passage. Take a straight line course for Dodd Narrows from the southwest tip of De Courcy island. Slower craft should wait for a drop in the speed of the current, which can run to 9 knots in Dodd Narrows. Be courteous to other boats. Faster boats avoid creating a wash for slow moving and smaller craft, sailboats and hull speed trawlers that may be negotiating the passage, particularly when the currents are still running.

Right: Gabriola Pass from Pylades Channel. To the right of the widening passage is Degnen Bay, a good, but limited anchorage.

Opposite: Silva Bay showing marinas and adjacent passages.

Right, bottom: Gabriola Island with Degnen Bay in the foreground and False Narrows to its left.

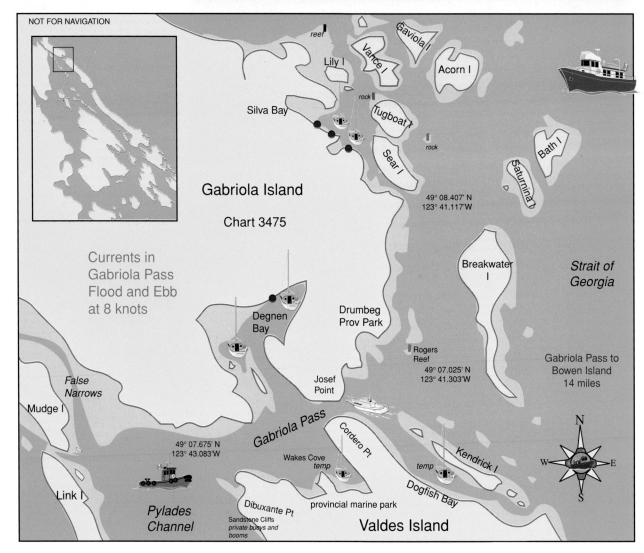

NOT FOR NAVIGATION

reef

Gaviola I

Vance I

Lily I

Acorn I

rock

Silva Bay

Tugboat I

rock

Bath I

Sear I

Saturnina I

Gabriola Island

49° 08.407' N
123° 41.117'W

Chart 3475

Breakwater I

Strait of Georgia

Currents in
Gabriola Pass
Flood and Ebb
at 8 knots

Degnen
Bay

Drumbeg
Prov Park

Gabriola Pass to
Bowen Island
14 miles

Rogers
Reef
49° 07.025' N
123° 41.303'W

False
Narrows

Josef
Point

Mudge I

N

W   E

S

49° 07.675' N
123° 43.083'W

Gabriola Pass

Cordero Pt

Kendrick I

Wakes Cove
temp

temp

Link I

Dogfish Bay

Pylades
Channel

Dibuxante Pt

provincial marine park

Sandstone Cliffs
private buoys and
booms

Valdes Island

Gabriola Passage

If you are heading for Gabriola Passage and Silva Bay from the De Courcy Group or beyond, plan your route through Ruxton Passage on the east side of Stuart Channel. Cross Pylades Channel and make for Dibuxante Point at the en-trance to Gabriola Pass. Or cross to the near shore of Valdes Island and slowly run parallel to it to take in a view of the magnificent sandstone cliffs.

Entering Gabriola Pass steer wide of the beacon marking

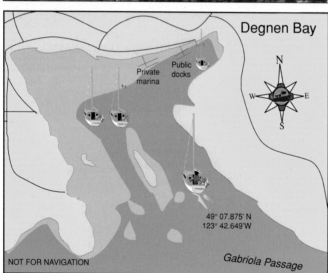

Degnen Bay

Private marina

Public docks

N
W   E
S

49° 07.875' N
123° 42.649'W

Gabriola Passage

NOT FOR NAVIGATION

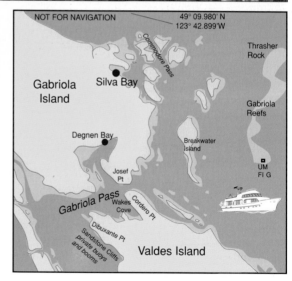

NOT FOR NAVIGATION

49° 09.980' N
123° 42.899'W

Gabriola Island

Silva Bay

Commodore Pass

Thrasher Rock

Gabriola Reefs

Degnen Bay

Breakwater Island

UM
FI G

Josef Pt

Wakes Cove

Cordero Pt

Gabriola Pass

Dibuxante Pt

Sandstone Cliffs private buoys and booms

Valdes Island

the protruding reef. The current floods east and ebbs west at a maximum of 8 knots. The pull from it is strongest at the 500 metre wide narrows between Cordero Point and Josef Point. This is a busy passage in summer and operators of slower boats especially should exercise caution. It is the narrowest passage into the Gulf Islands from the Strait and therefore one can expect tidal currents to run faster than the wider Porlier or Active passes.

Two anchorages which range from fair to good are at **Wakes Cove**, a provincial park on the inside of Gabriola Pass, and **Dogfish Bay** in the lee of **Kendrick Island**.

Wakes Cove is quite open and exposed to wind and passing traffic wash. A small dock gives access to the park. Dog-

fish Bay is narrow and subject to a fair amount of current due to the opening at the south end of Kendrick Island.

Degnen Bay

Many mariners travel to Silva Bay taking Gabriola Passage at the slack and completely miss the protected anchorage at Degnen Bay. That's perfectly acceptable as it leaves it less crowded for those who prefer to keep it that way.

If you are going into Degnen Bay take passage just off the south shore southwest of Josef Point. You can continue along the shore into the bay and drop anchor or carefully double back around the small island and reefs in the centre of the bay and anchor in the shallows. Do not use the south-

ern waters of the bay as a passage. A marina inside the bay is private with moorage for local residents only. The public dock farther in is available when space permits.

Degnen Bay is near Silva Bay by road as well as by boat through Gabriola Pass. It's a good, sheltered but small anchorage surrounded with private docks. There is not a great deal of room in the bay for anchoring and most yachtsmen simply forego stopping there in favour of the larger anchorage at Silva Bay. If you do get to anchor at Degnen Bay, however, go ashore by dinghy and tie up at the public wharf. There is quick and easy access to the road on the island for walking. Look for the killer whale petroglyph at the head of the bay.

After passing through Gabriola Pass, regardless of the tide and state of the current, turn to starboard and anchor off Kendrick Island. The island belongs to the West Vancouver Yacht Club and is private.

Tidal currents run between it and the Valdes Island shore with some rocks and reefs at the narrow end of the anchorage. It is possible for small boats to pass through at higher tides. It's best, however, to continue to Silva Bay from Gabriola Pass staying to the starboard side of Rogers Rock, clearly marked, and turning into the passage beyond, sheltered from the open Strait of Georgia by **Breakwater Island**.

Steer wide of Kendrick Island if you are heading out into the Strait and use a chart to navigate past the reefs and

Above: A sailboat heads out of Silva Bay through the shallow passage south of Sear Island. The opening faces Breakwater Island and the Strait of Georgia. Beyond Breakwater Island lies Gabriola Reefs. Opposite page: Degnen Bay. There is a public dock that is usually crowded and a private marina that has moorage for local boats. Anchorage is fairly well protected in the shallows of the outer bay.

shallows off Valdes and Breakwater Islands.

When headed across the Strait of Georgia in the direction of Howe Sound or Vancouver, or if you are continuing north directly up the coast of Vancouver Island you might want to stop in sheltered waters at the edge of the Strait to await suitable weather. Degnen Bay or Silva Bay are suitable places to wait, either at anchor or at a marina.

Silva Bay

Most people know Silva Bay as it is also the first anchorage you arrive at when crossing the Strait from the lower mainland of BC. It is known for its marinas and stores, craft shops and one time bustling shipyards. The Royal Vancouver Yacht Club has a station in Silva Bay at Tugboat Island. There is a fuel dock at Page's Marina as well as one at Silva Bay Marina. And the shipyard, which still offers haul outs and repairs, is now the site of a wooden boat building school.

Silva Bay Resort and Marina

Entrance (Commodore Pass)   49° 09.080' N
123° 40.962'W

3383 South Rd, Gabriola BC V0R 1X7
Phone: 250-247-8662 Fax: 250-247-8663
Charts 3313, 3475, 3443, 3463   **VHF 66A**
www.silvabay.com

Marina and customer services: BroadbandXpress. The marina serves gas, diesel and outboard mix. Repairs and boat service are available. Washrooms, laundry and showers are available at the marina. There is moorage, a ways, a shipyard, water at the dock and power with 30 and 50 amp service. Other services include an off-sales liquor store and a restaurant overlooking the bay, the Silva Bay Bar and Grill, located on the property. It is open for breakfast during summer. Activities and services available include kayaking, boat charters, horseback riding, golf, biking, tennis, a children's park and a Sunday market in summer. The property is also the site of the Silva Bay Shipyard School. It is located at the resort property and offers a full time accredited six-month course in wooden boat building and repair. The school is the only one of its kind in Canada. Gabriola Island Visitor Information: 250-247-9332 *www.gogabriola.ca*

Silva Bay

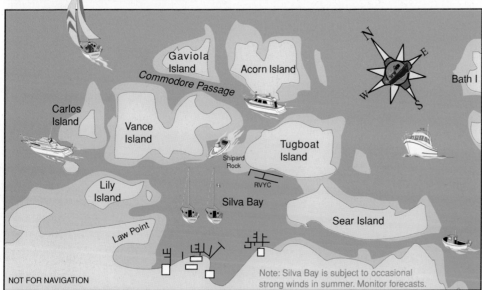

Gaviola Island

Acorn Island

Commodore Passage

Bath I

Carlos Island

Vance Island

Shipard Rock

RVYC

Tugboat Island

Lily Island

Silva Bay

Sear Island

Law Point

NOT FOR NAVIGATION

Note: Silva Bay is subject to occasional strong winds in summer. Monitor forecasts.

Top: A busy day at Silva Bay. The fuel dock at Silva Bay Marina is to the right and visitor moorage to the left.
Below: A view of Silva Bay Marina from the docks of Pages Marina.
Opposite page: Silva Bay showing the marinas and the Royal Vancouver outstation at Tugboat Island.

Above: Commodore Pass, seen beyond the anchorage, is the most common entrance to Silva Bay. Pass clear of Shipyard Rock in the entrance.

Above: Guests enjoying the patio at Silva Bay Marina.
Below: Launching two new boats at the Silva Bay Shipyard wooden boat building school.

Silva Bay anchorage and approaches

Approaching Silva Bay passage is often taken out of the Strait of Georgia by way of Gabriola Passage. Check the tables and avoid the swift flowing waters. Mariners wait for the tide at Degnen Bay or Wakes Cove. Those planning to head through Gabriola Passage from the Strait should time their arrival to coincide with slack water, or head into Silva Bay to wait.

Enter the anchorage cautiously to avoid Shipyard Rock off the north end of Tugboat Island. The best course is to aim for Law Point after passing north of the beacon at the entrance. There is lots of room for many boats to anchor in the bay in depths to 7 metres. However, keep a wary eye on the weather as winds can cause anchors to drag. Those who arrive early may have a choice of shallower, more protected anchorage in the lee of Law Point just off Lily Island.

A cove to visit at slack tide is Dogfish Bay in the lee of Kendrick Island. The bay is subject to tidal currents. Anchoring in it requires a careful watch on the currents and therefore overnight anchorage is not recommended. However, members of the West Vancouver Yacht Club sometimes use it as an anchorage. At high tide it is possible to slip into or out of Dogfish Bay, carefully, through the narrow passage at the south end of Kendrick Island. Valdes Island is the largest Gulf Island with no ferry service. It is sparsely populated and has little to offer by way of anchorage and shelter.

G&S Quality Meats and Grocery (Silva Bay Inn)
3415 South Rd, Silva Bay, Gabriola BC V0R 1X0
Phone: 250-247-9351
Shallow water moorage for smaller boats. The grocery store sells fresh produce and an outstanding selection of cheese, meats and home made sausage. It also carries hardware, ice and propane. Accommodation is available at the Silva Bay Inn, which offers self-contained kitchenette suites.

Top and centre: A view across Silva Bay from the docks at the far northwest end. These docks, which were being rebuilt in 2006, give access to the waterfront grocery and meat store and Silva Bay Inn. The Royal Vancouver Yacht Club on Tugboat Island is a private facility.
Right: Sketch shows location of marinas and store in Silva Bay.

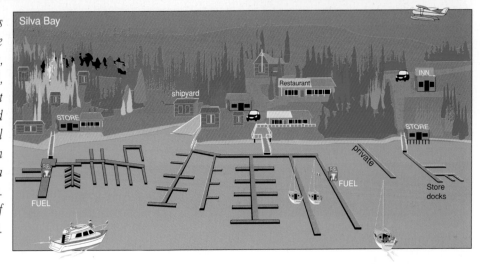

Above: Page's Marina is located at the north end of the passage between Gabriola Island and Sear Island. Watch depths at low tide and use a chart when navigating. Centre: Page's has books and art at the office ashore. Bottom: Page's fuel dock is large and easy to access.

Mariners crossing the Strait of Georgia head for Silva Bay via Thrasher Rock at the north end of Gabriola Reefs, or for Gabriola Pass around the south end. Be wary of the drying rock off the southern tip of Breakwater Island. Pass north or south of the privately owned Flat Top Islands.

Approach Silva Bay from the northeast after passing well clear to the north of Thrasher Rock. Continue between Bath Island and Acorn Island keeping clear of Brant Reef north of Acorn Island. Keep Acorn Island well off to your starboard. Use the channel marker on the outside of Tugboat Island as a guide to the Silva Bay entrances. The popular entrance to the bay is through the passage between Tugboat Island and Vance Island. Alternative passages can be made between Acorn and Gaviola (small boats) if you are approaching from a more northerly direction. Beware of the reefs well to the east and north of Acorn Island. Alternatively go between Gaviola and Vance or around the west side of Vance Island, passing outside of Carlos Island and entering the narrow passage past the marker PA between Lily Island and Vance Island. All of these alternative passages are narrow and mostly shallow so favour the main entrance between Tugboat and Vance Islands.

When entering Silva Bay through the Tugboat northern route remember be mindful of Shipyard Rock marked by buoy U39 just inside the entrance. It needs to be cleared before turning into the bay. Many have turned too soon and run aground. It is clearly shown on local charts.

| Entrance (Commodore Pass) | 49° 09.080' N |
| Chart 3313, 3475, 3443, 3463 | 123° 40.962' W |

Page's Resort & Marina

3350 Coast Road, Gabriola, BC V0R 1X7
Phone: 250-247-8931 Fax: 250-247-8997
www.pagesresort.com

Moorage and Services: Fuel–gas, diesel, outboard oil. Moorage mostly to 30 feet, some larger. Water is available at the docks–limited supply. Power supply is 15 amp. Comfortable year round rental cottages with an adjacent picnic area. The office and store has charts, art, books, gifts and crafts. Regular music concerts and art shows are held at the home of the owners, Ted and Phyllis Reeve. For marina guests there are showers, laundry and washrooms. Road access from the marina provides good opportunity for walks. Fishing charters can be arranged. Some supplies are available and more at the grocery store at Silva Bay Inn. There is a taxi service to the golf course and shopping centre. Gabriola Island Visitor Information: 250-247-9332 Toll Free 1-888-284-9332 *www.gogabriola.ca*

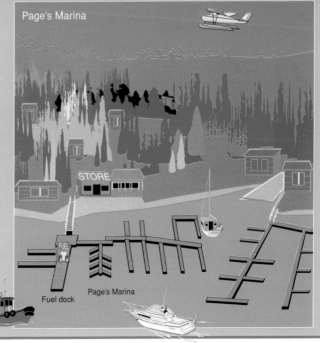

Page's Marina

STORE

FUEL

Fuel dock

Page's Marina

Top: Entrance Island from Forwood Passage. There is a shallow shelf that extends well into the passage. It is marked by a spar buoy. Right: From the air Forwood Passage separates Orlebar Point from Entrance Island. In the foreground is Leboeuf Bay with an unnamed 12 metre high islet a short way off shore. Seas are often choppy, with swells from the northwest at this point. The view across the Strait of Georgia includes the entrance to Howe Sound.

Vessels approaching from Gabriola Passage (Degnen Bay) can slip into Silva Bay via the narrow, shallow waterway between Gabriola Island and Sear Island. This is the south entrance, which is shallow with depths of 2 metres or less at low tide, and narrow at places.

Anchoring in Silva Bay is popular. Beware of strong northerlies or northwesterlies that tend to howl into the bay at times causing the need for a watch during the night when, all too often, anchors drag.

Page's Resort and Marina, which has been around a long time, has fuel at the dock and a store with some interesting works of art on display as well as casual supplies, books and crafts. The facility is popular as a transient marina.

Adjacent to Page's Resort and Marina is the larger Silva Bay Marina which has a large restaurant on site. It also has fuel at the dock and lots of transient moorage space.

During summer there are functions and events that have a

Note: Pilot Bay–This is a no black water discharge zone. The bay abuts Gabriola Sands Provincial Park and is used by bathers.

local flavour but appeal to visitors. Take in the Maritime Festival and wooden boat launch, the Dancing Man Music Festival, the Gabriola Art Theme Show in April and the first of the season's Salmon Series Derby in May. This is also when the Gabriola Farmers Market begins for the season. The Salmon Series continues each month during summer. In August there is a Beat the Heat Summer Fest and non-marine boat race and in September another music festival. Some events are centred away from Silva Bay including places such as Gabriola Sands Provincial Park at Taylor Bay. If you want to take part transportation can be arranged through the marinas.

Adjacent to Silva Bay Marina is the Silva Bay Inn, known to many long-time mariners as the Boatel. Here you will find

Left: Taylor Bay and Pilot Bay. Entrance Island lies in the distance. Pilot Bay and Taylor Bay are popular for swimming. The isthmus lies adjacent to Gabriola Sands Provincial Park. Below: The small, private cove at Descano Bay mostly dries at low tide. Note the ferry landing.

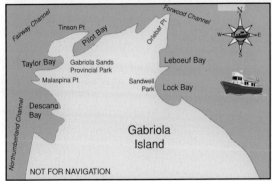

Left: Snake Island with a flotilla of small craft and a ship of the BC Ferries carrying spectators at the sinking of the former Canadian naval destroyer escort Saskatchewan. It was scuttled by the Artificial Reef Society of BC in 1997.

Photo by Jeanne Karcz

The classic yacht Euphemia *in Commodore Pass approaching Gabriola Passage en route from Silva Bay to Pylades Channel.*

a well stocked store on the waterfront. It is accessible by boat, preferably a small boat or dinghy as the docks are in very shallow water at low tide. The store carries groceries and fresh produce as well as dairy products and fresh meats from their butchery. All so well priced that boaters travelling to Silva Bay are advised to stock up for their boating excursions on arrival there rather than in advance of leaving home.

Tinson Point

Passing through Forwood Channel that separates Entrance Island from Gabriola Island, head west along Fairway Channel to Tinson Point (diagram page 193). **Pilot Bay** lies to the east of this headland while **Taylor Bay** lies to the west. Taylor Bay is a popular swimming area. Gabriola Sands Park abuts both bays and Malaspina Galleries sandstone cliffs is along the shore to the south of Taylor Bay. Temporary anchorage may be taken off the beaches in either bay. Westerlies affect Taylor Bay. Pilot Bay is sheltered from northeasterlies. There is a small shopping centre at Gabriola Sands Provincial Park.

Descano Bay opens to the south of Malaspina Point and is not a suitable anchorage. BC Ferries run between Nanaimo and Descano Bay off Fairway Channel. Passengers include both those who live on the island and those who come to visit Gabriola's fine parks. There are campsites at Descano Bay Regional Park near the ferry landing, a beautiful sandy beach at Sandwell Provincial Park, Lock Bay, and an array of petroglyphs at Petroglyph Park.

Gabriola Sands Provincial Park, adjacent the anchorage at Taylor Bay is a popular destination for landlubbers and mariners alike. This is where sand sculpture competitions are held every August long weekend, and where access is easy to the Malaspina Galleries with its sculpted sandstone features.

Approaches to Nanaimo

On the southwest side of Gabriola Island Northumberland Channel leads to Nanaimo Harbour. There you will find a large anchorage (bigger than at any other BC city), a spacious public marina and numerous private marinas, fuel and all services of a small city. Enter Northumberland Channel between Purvis Point and Joan Point and proceed west past the Harmac pulp mill and the ferry landing at Duke Point. Round Jack Point and turn west for McKay Channel off Protection Island.

When entering Nanaimo Harbour from the Strait of Georgia pass either side of Entrance Island keeping clear of the shallows that extend into Forwood Channel. Pass well off Tinson Point and take a heading along Fairway Channel for the south tip of Protection Island.

From a northerly direction use Rainbow Channel or Horswell Channel passing either side of Five Finger Island and keeping clear of Hudson Rocks. Continue south towards Newcastle Island.

Entrance to Nanaimo Harbour can also be made either side of **Snake Island**. Watch for the reef marked with the red channel marker P2. Another substantial, marked reef abuts Snake Island and there are two sunken vessels as artificial reefs in close proximity to the island. They are well marked with buoys. (Nanaimo–see page 85).

Northern Gulf Islands

Marinas, passages and anchorages from Nanaimo to the Comox

Charts 3313, 3447, 3458, 3443, 3463. 3458, 3459, 3527, 3512, 3513

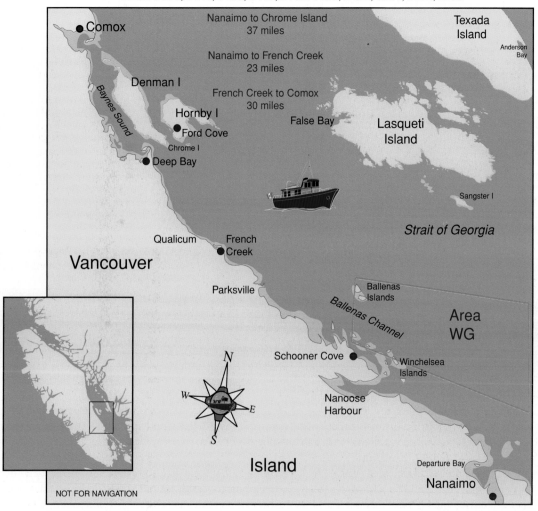

NOT FOR NAVIGATION

The Northern Gulf Islands include areas every bit as fascinating as some of the Southern Gulf Islands. Denman and Hornby Islands and Lasqueti Island make up the group of the northern Gulf Islands. They are popular destinations with marine parks, wide sandy beaches and lots of charm and ambience. Places like Tribune Bay on Hornby Island and the marine park at Sandy Island attract many mariners as well as sun worshippers and overnight campers throughout summer. Adjacent waterways lead mariners in protected passages to

coves and anchorages such as False Bay on Lasqueti Island. Resident artists and craftsmen and women produce fine work and their products can be found at galleries and community centres on the islands.

Getting there from the Southern Gulf Islands requires passage along a coastline that can be as calm as it can be inhospitable and care should be taken monitoring weather conditions and predictions. Leaving Nanaimo by way of Departure Bay pass Tyne Point on Newcastle Island after

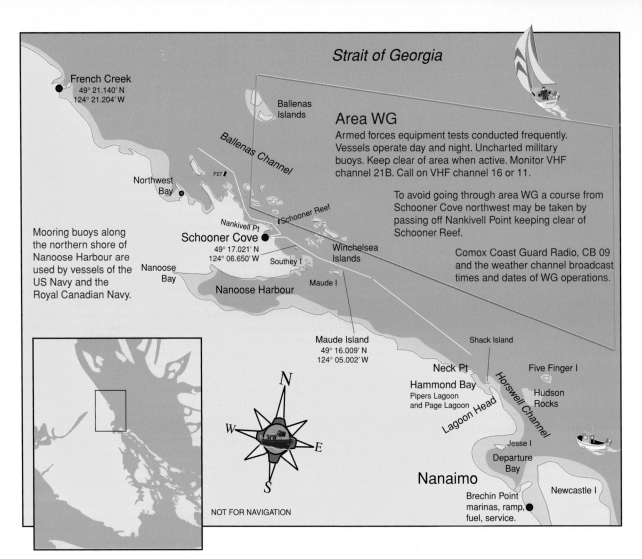

Strait of Georgia

French Creek
49° 21.140' N
124° 21.204' W

Ballenas
Islands

Area WG

Armed forces equipment tests conducted frequently.
Vessels operate day and night. Uncharted military
buoys. Keep clear of area when active. Monitor VHF
channel 21B. Call on VHF channel 16 or 11.

To avoid going through area WG a course from
Schooner Cove northwest may be taken by
passing off Nankivell Point keeping clear of
Schooner Reef.

Comox Coast Guard Radio, CB 09
and the weather channel broadcast
times and dates of WG operations.

Ballenas Channel

P27

Northwest
Bay

Nankivell Pt

Schooner Reef

Schooner Cove
49° 17.021' N
124° 06.650' W

Southey I

Winchelsea
Islands

Mooring buoys along
the northern shore of
Nanoose Harbour are
used by vessels of the
US Navy and the
Royal Canadian Navy.

Nanoose
Bay

Nanoose Harbour

Maude I

Maude Island
49° 16.009' N
124° 05.002' W

Shack Island

Neck Pt

Five Finger I

Hammond Bay

Pipers Lagoon
and Page Lagoon

Lagoon Head

Horswell Channel

Hudson
Rocks

Jesse I

Departure
Bay

Newcastle I

Nanaimo

Brechin Point
marinas, ramp,
fuel, service.

N
W   E
S

NOT FOR NAVIGATION

Hammond Bay
49° 17.341' N
124° 07.868' W

Neck Pt

Hammond Bay

Five Finger I

Vancouver
Island

Pipers Lagoon

Page Lagoon

Horswell Chanel

Clarke Rk

Hudson
Rocks

Lagoon Head

Brandon
Islands

Jesse Island

Departure Bay

BC Ferries

Newcastle
Island

N
W   E
S

NOT FOR NAVIGATION

Nanaimo

Texada
Island

Denman Island

Hornby Island

Lasqueti Island

Strait of Georgia

N
W   E
S

Vancouver
Island

Area shown at top

Schooner Cove

Nanoose Harbour

Nanaimo
area shown to left

NOT FOR NAVIGATION

Left: A temporary stop in Hammond Bay will afford an opportunity to view Shack Island. These rustic dwellings were built by squatters during the Second World War and have been occupied ever since.

clearing Brechin Point and then pass between Pimbury Point and Shaft Point. Watch for BC Ferries operations in Departure Bay with vessels leaving the terminal regularly on the hour every two hours and arriving on the half hour approximately every two hours. Stay well off the shoal on the Newcastle Island shore.

Anchorage in the lee of the Brandon Islands in Departure Bay is prohibited due to submarine cables. Stay clear of the Pacific Biological Station, located on the shore opposite the Brandon Islands. Pass between Nares Point and Jesse Island and head for the open Strait past the buoy at Horswell Rock that lies well off shore from Horswell Bluff.

A serious note of caution: As you leave Nanaimo you will be approaching the area WG. It is an Armed Forces equipment testing area and cannot be transited during exercises. Avoid the area at all times because there may be uncharted buoys and other navigational hazards.

The WG area lies across a large section of the Strait of Georgia off Nanoose Harbour. It extends from a point between Entrance Island and the Trail Islands off the Sunshine Coast, cuts through part of the Winchelsea Islands and includes the entire Ballenas Channel. Verify that it is not operational before entering the area. Listen on VHF channel 21B or call on channels 16 or 11.

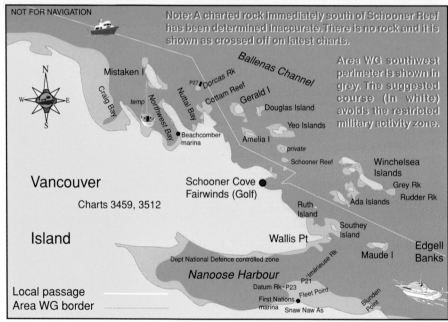

Schooner Cove has good, sheltered moorage and is located a short distance north of Nanoose Bay. The Winchelsea and adjacent islands are farther apart than appears on smaller scale charts. The indicated passage can be easily navigated with care and attention and using the large scale chart 3459. This diagram illustrates the approximate course local mariners use to avoid area WG.

NOT FOR NAVIGATION

Note: A charted rock immediately south of Schooner Reef has been determined inaccurate. There is no rock and it is shown as crossed off on latest charts.

Area WG southwest perimeter is shown in grey. The suggested course (in white) avoids the restricted military activity zone.

Ballenas Channel

Mistaken I

temp

Craig Bay

Northwest Bay

Nuttal Bay

P27 Dorcas Rk

Cottam Reef

Gerald I

Douglas Island

Yeo Islands

Amelia I

Beachcomber marina

private

Schooner Reef

Winchelsea Islands

Vancouver

Charts 3459, 3512

Schooner Cove
Fairwinds (Golf)

Ruth Island

Ada Islands

Grey Rk

Rudder Rk

Southey Island

Island

Wallis Pt

Maude I

Edgell Banks

Dept National Defence controlled zone

Nanoose Harbour

Impérieuse Rk

P21

Local passage
Area WG border

Datum Rk - P23

First Nations marina

Fleet Point

Snaw Naw As

Blunden Point

Follow Horswell Channel between Lagoon Head and Hudson Rocks to Neck Point. Keep clear of Clarke Rock to your port. In calm conditions, a temporary stop in **Hammond Bay** will be rewarded with a view of **Shack Island**. This crescent-shaped little island lies just outside Pipers Lagoon off Lagoon Head and Page Lagoon. The island comprises an outcropping of low bluffs overhanging a rocky beach. It lies in the shallow waters between Pipers Lagoon and Neck Point. Shack Island's very interesting history has it that the shacks were probably Japanese fishermen's cabins. Today there appears to be a number of occupants, possibly weekend fishermen.

Beyond Hammond Bay, from Neck Point to Nanoose Harbour is a featureless stretch of water. It starts out with a fairly uninterrupted shoreline and extensive shallows and continues past Nanoose Harbour into the **Winchelsea Islands** where it becomes a lot more interesting. The Strait along this shore can become rough, particularly in northerly winds, so if you are not in the mood for a bumpy ride stay in the shelter of Nanaimo until better conditions prevail.

Winchelsea Islands

Continue into **Nanoose Harbour** which requires keeping well to the north in its entrance to avoid a substantial shallow area that extends well across the entrance and shelters Snaw Naw As, a private marina at Fleet Point. Pass the marker P21 at Impérieuse Rock and P23 west of Datum Rock to reach the marina. This First Nations operated marina has little to offer

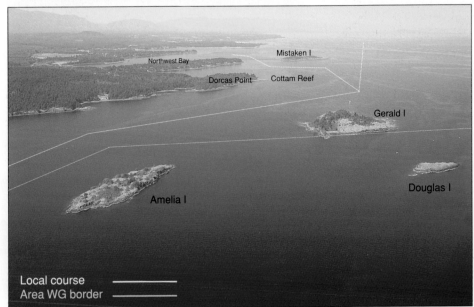

Heading north from Schooner Cove pass between Vancouver Island and Amelia Island (left foreground. Then pass Gerald Island avoiding area WG completely by favouring a course slightly closer to the Vancouver Island shore. The northwestern corner of WG reaches midway in the local passage. Beyond that point head in a more northerly direction to pass around Cottam Reef. Pass P27 at Dorcas Rock and enter Nuttal or Northwest Bay between Cottam Point and Mistaken Island.

at present and most mariners looking for moorage will continue to Schooner Cove. Naval vessels and other large craft can often be seen anchored in Nanoose Bay and it is not recommended for small vessels. Continue rather to the more interesting navigational waters of the Winchelsea Islands.

Enter Ballenas Channel and pass the **Ballenas Islands** to their south and west, or to their north if you are travelling to Lasqueti Island. You can bypass the Winchelsea Islands to the north when the Department of Civil Defence restricted area WG is not active. Continue west past the Winchelsea and Ada Islands to Schooner Cove.

Schooner Cove

This is a sheltered, protected cove that has a large marina with lots of space for visitors. It is served by a large hotel with accommodations, moorage, marine supplies, launch ramp, restaurant/pub and coffee shop.

Beyond the entrance of Nanoose Harbour, passage may be taken either side of Maude Island. Stay north of Southey Island keeping well off its northern side to avoid a reef that dries one metre at low water. Proceed through the passage, noting some shallow areas (5.5 to 7.4 metres at low tide) which are of little concern to most pleasure craft, and pass the north side of Ruth Island and a nearby kelp covered reef as you head for the breakwater at Schooner Cove Marina. While there enjoy a round of golf at the popular nearby Fairwinds golf course. Later, continue along the Vancouver Island shoreline to Denman Island and Hornby Island. Alternatively, at this juncture, cross through area WG if not active and go directly to Lasqueti Island and Texada Island.

From Schooner Cove, round Nankivell Point being cautious of the shallows and rocks near shore and find the channel inside Schooner Reef, Amelia Island and Gerald Island as you head north along the Vancouver Island shore. Pass close to Gerald Island to avoid the reefs off Dorcas Point. Pass around the Dorcas Rock marker P27 at Cottam Reef. Local small craft are familiar with other channels, but use them only if you too, know them well. Pass Nuttal Bay.

Continue between Mistaken Island and Cottam Point and

PV photo 2005

Fairwinds Schooner Cove Resort & Marina

3521 Dolphin Dr
Nanoose Bay BC V9P 9J7   **VHF 66A**
Marina Phone: 250-468-5364 Fax: 250-468-5744
www.fairwinds.ca
Hazard: Drying rock in entrance to marina.
Keep marker to starboard and keep close to floats.
Marina services: BroadbandXpress wireless internet.
Gas, diesel and oils. marine service is available and can be arranged at the dock. 360 permanent and transient berths. Water is available at all berths. Power is 15, 30 and 50 amp. There is a pumpout station at the end of G dock. Hotel accommodation, restaurant, lounge, pub are located at head of the marina. For guests there is a coffee shop as well as laundry, showers and washrooms, an outdoor pool and a hot tub, tennis court, scuba shop and a fitness centre. Marine supplies, fishing gear, licences, charts, bait, ice, books, gifts and snacks are available at the hotel marine office. There is a cold beer and wine store on site. A courtesy shuttle operates to the Fairwinds 18 hole course golf, post office, banks and the grocery store. Nearby parks and road access provide walking or cycling. Mountain bike rentals. 1300 acres of trails.

Charts 3459, 3512   49° 17.238' N
                                     124° 08.003' W

Small bus tours to local attractions.
Fishing is excellent near the marina. Horseback riding, nature walks. Sail charters and fishing charters.
Group facilities. A launch ramp and picnic area overlook the marina. An activities dock is available. Boat rendezvous welcomed and catered.

Fairwinds Golf & Country Club
Toll free 1-888-781-2777 Phone: 250-468-7666

Schooner Cove Marina

214

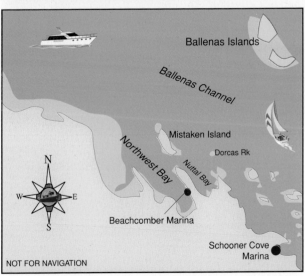

Ballenas Islands

Ballenas Channel

Mistaken Island

Dorcas Rk

Northwest Bay

Nuttal Bay

Beachcomber Marina

Schooner Cove
Marina

NOT FOR NAVIGATION

Continuing north to Comox

"From Nanaimo go along the coast to Campbell River with a stop possible at Schooner Cove, one of the largest and finest facilities anywhere with hotel and all amenities including golfing nearby, good fishing and good scuba diving. Farther north up Vancouver Island's east coast is Comox with a vast set of docks, private and public. Comox Marina or those adjacent have lots of transient moorage and restaurants ashore, a park and nearby stores and other facilities along with events such as the Filberg Festival and Nautical Days each August to keep you entertained and enthused about the stopover. En route you will find sheltered facilities at Deep Bay or French Creek."   —*Docks and Destinations.*

Beachcomber Marina

1600 Brynmari Rd, Nanoose Bay BC V9P 9E1
Phone/Fax: 250-468-7222   VHF 66A
Water. Power at the dock is 15, 30, 50 amp. Store with marine supplies and some groceries.
Limited guest moorage. Charts 3459, 3512

Refer to charts for reefs. Enter the bay and marina between the red and green buoys.

on along the shore northbound. There is temporary anchorage and a small, private marina in the lee of **Cottam Point**. Beachcomber Marina accepts overnight visitors when space is available. Temporary anchorage is recommended when winds are calm and not blowing from the northwest.

Choose your ideal weather conditions for the open waters along the Vancouver Island shore. Strong northwesterly winds can make this area quite uncomfortable and entering shelter during strong winds can be a challenge.

Avoid the shallows off the long sandy beaches of Parksville and Qualicum Bay and if time and weather permit, stop for

Above: Approaching the Winchelsea Islands from the south. Note Grey Rock to starboard of the vessel. Southern tip of Lasqueti Island in the background.

Above and below: Schooner Cove entrance and departing Schooner Cove northbound. Gerald and Douglas Islands lie ahead.

*Top: Sailing towards the Winchelsea
Islands past the Ada Islands.
Above left: Wallis Point and the
entrance to Nanoose Harbour.
Above right: The Ballenas Islands.
Left: Winchelsea Islands in the
foreground with Ada Islands in the
centre and Southey Island off Wallis
Point at the Nanoose Harbour
entrance.*

The large well-protected French Creek basin has been carved from the shoreline to provide protected moorage at this midway point between Schooner Cove and Baynes Sound. When seas are picking up and getting rough, it may be best to bypass this shelter to avoid a difficult entrance. Inside, mariners are protected from the seas that roll past in windy conditions.

French Creek is a refuge for mariners travelling up the coast. If the weather kicks up and a place is needed for shelter this large public harbour is well protected by a substantial breakwater.

Once inside there are numerous docks, mostly occupied by commercial vessels. A recreational boat will always find a place to tie up. Sometimes rafting to another vessel is necessary.

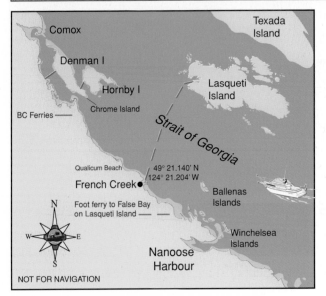

supplies or a visit to the fresh fish market at French Creek. This is primarily a commercial boat harbour. Entrance to the harbour is between the breakwater arms. A northwesterly or northerly wind may make the passage into the French Creek Harbour intimidating as the waterway begins to feel very narrow as you enter. Avoid entering in rough seas.

A straight run from French Creek towards Chrome Island at the southern tip of Denman Island will take you to the entrance to Baynes Sound or Lambert Channel.

French Creek

Harbour Authority dock Phone: 250-248-5051
A substantial breakwater offers shelter from the open Strait and moorage is available at the public docks. There are restaurants and stores nearby. The marina has facilities for visitors including laundry, showers and washrooms. Power and water are provided on the docks.

Deep Bay to the Comox Bar

Baynes Sound and adjacent Vancouver Island

Charts 3527, 3513

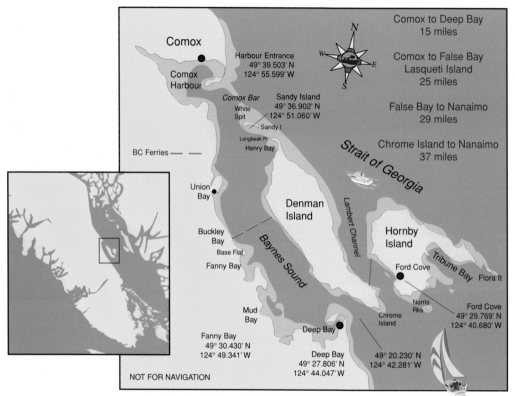

When you arrive at the south end of Baynes Sound you will soon gain shelter from the open waters of the Strait of Georgia, at Deep Bay or Ford Cove. Winds down the Sound can be adverse so choose a destination that offers shelter. If it is calm and you are headed for Comox continue up this beautiful waterway but do not overlook some of the interesting stops along the way. These include Union Bay and Sandy Island Marine Park, and the lighthouse on Chrome Island.

The prominent lighthouse located on Chrome Island has played a significant role in weather reporting over the years. Weather reviews detailing the Strait of Georgia sea conditions include this point as a major reporting station. Take a small boat, preferably an inflatable, from a nearby anchorage or from the public dock in Deep Bay or at Ford Cove on Hornby Island and visit the lighthouse. A small landing allows access

onto Chrome Island. If you examine the rock faces on the south side you will find petroglyphs.

Tides flood northwards into Baynes Sound. Pass between the channel markers P39 off Mapleguard Point and P40 at Repulse Point, green and red respectively. Swing wide around Mapleguard Point to enter Deep Bay harbour and slow down on approach to the marina and docks. There is good anchorage in deep water in Deep Bay.

If you are continuing through Baynes Sound pass to the south of red marker P42, indicating shallow water off Denman Island. Equally shallow are the waters in Mud Bay on the opposite shore and from Fanny Bay to Buckley Bay farther into the Sound. These shallows extend throughout Mud Bay and off the shores of Ship Peninsula and a smaller peninsula called Base Flat, all clearly marked on the large scale chart.

Top: The Chrome Island lighthouse marks the tip of Denman Island and the entrance to Baynes Sound. Above: Deep Bay has a large private marina and yacht club. It also has a public dock, located on the west side of the wharf. A general store, cafe and RV park serves as an accessway to small pleasure craft launched down a tidal ramp. Fuel is available at the general store. This is the only fuel supply between French Creek and Comox.

Above: The Deep Bay general store, cafe and RV park serves fuel to launching customers and by portable means to the marina.
Top, right: The east side marina is close to the shallows of the bay. Visitors should be cautious approaching the docks.
Right: The public dock at Deep Bay is located on the west side of the wharf, nearest the bay entrance.

Deep Bay and Ship & Shore Marine

Harbour Authority dock Phone: 250-757-9331
There is a launch ramp, marina and public docks in the shelter of a curved bight. Shallow areas are found on the approaches. Pumpout, 15 amp power at the dock. Water, washrooms, showers. Adjacent store and coffee shop.

Base Flat shallows are marked by the green buoy P43.

There are campsites with launching ramps at **Mud Bay** and **Buckley Bay** and a small public dock at **Fanny Bay**. These ramps provide access for small trailerable boats from the Vancouver Island shore into Baynes Sound. The channels through the muddy shallows are no problem for them.

Mud Bay has some depths suitable for careful navigation, identified at low tide when the mud banks are exposed. A large drying bank sits in the middle of the bay and a large drying rock at its south side. It is possible to find a suitable depth to drop the hook in the lee of the muddy island.

The ferry landing for Denman Island is located at Buckley Bay. From here until it emerges near the north end of Denman Island, Baynes Sound is clear of any substantial shallows.

Union Bay

Union Bay affords a magnificent view over Sandy Island towards Texada Island and the Sunshine Coast beyond. As a marine destination it has some protection but little access for those wanting to stop there. The public dock is somewhat sheltered from southerly winds but the predominent summer breezes from the northwest tend to cause minor discomfort, although the tiny bay is fairly protected. There is a launch ramp in the protection of the breakwater and Union Point. Temporary anchorage may be taken in the lee of the bay where its northern finger protrudes into Baynes Sound alongside the wharf. Stay well away from the indicated shallows. Much of the launch area and the bay dries at low tide. Four kilometres across Baynes Sound, anchorage can be taken at the north end of Denman Island in Henry Bay.

Going ashore at Union Bay one can find remnants of the past by way of the beautifully restored 1913 post office building and the jailhouse. It is worth seeing.

Continuing north towards Comox, shallows emerge once more and are indicated by the green channel marker P45. Keep to the east of it and stay off shore enough to pass east of P47 on the approaches to Comox Harbour.

Above: The private marina and yacht club at Deep Bay has reciprocal arrangements with other yacht clubs.

The Flying Dutchman

Union Bay was a fairly substantial town in the early 20th century and one of many stops for a notorious pirate of sorts. Known as the Flying Dutchman, he and his band of followers would raid places throughout the Strait of Georgia including Union Bay.

What made him so loathesome among the communities was his fearsome gang and his fast, quiet motor launch that enabled quick escapes from the law.

On the opposite shore, Denman Island's Longbeak Point marks the beginning of another massive shallow area. This continuation of Denman Island is sometimes partially submerged during high tides. It is broken up with several islands including Sandy Island and the **Seal Islets** with Sandy Island Marine Park in the centre and White Spit at the tapering north end.

Sandy Island Marine Park is a favourite destination for local boaters. Its white sandy beaches and adjacent tidal mud banks are popular among those who love to stroll barefoot along the shore watching birds and enjoying the antics of the numerous creatures that make their home in the sand.

Comox Harbour

Goose Spit and the Comox Bar

Charts 3527, 3513

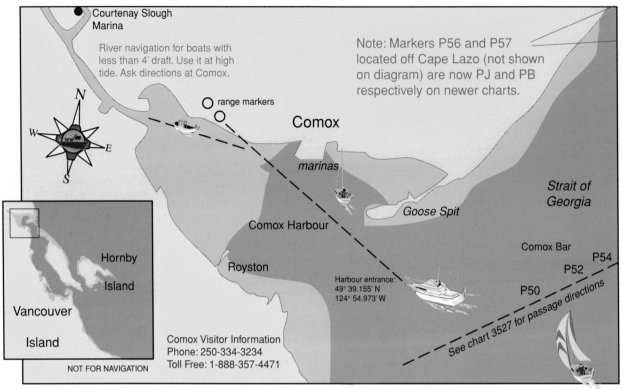

Courtenay Slough Marina

River navigation for boats with less than 4' draft. Use it at high tide. Ask directions at Comox.

Note: Markers P56 and P57 located off Cape Lazo (not shown on diagram) are now PJ and PB respectively on newer charts.

range markers

Comox

marinas

Goose Spit

Strait of Georgia

Comox Harbour

Comox Bar

P54

P52

Royston

P50

See chart 3527 for passage directions

Harbour entrance:
49° 39.155' N
124° 54.973' W

Hornby Island

Vancouver Island

NOT FOR NAVIGATION

Comox Visitor Information
Phone: 250-334-3234
Toll Free: 1-888-357-4471

Before visiting Denman and Hornby Islands and Texada, Lasqueti and Sangster Islands in the middle of the Strait of Georgia, a visit to Comox is in order. If you are arriving at Baynes Sound (that separates Denman Island from Vancouver Island) from the north, you will have passed the red buoys PB and PJ (formerly P57 and P56) in turn off Cape Lazo and arrived at the red bell buoy P54. Keeping it within 30 metres to your starboard take passage across the **Comox Bar** passing close to red spar P52 and red cone buoy P50. There are no green markers, so stay close to the red ones. Two range markers on the shore are in alignment when you are in the correct channel, but are very difficult to identify in daylight.

After passing P50 you can turn on a northwest bearing for **Goose Spit**. This is the location of a Canada Sea Cadet camp. Pass around Goose Spit and drop anchor in about 10 metres in its lee, being cautious of the shallows that extend a fair distance into the bay at low tide. Otherwise continue to the marinas nearby keeping off the harbour's north shore shallows by running a fairly straight line between the top of Goose Spit and the breakwater at the marinas.

A substantial public dock protrudes into the bay and overnight visitors will find space at fingers on the east side of the breakwater wharf. The other marinas in the complex can be reached by cruising past the breakwater and entering at its west end. Immediately ahead is the fuel dock. The long dock west of the fuel dock is part of Comox Bay Marina where overnight moorage is available to all including large vessels. Make reservations in summer. If you are directed to a slip on the west side of this marina stay within 10 metres (30 feet) of the docks to avoid the shallows.

Facilities in the harbour include a large launch ramp, restaurants, pub, park area and nearby shops including marine supplies. Visit the Filberg Heritage Lodge and Park. In Courtenay visit the Courtenay and District Museum. Get there by taxi or run your dinghy up the river at high tide.

The marinas at Comox include the base of operations for Desolation Sound Yacht Charters. This is a jumping off point for many heading to Desolation Sound. Comox is also, and more notably, a base for the military.

Small sailing craft can often be found plying the waters of

Top: Small boats beached on Goose Spit. They can be seen plying the waters of Comox Harbour on balmy summer weekends.
Above: The public overnight visitors docks are located at the east side of the breakwater.

Above: The busy commercial wharves at Comox. The rock breakwater can be seen beyond it. Entrance to the fuel dock is at the end of the wooden breakwater. A short walk takes you to stores, the local marine store and book shop and a variety of restaurants.
Right: The fuel dock has a convenience store and possible moorage.

Comox Harbour on hot weekends in summer and breezy evenings during the week. Light northerly and northwesterly winds are common and the harbour and adjacent Baynes Sound is a sheltered playground for small recreational boats.

Southeasterly winds can cause discomfort, even distress, out in the Strait of Georgia. Desolation Sound Yacht Charters rents out a good number of boats each summer and they have prepared a check list for their customers. It includes some sage advice for entering or leaving Comox Harbour.

They say you should never guess at the wind forecast. Keep a close ear to the weather channel and do not second guess southerly or southeasterly winds. If a southeast wind is in the forecast and you are in Desolation Sound or Campbell River stay put. An early morning start may favour a crossing of the northern waters of the Strait of Georgia. This applies also to leaving Comox for those destinations.

When approaching Comox from the northern part of Texada Island locate the bluffs of Cape Lazo. Just south of these are Willemar Bluffs. Sandy Island is just southeast of Willemar Bluffs and marks the south side of the Comox Bar. Head for a point midway between Willemar Bluffs and Sandy Island and this will bring you to the cardinal buoy PJ

which will lead you on to the Comox Bar bell buoy P54.

Approaches from Campbell River along the Vancouver Island eastern shore requires passage to the east of cardinal buoy PB (formerly PK and P57) and PJ (formerly P56). Keep well clear of Cape Lazo and avoid it during windy conditions.

If you find yourself entering Comox Harbour after dark stay well out to sea until you pick up the bright, yellow flashing range lights–both of them. Trees obscure them until they are lined up. Once you have both in view follow them in and do not wander as you have to pass close to P54, P52 and P50. Approach the harbour by heading for the flashing light at Goose Spit.

The diagram above shows the layout of the marinas, location of the fuel dock, launch ramp and office. Tidal grids are not available.

The overnight visitors' docks are at the far right (east side of the marina complex). The Black Fin Pub is to the right (pictured).

Below left: The launch ramp alongside the Edgewater Pub. Water access to it is past the fuel dock. Below, right: Comox Municipal Marina.

Comox Bay Marina

1805 Beaufort St, Comox V9N 1R9
Phone: 250-339-4664 *www.town.comox.bc.ca*
Transient and permanent moorage. Laundry, showers, washrooms, power at dock 15, 30, 50 amp.

Gas n Go Marina and fuel dock

PO Box 1296, Comox V9M 7Z8 Ph/Fax: 250-339-4664
Gas, diesel, ice. Convenience store. The Edgewater Pub is located ashore alongside the launch ramp. Limited visitor moorage– 2 or 3 slips available.

Comox Municipal Marina

127 Port Augusta, Comox V9N 2K9 Ph: 250-339-3141
www.town.comox.bc.ca
Permanent moorage and overflow from other marinas. Launch ramp and park area. Nautical Days on Canada Day with fireworks, parade etc. Black Fin Pub adjacent.

Fisherman's Wharf

Comox Valley Harbour Authority
121 Port Augusta St, Comox V9M 3N8
Phone: 250-339-6041   VHF 66A
www.fishermanswharfmarina.com
Office on the wharf has BroadbandXpress internet and lounge. Transient moorage is available at the east docks. Laundry, showers, washrooms and power at the dock. Near all services. Adjacent to Comox Municipal Marina.

Courtenay Slough

Public fishing dock–Comox Valley Harbour Authority
121 Port Augusta St, Comox V9M 3N8   VHF 66A
Phone: 250-339-6041 VHF 66A
www.fishermanswharfmarina.com
Located up the river–shallow draft boats at high tide–use the dredged canal to reach the river. Turn before the Lewis Bridge. Permission/key is needed from Harbour Authority.

The communities of Courtenay, Comox, Denman Island and Hornby Island are included in Comox Valley. Some 50 kilometres of coastline from Fanny Bay to Oyster River are also part of the Valley.

Top: Scenic Comox Harbour is protected by low lying Goose Spit. Anchor beyond the shallows and monitor strong wind forecasts.
Right: Uptown Comox is a quiet place with hospital, library, restaurants and shops catering to most needs.
Bottom: The Courtenay River is shallow and navigable by small boats at high tide. Enquire at Comox Marina. A dinghy ride into Courtenay provides access to more and bigger shopping centres. A big event at Comox is the Filberg Festival in August. Phone 250-339-2715. www.filbergfestival.com

Denman and Hornby Islands

Sandy Island, Ford Cove and Tribune Bay

Charts 3527, 3513

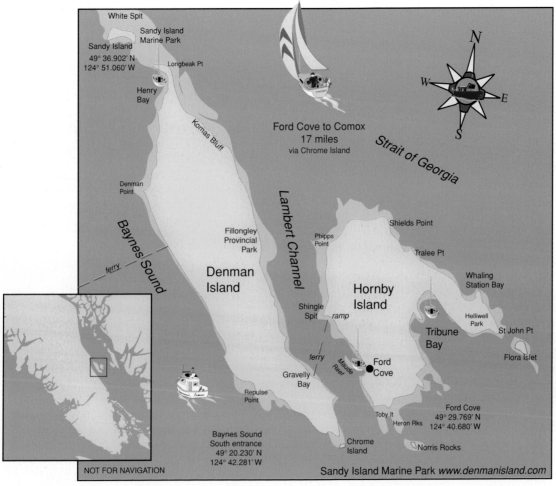

Sandy Island Marine Park www.denmanisland.com

NOT FOR NAVIGATION

Sandy Island is part of a provincial park that includes the Seal Islets. It serves the mariners of Comox and Courtenay as a boating destination much as Newcastle Island serves Nanaimo. But this is where the similarity ends. Where Newcastle Island is developed and has docks and shore facilities the only semblance of civilization you will find at Sandy Island are pit toilets and picnic tables. The park includes camping facilities, picnic sites, hiking trails, fishing, long sandy beaches and swimming.

Anchor during the day but do not stay overnight. The shallows are not necessarily as shown on the chart and tidal changes have currents running past the beach that would leave an anchored boat washed ashore or stranded in the shallows. Anchor instead at **Henry Bay** in the lee of Longbeak

Point at the northern tip of Denman Island.

From Sandy Island Park southwards down Baynes Sound the west shore of Denman Island has no features for boaters other than the ferry landing, a small dock and a launch ramp opposite Buckley Bay on Vancouver Island. Access to the east shore requires leaving Comox by way of crossing the bar, steering well out into the Strait of Georgia to avoid shallows and reefs extending off White Spit and Sandy Island as well as the north end of Denman Island and following a course down Lambert Channel.

There is no shelter on the east side of Denman Island so cross over to **Shingle Spit** or Ford Cove on Hornby Island. The shallows off the Komos Bluffs and **Fillongley Provincial Park** beach on the Denman shore are popular areas for

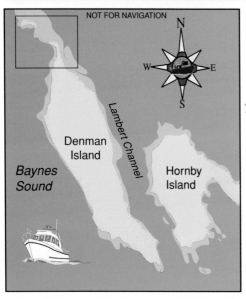

N
W · E
S

Denman
Island

Lambert Channel

*Baynes
Sound*

Hornby
Island

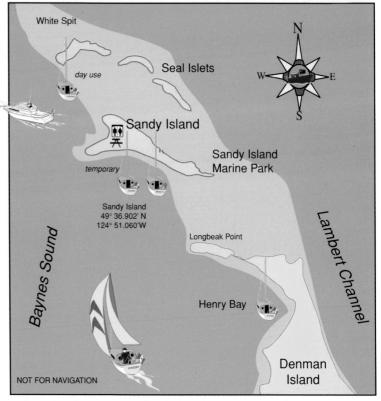

White Spit

day use

Seal Islets

Sandy Island

Sandy Island
Marine Park

temporary

Sandy Island
49° 36.902' N
124° 51.060'W

Longbeak Point

Baynes Sound

Lambert Channel

Henry Bay

Denman
Island

NOT FOR NAVIGATION

N
W · E
S

*Top: Sandy Island Provincial Marine Park stretches
from the north tip of Denman Island towards
Comox Harbour.
Diagrams show the proximity of Sandy Island park to
Denman and Hornby Islands.*

Denman Island

There is a grocery store , general store, post office and liquor store near the ferry terminal from Vancouver Island. There is no landing for small craft.

Apples were the product of early settlers at Denman Island. After the industry waned for a period it resurfaced to become a strong contender in the local market, particular for the juices. The island is also a haven for recreational home owners.

Above: A sailboat arrives at White Spit during low tide and prepares to anchor in the shallows. Children and adults alike enthusiastically slip over the side to play in the water.

Above and right: Sandy Island Provincial Marine Park attracts many boaters, especially from nearby locations, in the summer months. During calm days the anchorage is good and the shallow waters provide safe, warm bathing. Campsites and picnicking are available on this pristine island. Long sandy beaches extend all the way from Longbeak Point and Henry Bay on Denman Island along White Spit at low tide.

paddlers. Vessels should pass about one kilometre off shore to avoid rocks and sandbars extending from the shoreline. Sections of sandstone formations were relocated from this shore to Victoria where they were used in the Provincial Museum rock gardens.

Ford Cove

Public dock Phone: 250-335-2141   Charts 3527, 3513 *www.hornbyisland.com.* Wharfinger Una Keziere will enthusiastically greet you when visiting the large, improved docks. Garbage disposal, washrooms, store and arts and crafts are available. 15 and 20 amp power at the dock.

To reach Ford Cove, enter Lambert Channel from the south after passing Chrome Island off Boyle Point. Ford Cove is the most protected moorage in these islands. The public marina is small and invariably full with local vessels. There is no fuel and the nearest available gas or diesel supplies are at Comox, French Creek or Deep Bay. A few stores on shore include a small grocery store and a craft shop. If there is no moorage at the docks anchor a short way out in the protection of Maude Reef. This reef runs parallel to shore in line with the breakwater at the cove. Beacons mark the waterway and reef. Windy conditions sometimes disturb the anchorage so check forecast and tidal data before settling in for the night.

Hornby Island's population is made up of permanent

Ford Cove at Hornby Island. The above photo shows the extended breakwater and docks as they were expected to be on completion. Right: Behind the breakwater at Ford Cove in summer 2005. Major changes were in progress including the addition of another finger and extension of the breakwater. The fuel supply has been discontinued leaving the nearest available fuel at French Creek or Comox. Nearby Deep Bay has gasoline that can be dispensed by limited portable means at the dock.

residences and vacation homes. This island has a large community of artists. A trip into the village would reveal their presence by the number of art and craft stores and vendors. Best to have friends on the island who could run you into the village, or enquire about transportation at the store or from the wharfinger at Ford Cove.

A hike up the 300 metre Mount Geoffrey that overlooks Lambert Channel provides spectacular vistas across the Strait of Georgia and of the distant shores and islands.

Tribune Bay

This is a popular day anchorage. It washes an expansive white sandy beach, one of the finest on the coast, which is protected as a provincial park. Travelling from Ford Cove to Tribune Bay entails leaving the breakwater at the marina, steering wide of a submerged rock a short distance to its south and passing clear of Toby Island off Norman Point. Pass either side of Norris Rocks staying clear of Heron Rocks then continue well off Downes Point past the green marker P35 at Nash Bank. Enter Tribune Bay and anchor in 6 to 10 metres in the shallows north of Spray Point. Some yachtsmen choose to remain anchored in the bay overnight. In summer northwesterlies prevail so the bay is sheltered at most times.

Nevertheless be safe and check wind forecasts before committing to an overnight stay. Helliwell Provincial Park is adjacent to Tribune Bay.

Whaling Station Bay

The north shore of Hornby Island has little to offer by way of coves or nooks other than Whaling Station Bay immediately beyond Cape Gurney. From here to Tralee Point there are petroglyphs of leaping whales, birds and arrows in the sandstone ridges along the shore. These are best reached in a small boat that can be beached during calm weather.

Whaling Station Bay has a white sandy beach that is easily the equal of the the beach at Tribune Bay, but smaller. It is a picturesque bay but not a suitable place to anchor although at times it is calm for long stretches and very tempting to drop the hook. The bay is named for the whaling activities that continued there for many decades. Local residents say the occasional mariner anchoring overnight has invariably had a very uncomfortable stay. Anchor rather in Tribune Bay or Ford Cove.

Above: Anchorage at the Shingle Spit ferry landing on Hornby Island.
Left: The general store and arts and crafts shop at Ford Cove. Hornby Island has many well-known artists and craftsmen and their products are usually available at local stores.
Bottom: At low tide Ford Cove dries substantially. Anchorage has good depth but note wind forecasts.

Vancouver Island Comox Events

Comox Nautical Days July/August Phone: 250-338-1120. Vancouver Island Music Festival July: 250-336-7929. North Island Hot Jazz Festival June Phone: 250-334-3499. Filberg Festival July/August Phone: 250-334-9294.

Comox Airforce Museum
West coast military aviation includes research library, gift shop and heritage park Phone: 250-339-8162.

Comox Archives & Museum
The maritime history of Comox. Tours appointment Phone: 250-339-2885.

Hornby Island

The anchorage at Tribune Bay attracts many boats during summer. It is protected from most summer winds. Visitors arriving at Hornby Island by way of the ferry service boost the population numbers significantly during the season.

The BC Ferries offload about 1,000 visitors a day. Helliwell Park, at St John Point, includes Flora Islet and is a bird watching haven. Scuba divers visit Flora Islet to view large six gill sharks at recreational depths.

Above: The lighthouse at Chrome Island looks out over Baynes Sound and the Strait of Georgia. Right: Chrome Island light from the south end of Lambert Channel. Bottom: The ever popular Tribune Bay has white sandy beaches and a temporary anchorage that is usually protected from prevailing summer winds. The shopping centre is not far from the beach.

Scuba diving is very popular in the waters off Hornby Island. Norris Rocks attracts many divers for the vast array of marine life, and Flora Islet (**Helliwell Park**) at the eastern tip is renowned for its population of deep dwelling six-gill sharks. Watch for divers in the water, noted by their flying of a red flag with a diagonal white stripe.

Heading north out of Lambert Channel avoid Savoie Rocks on the approaches to the ferry landing at **Shingle Spit.** Steer clear of ferry activities. Temporary anchorage is possible in the lee of the Spit. A small basin south of the ferry landing is shallow and dries at low tide.

For those with trailerable boats there is a launch ramp alongside the ferry landing on Hornby Island as well as at **Gravelly Bay** on Denman Island near the ferry landing on the east side of Lambert Channel. The Hornby Island village used to be at the ferry landing but the island's village centre is now located inland. There is still a bank, restaurant and store as well as a hamburger stand at the terminal.

Lasqueti Island
Sheltered bays and coves in the middle of the Strait of Georgia

Charts 3536, 3312, 3512, 3513

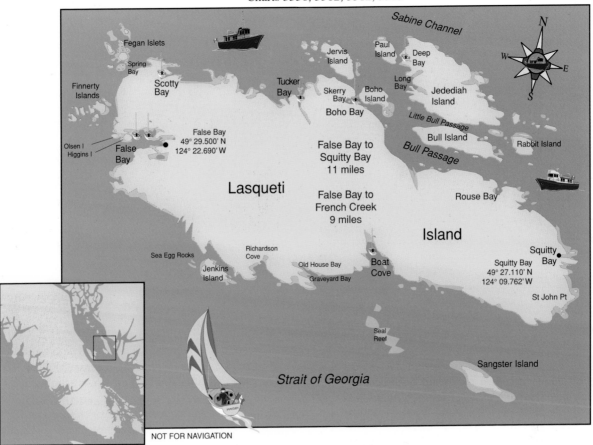

NOT FOR NAVIGATION

Approaching Lasqueti Island from Tribune Channel on Hornby Island requires simply passing well off Flora Islet and setting a course for the **Finnerty Islands** beyond Sisters Islets. In a straight line, you will pass well to the north of Sisters, a significant weather reporting station. The Finnerty Islands, near the entrance to False Bay, have several passages among them that can be navigated in a small boat. There are one or two nooks in which to anchor, usually for temporary durations. Longer stays are more common in False Bay.

False Bay

False Bay is a large bay opening on the west side of Lasqueti Island. It can be approached directly across the Strait of Georgia from the direction of Vancouver Island. Many vessels travelling up the Strait from Vancouver and Howe Sound make their way to the bay via Sabine Channel between Lasqueti Island and Texada Island.

From Stevens Passage enter False Bay past Olsen Island and **Higgins Island**. Anchoring is favoured in the northern part of the bay to the east of Higgins Island. The favoured spot is in the northernmost cove where there is room for numerous boats to anchor. The *BC Sailing Directions* says to watch out for the Qualicum winds which blow strongly from the west into False Bay. There are rocks off Olsen Island and Higgins Island. Enter False Bay with caution, using the large scale chart 3536. There is a drying reef in the middle of the

Lasqueti landing in False Bay. Enjoy a leisurely walk along the island road between False Bay and Scottie Bay.

Top: False Bay opens to the northwest at the north end of Lasqueti Island. It offers sheltered anchorage to a large number of boats. The Finnerty Islands can be seen beyond the entrance.

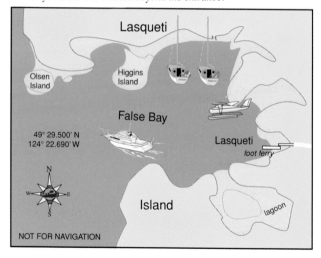

cove so remain close to the island or directly north of it. Do not attempt the passage to its northwest as this dries at low tide as does the cove west of that.

Across False Bay there is a small dock that accommodates a few boats, mostly coming and going constantly. This includes the passenger ferry from French Creek. There is a hotel with a pub/restaurant and convenience store at the head of the dock. No fuel or marine services are available.

False Bay

Lasqueti public dock   Charts 3312, 3536, 3513
No facilities at 36 metre dock. Used also for seaplanes and passenger ferry from French Creek. Hotel ashore.

Opening off the south shore of False Bay is a lagoon with a passage that dries at low tide and therefore admits mostly smaller boats, although fishboats are known to use it regularly. A reef lies in the middle of the entrance to the lagoon and passage should be made close to Prowse Point and following the northern shore. But be mindful of shelving reefs that protrude into the channel farther along.

In addition to False Bay, most mariners who know Lasqueti Island use the bays and coves on its northeast shore

Left: False Bay offers anchorage to a large number of boats in most wind conditions. A small dock serves to access the local hotel but no facilities are available for overnight mooring. In the distance is Sisters Islets.

Lower: False Bay with an expanded view showing the lagoon. Entrance is shallow at high tide and mostly dry at low tide. Enter along the north side of the channel to avoid the large rock midway and be cautious of the other rocks and shallower areas.

Lasqueti Island

A walk across the island could reward you with a viewing of the swamps and forests. The roads wind through rugged terrain with pine covered ridges and homes dotted among the trees without specific definition of property borders.

Jedediah Island

Walk the island trails. There are sandy beaches, archaeological sites, an old homestead and much wildlife to be seen.

for overnight anchorage. The south shore has a number of coves and small inlets, including Boat Cove, beyond Jenkins Island. None of these is particularly useful as extended anchorages. Temporary stops may be made in Boat Cove or the one just west of it and some protection is available in the small bight directly north of **Sea Egg Rocks**.

Old House Bay

If you must stop on the exposed southwest side of Lasqueti Island, Old House Bay is a protected anchorage from northwest winds. It lies beyond Jenkins Island. **Richardson Cove**, just before it, is sheltered from westerlies and makes a suitable anchorage in fair weather. Jenkins Island itself does not afford much shelter, although there are coves at the north and south ends that offer protection from westerlies and southeasterlies respectively.

Boat Cove

From Old House Bay it is an easy cruise into nearby Boat Cove. Here anchorage is protected from westerly winds. Be mindful of the reefs along the east shore as you leave for Sangster Island or Squitty Bay beyond Young Point.

Squitty Bay has a narrow entrance, but as can be seen in the aerial photo on the opposite page, it is adequate for small to medium sized vessels. The small dock can accommodate several boats, sometimes rafted up.

Sangster Island

The passage north of Jenkins Island is navigable but stay well over towards the Lasqueti shore as you emerge south of it. Beware of Seal Reef on the approaches to Sangster Island and stay well off its north end and northeast shore if you are heading for Young Point and Squitty Bay on the southeast corner of Lasqueti. Sangster Island has a possible temporary anchorage located at the southwestern end of the island. There are rocks around the bay formed by the bight and one drying rock at the entrance. Bill Wolferstan, noted author of *Cruising Guide to the Gulf Islands*, says the anchorage is temporary and protected from westerly and northwesterly breezes but only when they are light. It is best to use this as an anchorage only in calm conditions.

Squitty Bay

Enter Squitty Bay off Sabine Channel west of Texada Island. The bay is located near the southeastern tip of Lasqueti Island to the north of Young Point and not far from the southern entrance to Sabine Channel. It looks out onto the open waters of the Strait of Georgia. Favour the southwestern shore as you enter, and use a large scale chart for reference to the reef in the centre of the entrance.

Squitty Bay is a marine park but has no facilities as camping is not permitted. There is a small dock attached to the

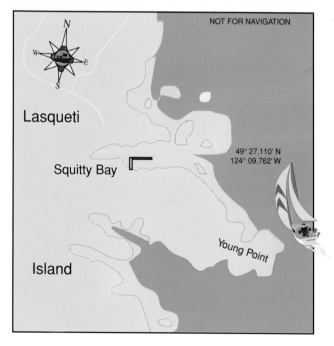

NOT FOR NAVIGATION

Lasqueti

Squitty Bay

Island

Young Point

49° 27.110' N
124° 09.762' W

southwest shore in a very narrow bay, and it is possible for a small boat to anchor in the bay near the dock. In summer time this cove is generally protected from prevailing winds. Year round it receives only a gentle residual swell caused by strong winds and big offshore seas. The wind may help control the presence of mosquitoes but make sure you have Deet on board as this little cove is aptly named considering the abundance of the pesky little insects encountered there.

Good gunkholing and some small bays and anchorages can be found nearby. This area has long been known for its good oyster yield. Watch for notices regarding red tides.

Squitty Bay

Lasqueti Island public dock Charts 3312, 3512
Unmanaged 47 metre dock with rafting allowed. Walking trails and island roads. Enter close to south side.

Squitty Bay with its narrow entrance and small public dock.

Sabine Channel Provincial Park

Use the large scale chart and navigate these rocky and reef strewn waters with care. The main channels are quite easy but watch out for the lesser used waterways. Furthermore during high winds from the northwest or the southeast, especially against a tidal current, steep seas wash the channel making it uncomfortable, even dangerous for small craft. Find anchorage early in the day and let the windy periods pass before venturing out again. Evenings are usually calm.

Vessels approaching Lasqueti Island from the south may enter Sabine Channel by way of Bull Passage, a short distance north of Squitty Bay. It is an easy entrance, passing between Lasqueti Island to the south and Rabbit Island, then Bull Island and Jedediah Island to the north. Two islands in the channel are part of the provincial park reserve. They are Jervis and Bunny Islands. They lie to the northwest of Jedediah Island which is a designated marine park. These islands have an adjacent cluster of smaller islands, islets and rocks, mostly off the northwest shore of Jervis Island.

Although no provision has been made for overnight visitors, camping on Jervis and Bunny Islands is permitted. You will find numerous paddlers in the area during summer. Sabine Channel is named for General Sir Edward Sabine of the War of 1812 Niagara campaign.

Rouse Bay

On the Lasqueti Island shore Rouse Bay offers protected anchorage. Enter Rouse Bay carefully, avoiding the shallows at the head of the bay that dry at low tide. Anchor in the lee of the small islet in the bay entrance. Rouse Bay is one of several anchorages along the Lasqueti Island shoreline. These include the anchorages at Boho Bay and Scotty Bay.

Boho Bay

Boho Bay lies to the south of Boho Island. Although the bays and coves along the Lasqueti Island shore are protected by Jervis Island and Boho Island from northwesterlies, you may be disturbed at times by the affect of southeast winds. For anchored boats, the best protection from such wind can be found in **Skerry Bay**. This good, protected anchorage lies to the west of Boho Island.

Access to Skerry Bay is through Boho Bay of which it is an appendage. Anchor in Boho Bay or Skerry Bay. The anchorage opens also off Sabine Channel east of Scottie Bay through a passage that has a drying rock almost blocking it at the south end. Skerry Bay is a sheltered overnight anchorage and offers more protection from the rare summertime southeasterlies than Boho Bay. It has some shallows to watch for as well as a drying rock at the entrance.

The small cove between Paul Island and Jedediah Island is known as Deep Bay. It has cleats in the rocky shore for stern tying. It is generally used as an anchorage by no more than one or two boats at a time. Many mariners use the shallow bay on the north side of Lindbergh Island as a temporary anchorage. The most sheltered spot is inside Scottie Bay. Be cautious entering the tiny, confined bay as the entrance is partially obscured by a reef on Lindbergh Island.

The first time we dropped anchor there we first did a widening circle to check depths. It is best to anchor close to Boho Island to avoid the reefs on the Lasqueti side of the bay. The entrance on the north side of Boho Island is obscured by a large drying rock.

Jedediah Island

All of Jedediah Island is a designated marine park. It abuts Sabine Channel opposite the southwest side of Texada Island. **Deep Bay**, on the northwest side offers protected anchorage. This cosy little anchorage is located in the narrow channel between Jedediah Island and Paul Island and is a popular place for those who know it. It is a small cove suitable for two or three boats stern tied to chains placed on a steep wall. It's the type of anchorage that is yours to enjoy if you are first to arrive. I favour leaving it to one or two boats if they are already there. Once anchored and settled in, you can poke around in your dinghy, exploring the passages, shoreline and nooks around the adjacent islands. If there is no red tide warning and you have your harvesting licence in order, check out the beaches for oysters.

Jedediah Island offers little in the way of anchorage as the two most prominent bays known as Log Boom Bay and Long Bay are too shallow. They are suitable as a temporary stop, and then only in their outer waters, during medium to high tides. Mind the drying shallows deeper inside the arms.

Jervis Island and Bunny Islet

There is a small cove on the west side of Jervis Island with Bunny Islet being a protective breakwater against most winds for those who choose to anchor there. The islands are part of the marine park system but have no facilities or moorage. Paddlers use them as a landing and camping area.

Tucker Bay

Tucker Bay has some protection with conditional shelter just off Potter Point or in the lee of Larson Islet or inside the narrow finger off the bay. It is located east of Boho Bay on the north side of Lasqueti Island. A peninsula at the northwest end of Tucker Bay forms a natural breakwater for the tiny, shallow **Lenny's Lagoon** that opens into its western shore. It is accessible by dinghy or kayak and should be entered only on a rising tide.

Jelina Island just to the south of the entrance provides shelter for temporary anchoring. Drop the hook in its lee and go ashore at **Marshall's Beach**, a beautiful sandy stretch that links the islands at low tide. As you proceed along the shore towards Scottie Bay pass **Barnes Cove** where temporary anchorage may be taken. Mining operations in the early days rendered the landfall in this cove hazardous for walking around. It is also known as Mine Bay.

Scottie Bay

Scottie Bay is tucked behind Lindbergh Island near the north end of Lasqueti Island. It is an easy entrance off Sabine Channel. Favour the port side of the narrow opening into the cove to avoid the reef that protrudes from the southeastern shore of Lindbergh Island. There is room for a good number of boats to anchor in the bay although the presence of private enterprise makes it restrictive at times. Over the years com-

240

Anchorages off Sabine Channel offer a fair amount of protection from windy conditions. There is moorage in tranquil surroundings such as Scottie Bay (left), Tucker Bay and Boho Bay in the lee of Jervis Island and Jedediah Island.

Below: Scottie Bay entrance looking out towards Sabine Channel.

PSP Precaution

When there are red tide warnings take them seriously. PSP (paralytic shellfish poisoning) is a very serious condition. It has been said that you can make your own test for PSP by tasting the tiniest morsel of shellfish, about the size of a grain of rice, wait about ten minutes and if you experience a slight tingling sensation around the mouth or lips, leave it alone. I suggest you don't even attempt this because if you have any allergy the reaction might be serious.

mercial mariculture has encroached increasingly on some favourite anchorages and boating destinations. Scottie Bay is one that has lost much of its appeal as a destination because of fish or oyster farming. If the bay is too busy try False Bay or Boho Bay.

A temporary anchorage may be taken outside of **Lindbergh Island** in the cove protected by the island that extends into Sabine Channel north of the entrance to Scottie Bay. Spring Bay is open to the northwest and not a suitable anchorage even though it is sheltered somewhat by the Fegan Islets. While there is no suitable anchorage in the Fegan Islets shelter is possible in the Finnerty Islands, as previously indicated. On the north end of Lasqueti Island, the Finnerty Islands offer tight but protected anchorage and Spring Bay has temporary anchorage.

Above: Sandstone cliffs at the entrance to Scottie Bay.

Above: A view of Scottie Bay. There is limited space inside for anchoring and no docks for public use. The entrance is narrow with a reef that protrudes well into its centre from the north shore.

Texada Island

South Texada Island is a Provincial Park Reserve area. However, it has little possibility of sheltered anchorage.

If you are travelling around the south of Texada Island you will find good anchorage in **Anderson Bay** just as you head north up the east side of the island. It is also a park and is separate from the larger South Texada reserve. Our good friend the late Corporal Bob Teather of the RCMP said he found excellent shelter in the bay and going ashore encountered good walking on trails with breathtaking views. Some reports say to keep an anchor watch for wind from the southeast.

The park offers no facilities and can be reached only by small boat. Paddlers who are looking for land-based wilderness adventure will find it in activities such as climbing the 885 metre Mount Shepherd.

A cruise up the east side of Texada Island will bring you to Vananda and Sturt Bay. This falls into the Sunshine Coast region and is covered in detail in cruising guides to the Sunshine Coast and Desolation Sound.

Note: There are magnetic disturbances off Texada Island.

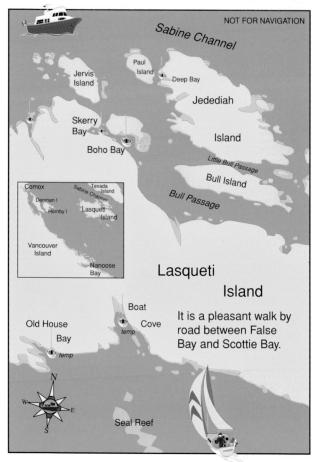

It is a pleasant walk by road between False Bay and Scottie Bay.

Above: Bull Passage with Bull Island in the centre right and the shore of Lasqueti Island on the left. Little Bull Passage runs between Bull Island and Jedediah Island, far right. Boho Bay lies beyond the tip of Bull Island. Jervis Island can be seen in the background.

Above: Yachtsmen find a sheltered anchorage among the Finnerty Islands off the northwest end of Lasqueti Island.

View across Comox Harbour from Goose Spit.

More exploration of the coast can be found in the author's best selling **North of Desolation Sound** guide to the Broughton Islands. A similar guide to the ever popular Desolation Sound is in the works. *www.marineguides.com*

INDEX

This index provides primary and some secondary reference to names of anchorages, marinas, passages, islands and features of the coast deemed to be notable. Most are found as headings, titles, subtitles and in bold typeface. Some appear only on the diagrams and/or in plain reference in the text. They may appear also elsewhere in the guide, not indexed as such, in a less notable reference.

Index References

The pages indexed in the foregoing list are referenced to the names of places that appear in the text or the diagrams or both. Where the names recur the index references indicate the first or primary use of the names.

Use of metric in this guide:

Metric has been used throughout the guide, in keeping with Canadian hydrographic charts. Therefore depths are in metres. Distances are approximate, and have been shown in nautical miles depending on the circumstances of the acquisition of the information and whether it refers to statute or nautical measurements. Canadian English is used for the spelling of metric measurements.

Bibliography and recommended marine books on the areas covered in this guide

151 Dives in theProtected Waters of British Columbia and Washington State. Betty Pratt-Johnson

Anchorages and Marine Parks: Guide to anchorages and marine parks in British Columbia and the San Juan Islands. Peter Vassilopoulos. Seagraphic Publications. 2000.

BC Marine Parks Guide: The official guide to BC's coastal marine parks. OP Publishing. 2004.

Birds of Southwestern British Columbia. Richard Cannings, Tom Aversa and Hal Opperman. Heritage House. 2006.

Cruising Guide to British Columbia: Vol. 1 Gulf Islands. Bill Wolferstan. Whitecap Books. 1994.

Canada's False Prophet: The Notorious Brother Twelve. Herbert Emmerson. Wilson Simon & Schuster. 1967.

Canadian Tide and Current Tables: Vol. 5 Juan de Fuca Strait & Strait of Georgia. Canadian Hydrographic Service.

Docks and Destinations: A guide to marinas in British Columbia and Puget Sound, Wash. GPS coordinates included. Peter Vassilopoulos. Pacific Marine Publishing. 2005.

Evergreen Pacific Cruising Atlas: Olympia to Queen Charlottes. Evergreen Pacific. 1990.

Exploring the San Juan and Gulf Islands. Don Douglass, Réanne Hemingway Douglass. Fine Edge. 2003.

Exploring the South Coast of British Columbia: Gulf Islands and Desolation Sound to Broughton Archipelago and Blunden Harbour. Don Douglass, Reanne Hemingway-Douglass. Fine Edge. 1999.

Dreamspeaker Guide: Vol. 1 Gulf Island & Vancouver Island. Anne & Laurence Yeadon-Jones. Fine Edge.

Edible Seashore: Pacific Shores Cookbook and Guide. Rick Harbo. Hancock House. 2005.

Hiking the Gulf Islands: An Outdoor Guide to BC's Enchanted Isles. Charles Kahn. Harbour Publishing. 2004.

High Boats: A Century of Salmon Remembered. Pat Wastell Norris. Harbour Publishing. 2003.

Islands in the Salish Sea: A Community Atlas. Edited by Sheila Harrington and Judi Stevenson. TouchWood. 2005.

Journeys Through the Inside Passage: Seafaring Adventures Along the Coast of British Columbia and Alaska. Joe Upton. 1998.

Local Knowledge: The Skipper's Reference-Tacoma to Ketchikan. Kevin Monahan. Fine Edge. 2005.

Marine Weather Hazards Manual: A guide to local forecasts and conditions for the West Coast. Environment Canada. 1999.

Naturally Salty: Coastal Characters of the Pacific Northwest. Marianne Scott. TouchWood. 2003.

Navigating the Coast: A History of the Union Steamship Company. Edited by Peter Chapman. 1977.

Newcastle Island, A Place of Discovery. Bill Merilees. Heritage House. 1998.

Oceanography of the British Columbia Coast. Richard E. Thomson. Canadian Special Publication of Fisheries and Aquatic Sciences. 1981.

Once upon an island. David Conover. Crown Publishers.1968.

One Man's Island: The Intimate Journal of a Family's Four Seasons on Their Wilderness Isle. David Conover. Crown Publishers. 1972.

Pacific Reef & Shore. Marine Life of the Pacific Northwest. Rick Harbo. Harbour Publishing. 2003.

Ports and Passes. Tides, currents and charts. Olympia to Prince Rupert. Chyna Sea Ventures. Annual.

Proven Cruising Routes: Vol. 1. Precise courses to steer Seattle to Ketchikan. Kevin Monahan. Fine Edge. 2000.

Sailing Directions: Pacific Coast, General Information. Fisheries and Oceans Canada. 2002.

Sea Kayak the Gulf Islands. Mary Ann Snowden. Rocky Mountain Books. 2004.

Seven Knot Summers. Beth Hill. Horsdal & Schubart. 1994.

Southern Gulf Islands. David Spalding & Andrea Spalding. Altitude Publishing. 2000.

Spilsbury's Coast. Jim Spilsbury & Howard White. Harbour Publishing. 1991.

The Brother XII. The Devil of De Courcy Island. Ron MacIsaac, Don Clark, and Charles Lillard. Porcepic Books. 1989.

The Curve of Time. M. Wylie Blanchet. Whitecap Books. 1997.

The Promise of Paradise. Andrew Scott. Whitecap Books. 1997.

The Radar Book: Effective Navigation and Collision Avoidance. Kevin Monahan. Fine Edge. 2004.

Tidepool & Reef: Marine life Guide to the Pacific Northwest Coast. Rick Harbo. Hancock House. 1980.

Upcoast Summers. Beth Hill. Horsdal & Schubart. 1985.

Waggoner Cruising Guide: Puget Sound to Prince Rupert. Robert Hale. Weatherly Press. Annual.

Weatherly Waypoint Guides: Vol. 2 Gulf of Georgia, includes Gulf Islands, Jervis Inlet, & Princess Louisa Inlet. Weatherly Press. 2002.

Whelks to Whales: Coastal Marine Life of the Pacific Northwest. Rick M. Harbo. Harbour Publishing. 1999.

My wife Carla and I have cruised the area this guide covers over the past thirty years. We have visited all areas described in the book and have stopped at and anchored in most anchorages. There are numerous books on cruising the coast and these along with your charts and reference books should enable you to extend your cruising range substantially and safely. Safe and happy boating–Peter Vassilopoulos.

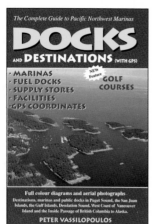

Docks and Destinations (Sixth edition)
ISBN 0-919317-36-7 2005 $29.95.
With GPS and Golf Course phone numbers.
Full colour throughout.

This is a complete guide to marinas on the coast of British Columbia and Puget Sound, Washington. It covers the inside passage to Ketchikan, Alaska from Olympia in Washington state in geographical sequence. The west coast of Vancouver Island is included from north to south. The book is filled with hundreds of aerial and ambient photographs and concise diagrams with pertinent information on marina services and facilities.
GPS Waypoints have been included for all entries in this popular marine guide.

Author Peter Vassilopoulos has travelled extensively throughout the entire area during nearly 35 years of boating in the Pacific Northwest, and provides up-to-date information on where to go, what to look for and why to visit the destinations included.

Anchorages and Marine Parks
ISBN 0919317-24-3 2000 b/w $19.95

A companion to Docks and Destinations, this book is a complete coastal guide to marine parks and anchorages. It covers the area from the San Juan Islands to Ketchikan following the coast in geographical sequence from south to north, returning down the west coast of Vancouver Island in a north to south progression. The guide is loaded with aerial and ambient photographs and concise diagrams clearly depicting location of anchorages and parks.
Foreword by Captain Ken Burton, RCMP, Marine Division.

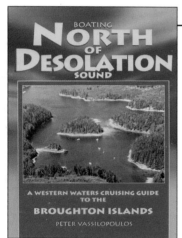

North of Desolation Sound
ISBN 0-919317-32-4 2004. $46.95

North of Desolation Sound– a coffee table styled full colour, Illustrated guide-book. This companion book to the Gulf Islands Cruising Guide is a comprehensive reference book/guide to the Broughton Islands area and routes from Stuart Island to Seymour Inlet. Filled with full colour photos, aerial pictures and diagrams. A must for serious mariners cruising the BC inland coast. Available at all marine stores and book sellers.

More guides and books from
Pacific Marine Publishing
PO Box 1310 Delta BC V4M 3Y8.
PO Box 984 Point Roberts WA 98281.

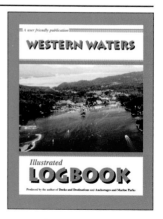

Western Waters Logbook
ISBN 0919317-30-8 2002.
Aerial and ambient photographs included.
Western Waters Logbook is a well-researched compilation of pages designed for convenient use by the astute west coast mariner. It recognizes specific record-keeping of experienced yachtsmen and has been assembled in collaboration with members of the marine community–in particular yacht club members who, like the author, have cruised local waters extensively and designed their own logbooks to record trips, maintenance, service, customs clearing and listing of guests and visitors who have been invited aboard.

This logbook is a companion to the above popular marine guides by the same author. They are widely acclaimed by experienced mariners on the west coast.